4/17

Always
By My Side

Life Lessons from Millie
and All the Dogs I've Loved

EDWARD GRINNAN

Foreword by Debbie Macomber

HOWARD BOOKS
AN IMPRINT OF SIMON & SCHUSTER, INC.

NEW YORK   NASHVILLE   LONDON   TORONTO   SYDNEY   NEW DELHI

An Imprint of Simon & Schuster, Inc.
1230 Avenue of the Americas
New York, NY 10020

First Howard Books hardcover edition February 2017

HOWARD and colophon are trademarks of Simon & Schuster, Inc.

For information about special discounts for bulk purchases, please contact Simon & Schuster Special Sales at 1-866-506-1949 or business@simonandschuster.com.

The Simon & Schuster Speakers Bureau can bring authors to your live event. For more information or to book an event, contact the Simon & Schuster Speakers Bureau at 1-866-248-3049 or visit our website at www.simonspeakers.com.

Interior design by Jaime Putorti

Manufactured in the United States of America

10 9 8 7 6 5 4 3 2 1

Library of Congress Cataloging-in-Publication Data

Names: Grinnan, Edward, author.
Title: Always by my side / Edward Grinnan.
Description: First Howard Books hardcover edition. | New York, NY : Howard Books, 2017.
Identifiers: LCCN 2016045211 (print) | LCCN 2016046141 (ebook) | ISBN 9781501156380 (hardback) | ISBN 9781501156397
Subjects: LCSH: Golden retriever—United States. | Human-animal relationships—United States. | Dogs—Therapeutic use—United States. | Grinnan, Edward. | Dog owners—United States—Biography. | Recovering addicts—United States—Biography. | Grinnan, Edward—Philosophy. | Compassion. | BISAC: BIOGRAPHY & AUTOBIOGRAPHY / Personal Memoirs. | PETS / Dogs / General. | BIOGRAPHY & AUTOBIOGRAPHY / Literary.
Classification: LCC SF429.G63 G74 2017 (print) | LCC SF429.G63 (ebook) | DDC 636.752/7—dc23
LC record available at https://lccn.loc.gov/2016045211

ISBN 978-1-5011-5638-0
ISBN 978-1-5011-5639-7 (ebook)

For Mike Emrick;
and for my nieces, Clare and Rachel,
who were taught to care.

FOREWORD

Debbie Macomber

You're going to love reading this book.

As you flip through the pages your appreciation and admiration for Edward Grinnan will quickly evolve. Edward is a writer with the gift of taking the most mundane story and turning it into a profound life lesson. He's a writer's writer, a role model, and a cheerleader to dozens of aspiring authors. As the editor-in-chief of *Guideposts,* he's wise, funny, honest, and endearing. I am fortunate to call him my friend.

If you're reading this book, you more than likely have had a dog touch your life. Edward writes about the dogs he's known and loved with chapters that detail his own life journey. And it seems that each step of his path included a dog walking by his side. The dogs Edward writes about are more than dogs, though. I am convinced that many were angels in disguise, canines who could easily have been mistaken as instruments of God. You'll meet Pete, the dog who helped him grieve the death of his brother with Down syndrome, and Rudy, who sat at his side during AA meetings. It was Rudy who introduced him to Julee, the woman who would become his wife. There's Marty and Sally and Millie . . . I defy anyone to read the story of Millie and come away with dry eyes. Interspersed with the stories of the dogs who have changed him, Edward weaves in tales of others who have experienced what can only be explained as the divine intervention of finding exactly the dog they needed and who needed them at exactly the right time.

I can say this with confidence because of the dogs that have been a part of our family. Over the years, Wayne and I have had several dogs. When our children were young, we took in a stray and named him Spot. He was a mid-sized dog of indeterminate breed who we should have entered into the Ugly Dog contest. White with one large black spot on his back, he loved our children, chased after sticks, and quickly knit his way into our home and into our hearts. He was loyal, trusting, tolerant as our little ones hugged and tried to ride him like a horse. At times, I wondered if God hadn't sent Spot as a babysitter and companion for me as I managed four toddlers.

Later there was Gypsy, the collie our neighbor found abandoned on the freeway. And then two dogs we named Peterkins, along with cats, guinea pigs, ducks, goats, a horse, chickens, and an assortment of other beasts.

The second Peterkins lived for seventeen years, and when he died, Wayne and I decided our time for pets was over. All the kids were grown and had families of their own. This was our time, we thought, and pets would only weigh us down. Our resolve lasted five years.

I was the one who gave in. We'd gone to visit friends, and their neighbor had a litter of puppies who needed good homes.

One look at Bogie and I couldn't resist. A few months after Bogie became a part of our family, our son Dale took his life. Only those who have buried a child can fully appreciate what that does to the human heart. The grief was overwhelming, the pain intolerable. For weeks, I wandered around in a fog of pain so deep it hurt to breathe. Through it all my constant companion was Bogie. It was as if he knew I needed someone to hold. I know beyond a doubt God sent Wayne and me this special dog. Bogie became our comfort dog.

Scripture states in Hebrews 13:2 that God sends angels in our lives and they often come disguised as humans and, I believe, as dogs. If you have any doubts, all you need to do is turn the page. The dogs/angels are there with tale upon tale from the talented pen of Edward Grinnan. As he reminds us in the subtlest of ways, *dog* is *God* spelled backward.

INTRODUCTION

An Instrument of Heaven

I can't imagine life without a dog to love and be loved by.

The love between humans and dogs is not the same as the love between humans. We love our own differently, sometimes better and sometimes worse than we love our dogs. The bond between man and dog is unencumbered by much of the baggage we bring to a human relationship. Some might say it is purer. I'll leave it as being something different.

Dogs love us in a fashion other humans can't. They love us in a way we can't necessarily love back. Their survival—from the time man and canine forged their unique and miraculous bond—has depended on them seeing deep inside of us, into our thoughts and emotions and desires. Into our very souls. I know my dogs have understood me better than most people do, better than I often do myself—like an instrument of heaven sent to guide me. The physically blind use Seeing Eye dogs to navigate their lives. But there are those of us who have been blind spiritually and emotionally, and who have discovered that a dog can help lead us into the light, a dog who grasps our deepest needs, who assuages our most profound anxieties, who uncovers both our faults and our virtues, a dog who *believes* in us. In short, a dog that makes us a better human being.

In my life, one such dog was Millie. And there is one fateful walk with her I will never forget, which is where this story begins.

MILLIE, AKA MILLIE JO McCALLISTER (born in the deep South), aka Millicent Johanna de Flanders (her sire was Flemish), aka Millicent!!! when she was bad (which was rarely) or just plain everyday MJ, was my eight-year-old "Devon cream" golden retriever, large and muscular, taking after her mother, but so decidedly feminine in deportment and temperament that it outraged me whenever someone mistook her for a boy.

Like all the dogs in my life, Millie seemed to be at my side the moments I needed her most, even if I didn't realize it at the time. On occasion Millie led me to a world only she and her kind are blessed to glimpse, a world of discernment and insight and intuition and knowledge that can defy human comprehension . . . endowed, I believe, by God. I never cease to be amazed, and never more so than on that muddy March day.

I hadn't planned to go to Massachusetts that weekend, but my wife, Julee, a singer, had back-to-back rehearsals for an upcoming performance, so Millie and I ventured north from New York City to check out our little weekend place in the Berkshires, some 120 miles as the proverbial crow flies (we drove). I was anxious to see how the house had fared over the rude winter.

We took the serpentine Taconic Parkway, which once we got out of Westchester County was largely devoid of traffic. Millie sat in back, staring at the colorless landscape, all grays and browns punctuated by a ragged patchwork of dirty white. I've often wondered how the world looks through the senses of a dog. Did it look as monochromatic to her? As dreary? What did she see that I didn't see? At one point, I had to brake hard at the sight of a highway patrol car lurking in the trees. Millie braced herself against the front seat.

"It would be nice if you could alert me to these things, Mil," I said with a laugh, reaching back to restrain her. I glanced in the rearview and saw her bright pink tongue drooping from the side of her mouth. We've taught dogs to do many things but not yet to detect sneaky New England speed traps.

A couple hours later we pulled up the steep dirt driveway to the house, the wheels of my Jeep spinning a little in the icy slush and Millie glancing around in mild alarm at the whining sound, ears perked. Julee and I bought the house fifteen years earlier to accommodate our cocker spaniel, Sally, and especially our somewhat crazed Labrador, Marty, who was hemmed in by city life. It was Marty who picked the house out. That is a story you will hear later. Millie certainly approved of his choice. She liked nothing more in the world than to hike the forested hills of Berkshire County.

For the moment, I was grateful the place was still standing, its roof intact. There was a ton of snow in the yard and covering the rugged hill behind, where a few trees had fallen since Christmas. Millie leapt from the Jeep and bulldozed some paths through the drifts, but it wasn't the same as being able to run free all over the place. I could tell she was a little downhearted as I hauled our stuff inside and turned up the heat. Later, when we went exploring, we found all our favorite mountain trails impassable without snowshoes. Millie might have had giant paws, but they were no match for the drifts, and it was dangerous for her to attempt, as I knew she surely would. *Easy for a dog to turn a leg in deep snow.*

"Sorry, girl," I said. I scratched her behind her ear. Her dense fur was already beginning to sop up the chill moist air. She looked at me plaintively. *You must find a solution! Why else have we come all this way?* her eyes said.

On an odd whim, I decided to try a woodsy little development on Stevens Lake where I'd never taken her before. It was just down the road. Most of the houses were closed for the season, but I knew they had a plowed road that went around the lake. It wasn't all that exciting except for a little stretch of undeveloped land that rose above the water. Still, we could get some exercise there. Millie jumped back in the car, upright and alert, eager to carry on.

Mostly what we got at Stevens Lake was muddy. The road was potted with mushy ruts. My Devon cream retriever soon looked more like hot chocolate. I would have much explaining to do when I got back to New York. And goldens, sweet as they are, can smell pretty sour when damp. I reminded myself to pick up a new air freshener for the car when we headed back in a couple of days. Probably several.

Millie was undeterred. She ran and splashed and occasionally threw herself on the ground. She didn't care how she smelled. I suspect she enjoyed it. Her breath preceded her in puffs, and she kicked up her hind legs like a colt when a breeze whipped off the lake. Every once in a while, she'd turn and pause, tail erect, waiting for me to catch up. *Come on*, her stance said, *I'm not going to wait for you all day.*

We turned around eventually, though it took a little coaxing on my part. "Come on, MJ. Time to go home. I'll cook you a burger on the grill." On the way back up the road, Millie, bored covering the same ground in reverse, ran off to check out one house or another, sniffing around for signs of life (and food, probably) but always galloping back at my whistle, splashing through the icy puddles and causing me more angst—almost deliberately, it seemed to me. She had a little of the devil in her, and I couldn't help wondering how long it would take just to get her clean enough to come inside.

Then, all at once, she took off up a barren hillside toward a darkened house I had not noticed before. I could barely see it through the naked trees and the lowering sun. Millie strode purposefully up the steep, curving driveway. I whistled. I shouted. She trotted on. Finally, I followed, more curious than perturbed as to why she would ignore me.

Millie disappeared around back. I was slipping and sliding at this point and calling her name, shocked she could be so oblivious . . . or willful. Then I thought, *Not a deer carcass!* and began running.

Actually, it was the main entrance to the house, tucked in the rear so as not to obstruct the lake view. Millie was sitting patiently on the little porch giving me a grave look.

"Millie, come on!"

She stayed.

"Now!"

Wouldn't budge. Suddenly a man opened the door. As soon as I recovered from the surprise of seeing that someone besides Millie and me was populating the area, I apologized profusely for my dog's behavior.

"That's all right. I have one myself. He's pretty sick right now, or I'd ask you in."

So we got to talking. He was a New Yorker, too, and like all New Yorkers we felt immediately compelled to trade neighborhood info. He lived in the Village, and I told him I lived in Chelsea.

"I have my practice in Chelsea, at Penn South. I'm the podiatrist."

Of course. I'd seen his sign a million times outside one of the buildings belonging to the sprawling apartment complex between Eighth and Ninth Avenues.

"Maybe your dog knows mine. I used to bring him to work with me all the time when he was young. Buzz. A mastiff mix."

I thought for a moment, realization dawning on me. Could it actually be? Buzz? Really? Buzz and Millie had the same walker when Millie was a puppy and they would stroll the neighborhood together or hang out at the dog run, sometimes for hours. I hadn't seen Buzz in ages, and certainly never dreamed I'd see him anywhere outside Chelsea, let alone in another state.

"This is Millie," I said. "They used to hang out." Millie edged forward.

"He's real sick," the man said, "and pretty frail." I peeked through the door and saw Buzz, gray and ancient now, inert on a pile of blankets, his chin resting on an old pillow. "I'd have Millie come in," he continued, "but I'm afraid she might want to play and Buzz's hips are shot. I thought he'd like it up here with the fireplace and all. It's so quiet this time of year."

He was telling me his dog was dying. I felt terrible for him. It's as bad as losing a person you love, worse sometimes, since some people don't seem to understand how painful it is. Some of them treat you like you just got rid of an old boat.

Millie nudged the door open a little wider and stared in at Buzz. She was very still. Silent.

"How 'bout I put her on her leash and let her say hello," I said softly, knowing hello would really be good-bye because dogs know these things in a way we humans never will. The man nodded, and I leashed Millie up. She padded over to Buzz, who had come slowly awake, his rheumy eyes blinking. He lifted his head, and it was obviously an effort. His breathing was short.

Millie glanced back at me. She wanted me to know. Then she leaned in and nuzzled his ear. Buzz's tail flopped against the old blankets. It was all he could manage.

Millie stepped back, turned, and gave me another look, eyes turned upward. *We can go now*, it said.

And so we went. I thanked the man and wished him luck and said a silent prayer for Buzz's peaceful passing. Millie was already quite a few paces ahead of me, head to the ground, following her nose, zigzagging down the hillside. I caught up to her, slipping and sliding as I did, and dropped to one knee, hugging her and not minding the wet and the mud and the golden aroma at all. I felt her lean in to me. She stayed perfectly still. That stillness, I eventually came to understand, that whole amazing episode in fact, was a message. A message that would break my heart, though I didn't know it then.

I think that's how it is supposed to be. Our dogs teach us great lessons and often at just the right moment. They teach us about love and much more: empathy, resilience, leadership, loyalty, compassion, humor, courage, joy, vigilance, forgiveness, serenity, respect. They teach us about life and about death.

Millie and I dried off in front of the woodstove, staring at the dancing flames. I didn't know what she was thinking but I wondered if someday all of this would be explained to me . . . probably in heaven. Not that it mattered. Nothing really mattered except that one moment, alone with my dog, soaking up the warmth and feeling so connected and content, so present. For that one all-encompassing moment, I was content to be amazed. I had no idea that I was being prepared for what was soon to come.

CHAPTER 1

————— 🐾 —————

Our golden girl Millie came to Julee and me on an airplane from Tampa, Florida, via Atlanta, on Memorial Day weekend, 2007, a hot, brilliant, backlit kind of morning, one of those days that stamp a vivid, practically surreal impression on your memory. I remember standing in the baggage claim area at Newark Airport, disembarking passengers streaming around us, waiting for the luggage handlers to bring out a ten-week-old puppy in a sturdy plastic travel kennel provided by her breeder. There were several false alarms, including a Dalmatian who was barking hysterically and a pug with its eyes bulging out of its head.

Then she appeared. Or at least her nose did, poking out of the wire mesh of her kennel door. The kennel was stacked precariously with a whole bunch of non-living luggage on a stainless-steel cart, which the man pushing it seemed determined to bash into everything that stood in its way. I ran over protectively and snatched the kennel. "This one's mine," I snapped. He didn't ask me for my baggage claim ticket. I think he knew better.

We liberated Millie immediately, Julee gently lifting her up in her arms and me taking pictures with my phone. We'd lost Sally, our sixteen-year-old cocker, a few weeks earlier while Julee was on tour in Europe. We waited until she got home to find another dog. It was the longest we'd ever been without a dog as a couple, and the longest Julee had ever been in her life. Julee is known to say that she was raised by golden retrievers and cocker spaniels, in a family that sometimes treated their dogs better than they treated one another. Sally had been at the center of our lives for so long we hardly recognized ourselves as a couple without her. She had lived a long, eventful life, but that didn't make losing her any less of a heartache. We needed another dog, not to replace her but to fill that void in our hearts.

This creamy, snuggly puppy was an answer to prayer. We had found a small, specialty breeder in Florida online. We'd seen video of the parents, Maggie and Petey, proudly standing with their litter. Immediately both Julee and I were attracted to a puppy with a kind of light in her eyes—Dark Pink Girl, named after the collar that identified her from her brothers and sisters. And now, finally, here she was. Millie.

Yes, she was a little rank and a little damp from her imprisonment, but that could be easily remedied by a quick bath when we got back to New York. Julee held her in her lap in the backseat all the way into Manhattan. I nearly got into several wrecks reaching back to pet Millie. We got to the apartment and carried her upstairs. We had everything ready—toys, bowls, treats, a bed, and wee-wee pads until she was old enough to go outside. I emailed the breeder as soon as we got in: "She's absolutely out-of-this-world beautiful!"

That night she slept in a brand-new kennel at the foot of the bed. In the middle of the night she cried. Julee started to get up. "No," I said. "It's like a baby—you have to let them cry it out. You can't go running." Reluctantly Julee went back to sleep. A few minutes later Millie cried again. I stared at the ceiling for about a minute then reached over, undid the door to her kennel and brought her into bed.

She was everything we dreamed of in a pup. We were ready to raise her to be a strong, confident girl, to love her until the ends of the earth and back. If she was traumatized by her time in the belly of a 747, she didn't show any signs of it. She was the happiest puppy I'd ever seen. Or so I thought.

But we'll get to that soon enough.

WHEN I AM NOT spending time with my dog, I am the editor-in-chief of *Guideposts* magazine, a publication featuring true, uplifting personal stories from people of all walks of life. It was a job I literally wandered into one day in 1986, a lost young man desperate to keep body and soul together. Would I be interested in using my writing background to help people tell their stories of hope and inspiration? Well, why not? I had nothing better to do and practically no place to live at the time, no "visible means of support," as they say. I liked the Midtown Manhattan location of the office. It made me feel like I was coming up in the world and my bottom was a long way down. I figured I'd give it a year, work on my resume, and use the office Xerox machine to make copies to send out. In any event, I wouldn't stay at *Guideposts* for long. It wasn't really my milieu, I told myself.

Things didn't quite work out like that. I kept staying. One year, then two, then five, until I couldn't imagine leaving this wonderful publication and the millions of people who are inspired by it every month. *They* inspired me.

One thing everyone knows about me as an editor is that I love a great dog story. My first cover story for *Guideposts* was with a man named Bill Irwin, who thru-hiked the Appalachian Trail in his fifties. No big deal? Well, Bill had never hiked anything in his life. In fact, up until shortly before the story takes place he was a sedentary, lifelong alcoholic. Did I mention that he was blind? And that he hiked the entire 2,000 miles of the trail from Georgia to Maine alone save for his amazing guide dog, Orient? All of this simply because he believed the Lord wanted him to, that a man as broken as Bill Irwin could be restored.

Bill was unforgettable and so was Orient. It was one of my biggest thrills when I finally got to meet them in person, though it was a totally random-rush hour encounter at Union Station in Washington, DC. Well, maybe not so random. Bill and Orient have supplied me with a lifetime of inspiration. I identified with Bill as a recovering alcoholic and a dog devotee. Bill and Orient's saga infused me with a love of the Appalachian Trail, many miles of which I have hiked with my own dogs, especially Millie. Sometimes I will close my eyes and try to take a few steps, just to feel what it was like to be Bill, but it is an impossible thing to imagine, like trying to imagine what it was like to be Neil Armstrong walking on the moon. No, I was wrong. Bill Irwin and Orient did not hike that great trail alone.

I have learned that some of the most powerful human stories are from people and their dogs. It is a dynamic that can produce great personal insight and change. No wonder then that our dog stories are among the most popular in our repertoire, and have been for more than seventy years. And why not? We've been talking about our dogs since we could talk. Prehistoric cave paintings attest to this. So do Minoan pottery and ancient Chinese statuary. Dogs hold an esteemed place in literature. Remember Argos from Homer's *Odyssey*? He is the only one to recognize Odysseus after his twenty-year wander, the first dog to appear in literature. Or Dora's Jip in Dickens's *David Copperfield*, who dies at the moment his mistress does.

Hard-living Jack London created two of the most memorable literary dogs—Buck in *The Call of the Wild* and the eponymous *White Fang* (technically a wolf-dog), two books I must have read a hundred times as a kid. Who can forget Old Yeller and Lassie? These dogs are canine archetypes—brave and noble and wise. And unforgettable.

I've worked on a lot of dog stories through the years and in a way, they are all unforgettable—but maybe that's just me. I hope it's you, too.

But my love of dogs started well before I came to *Guideposts*. For most of my life I have been in the company of a dog, sometimes multiple dogs, and in periods of involuntary doglessness I have sought them out wherever I could, if only for a transitory fix. If a friendly one came bounding down the street,

I'd squat and open my arms, I'm sure with a ludicrous expression on my face, even sillier than the canine in question. Many owners have had to tug their charges away from me. Occasionally, I would loiter in the vicinity of a dog park, just to watch them play. I remember sitting at a discreet distance in Manhattan's Madison Square Park, at dusk, observing a sleek Viszla named Ubu (after the Alfred Jarry character, I presume) chasing anything his owner could throw, leaping and snatching the item out of the air as if he could jump all the way to heaven. Ubu's joy was infectious. So was his human's.

My very earliest recollection of a dog at my side is almost completely obscured by the mists of memory. I was a colicky baby. I would wail and cry and scream for hours upon hours. I drove everyone to the edge of madness, to hear my family tell it. And with my mom coping with my brother Bobby, who had Down syndrome and was sensitive to disruptions, there was only one sensible thing to do.

The house on Hillcrest Avenue in Havertown, Pennsylvania, just a few miles west of downtown Philly, had a deep, narrow backyard with an empty lot bordering the end farthest from the house. That's where my playpen was relocated, with me placed in it. Oh, I'm sure my wailing could still be heard, especially by my mom, but it was now muted by the aural rhythms of the neighborhood, just another piece of the cacophony. And wail I did, alone in my pen.

Except for a visitor. It is such a vague fragment of memory, a deep brownish dog with alert ears that pointed to heaven, white markings, and beautiful dark eyes. There he would stand, seemingly for hours (but what did I know about time?), just staring at me, sometimes lying down and resting his chin on his forepaws. And his presence comforted me in my howling.

He could have been a figment of my imagination, possibly retrofitted at some point. But the thing about this mysterious comforter—he was to appear again in my life and somehow I recognized him.

The first dog I truly remember was Sparky, a sweet but at times unruly and errant beagle. I had been led to believe that Sparky had wandered off one summer in Philadelphia while under the care of my father, never to return. At the time of his disappearance the rest of us were down on the Jersey Shore in Stone Harbor, where we had a house.

I didn't learn the truth about Sparky until a large Grinnan-Rossiter-Gallagher family reunion somewhere in the Midwest—or was it in the Southeast?—sometime in the nineties. The eventual shock of what was revealed to me that summer day has obliterated the details. I was wandering around a spacious, sun-saturated yard squinting and introducing myself to people I'd never met and would no doubt never see again. I finally ended up in a little knot consisting of Julee; my brother, Joe; his wife, Toni; my sister, Mary Lou; and assorted cousins, nephews, nieces, and corresponding spouses, fiancés, boyfriends, and girlfriends.

The subject turned to dogs, as it often did since we all had them and loved them and loved to talk about them. I lapsed into a reminiscence about Sparky.

I'd long since accepted Sparky's fate, especially since there would be a far more devastating disappearance to strike my family several years later, a tragedy, and a cruel mystery, that would change everything, including leading me to my first real dog. And Sparky was, after all, a bit of a travelin' man, and I doubt if he was "fixed."

Yet I couldn't help noticing the looks on my siblings' faces as I fondly held forth at the reunion: bemused disbelief and maybe a little embarrassment that I had never been clued in, or maybe that I was so completely clueless. As in, you didn't *know*? You didn't know what Dad actually did with poor Sparky?

Technically Sparky was Mary Lou's dog, not mine. I want to be clear about that and that she loved Sparky. I was much too young for a dog. But he constituted the first canine presence in my life, and I would sometimes put him on a leash and pal around with him in the neighborhood, bringing him with me to the O'Malleys' or the O'Haras' or the Thompsons' or the Kennedys' (there's a reason they call Haverton the thirty-third county of Ireland).

Mary Lou was a freshman at Archbishop Prendergast High. A dancer, a cheerleader, an activity-consumed extrovert even for a teenager. How she talked my parents, especially my dad, into getting her a dog is a puzzle. She was devoted to Sparky but couldn't take care of him all by herself.

Worse, my father enforced harsh conditions, or tried to: he exiled Sparky—whose idea was that name?—to Mary Lou's bedroom when she wasn't there to watch him. That was the deal, a deal no adult should have ever made with a kid. When Mary Lou wasn't home, Sparky stayed locked in her bedroom, though I happen to know my mom violated this incarceration from time to time. But she had her hands full with Bobby, my brother who was a few years older than me and in school only half the day.

Before you denounce my father, remember that he was of a different generation, which is not to excuse him in any way, but that fact lends context to his view of pets. He saw a much larger gulf between animal and human, which was amplified by his orthodox Catholicism, Saint Francis notwithstanding (my mother was an entirely different story). It was a generational perspective. Pets were pets. Property not family. And Sparky was canine property. Moreover, Dad put an inordinate importance on the concept of obedience, and dogs are not necessarily naturally obedient, especially if they are not lovingly taught to be, and this holds especially true for beagles, like Sparky, who are known free spirits. My dad, I suspect, perceived canine misbehavior as willful defiance. He subscribed to the rolled-up newspaper school of discipline and dog training. And if you suggested that a dog or any animal might be in possession of something akin to a soul, he would have looked at you blankly. He may have even regarded the notion as heretical. Besides, my father came of age in the Depression, and to hear him tell it, he had to fight dogs for scraps of food to survive.

Now I found myself at the reunion staring at Joe and Mary Lou, the awful truth creeping up on me.

"What?" I demanded.

"Dad had Sparky put down," Mary Lou said. "You never figured that out?"

I flapped my mouth but no words came out. For more than thirty years I had accepted the perfectly plausible narrative that Sparky had simply given in to his wanderlust and lit out for better opportunities than being locked up in a teenage girl's room with occasional forays with the little brother. Maybe he'd assumed with all of us away at the shore he'd never see us again. From his point of view, *we'd* run off, except for my father who was working all day while Sparky was confined. That was no life for a dog. Who could blame him for bolting?

Occasionally, I'd indulged in fantasies, even in adulthood, as to what became of Sparky, the fascinating trajectory of his post-Grinnan life. Was he adopted by some jolly butcher? Given a job by a wise old farmer? Did he offer comfort and companionship to some sweet but lonely couple adrift in their golden years, romping with the grandchildren when they came to visit, increasing those visits by his lovable presence? "Mom, Dad, can we go see Sparky at Grandma and Grampy's house? Please?" Or did he end up at a Philly firehouse perched atop a hook-and-ladder truck racing to five-alarm blazes, ears flying, head high, smelling the smoke before anyone else?

No. Dad returned him to "the pound" whence he came and reported that the dog was incorrigible. Apparently, he peed all over and chewed the walls, though I don't remember it. And there was no way my father would ever tolerate that, probably not even from his own children. I imagine he saw it virtually as a moral failing on Sparky's part. Disobedience. Defiance. And no way Sparky was ever getting out of the pound again alive. Not now.

I didn't want to make a fool of myself blubbering and carrying on at the big family reunion about a dog I barely remembered and who wasn't technically mine. So I kept a stiff upper lip while Joe and Mary Lou laughed a little self-consciously, not at Sparky's end but at my naïveté. What did I think had happened?

I thought he'd run away because that's what everyone had told me. I accepted the explanation.

Walking back to the car Julee took my arm and said, "That really upset you, didn't it? You really didn't know?"

"No. I totally believed the cover story. I never doubted it. Why would I?"

"I remember my dad sobbing when he had to put one of our goldens down. He was inconsolable." Dr. Cruise may have had his failings, but he adored his dogs.

"I only saw Dad sob once, the day they found Bobby's body." Bobby's mysterious death at age twelve haunted us all.

"Sparky was a long time ago, Edward."

"They lied to me."

"Maybe they were trying to protect you."

"From what?"

"The truth?"

"Yeah, but the truth came out. It has a habit of doing that."

Driving back to New York, I brooded on Sparky's short, troubled history in our little home on Hillcrest Avenue. Why had everything gone so wrong? Why did I look back on it so bleakly, as if the memory hollowed out a part of me? I knew Julee was right. It was a long time ago and people were different. But I just couldn't see it that way.

Sometimes one memory dredges up another, and I found myself thinking about a dog that had long since migrated from my memory, whose name I could not even remember, if it even had a name.

Not long after Sparky was condemned, another dog appeared on the scene—a beautiful, purebred Kerry blue terrier pup. Maybe my father thought an Irish dog would work out better than a lowly beagle from the pound.

I think other forces were driving him as well, forces he himself may not fully have come to grips with. I think he felt bad about eliminating the family pet. Maybe even guilty. Perhaps he confessed it to a priest. Maybe the priest pointed him toward the Kerry blue breeder, or perhaps a business associate advised him. Maybe my mother was involved. In any event, one day a beautiful Kerry blue puppy appeared in our house.

I can't remember much about that dog's brief residence. I remember lots of vet visits and the poor thing not exactly thriving. I overheard conversations about how much the dog was costing to treat and that awful strain that came into my father's voice whenever things were boiled down to money, an echo from the depths of the Great Depression. Finally, one afternoon Dad came home from work early and collected the Kerry blue and carried him to the car.

"Eddie, come with me."

I climbed into the seafoam-green Pontiac Bonneville my dad was driving so proudly those days, the one with the miracle of power steering, and held the puppy on my lap. He dropped his head between my knees. I peeked down at his eyes. That's where the problem was. He was going blind and that blindness might lead to worse, more expensive problems, I had heard. There was an operation, but it was pricey, which made me wonder if it was about the dog or the money.

We brought the dog inside the clinic. Dad conferred with the vet in low, somber tones. I heard something about cost, saw Dad shake his head, then the dog was handed over to the vet, who disappeared in back with it, the last I was ever to see of him. My father explained the dog was sick and there was nothing to be done.

Why had I been brought along for this? Why not just deceived again? Upon many years of reflection, through what I pray is a lens of understanding and forgiveness, I believe it was an honest attempt to acquaint me with the truth of life, the truth of the world, the truth of death. It is, after all, a lesson all kids must come to learn and accept. My father was afraid of how confused I might be if yet another dog simply vanished. I think it broke his heart to euthanize the Kerry blue. I think he was trying to do the right thing and he failed.

But I did ask my father one question. "Will he go to heaven?"

Dad looked at me quizzically, maybe even a bit anxiously and said nothing. Just fired up the Bonneville.

It would be another five years before Dad got me another dog, after we moved to a bigger house in Michigan, a short time after they found Bobby's body floating mysteriously in a Michigan lake and it felt like my family was coming apart like something caught in a tornado. That dog would be with me for many years, yet he, too, was to meet an untimely end.

Bobby disappeared on a winter's day when I was at school, not long after my family moved from Philly to Birmingham, Michigan, just north of Detroit. The police and my family believed it was foul play and the Detroit media made a big deal about it. I remember their vans parked in front of our house on Pebbleshire Road. I remember my parents making an appeal on TV. I remember Annette Funicello, Bobby's favorite Mouseketeer, also making a broadcast appeal. People assumed he could still be alive. Abducted or maybe just lost and confused. Then, many weeks later, during the Michigan spring thaw, they found his body floating in a lake that had been searched many times. There was a lot of controversy about how to close the case. The detectives wanted to continue the search for whoever abducted him. The trail had gone cold and the DA didn't want an open case involving the disappearance of a child on the books. He was running for reelection. He closed the case, and the chief of detectives resigned in protest. And my parents tried to go on.

I don't know if what my family went through during that time accounted for the trouble with depression and drugs and alcohol and everything else I had later in life . . . and not that much later, really, since I started drinking when I was thirteen, just a few years after Bobby died. That is a different story than the one I am telling here about Millie and my other dogs, though. I wrote a book about my journey to sobriety and sanity and faith called *The Promise of Hope*, and it helped me come to terms with my life. I am convinced it is only by the grace of God that I found my way to where I am today, a God who sent dogs to guide my way from the darkness that once threatened to swallow me.

MY QUESTION THAT DAY about the possibility of that poor Kerry blue going to heaven did not come out of thin air. It came from something I saw Sparky do, something *in* him, something not completely explicable to me at the time. Just a hint of what I would discover throughout my life, like a curtain being inched aside for a fleeting reveal.

Before the Great Depression, my father's family was fairly well off, not rich but certainly well-to-do, as the expression was back then. Then the market crashed and the economy imploded and a wave of poverty swept over the country like a shadow. Dad's family had not protected their assets very wisely, and most of the money disappeared. Dad's father turned to drink, and Dad had to forgo medical school to support his family. Things turned even worse when the crooked family lawyer absconded with the last $250,000, aided and abetted by strong-willed but hopelessly naïve Aunt Blanche, my father's first cousin or second cousin, I never quite knew.

The episode was sordid and completed the financial demise of my father's family, its little sandcastle of wealth washed away by the tide of history and avarice. Years of struggle followed. Blanche disappeared. No one knew what became of her or the sticky-fingered lawyer, who was said to have swept Blanche off her poor spinster feet.

But the story finally came out as the Great Depression ground on. The lawyer had abandoned Blanche when he was through with her, dumped her like an old tire. He'd gotten what he wanted, which definitely wasn't her. Heartbroken and ashamed, her life ruined, Blanche lived in poverty and obscurity . . . until my father tracked her down decades later.

You see, he wasn't a heartless man. He was the only member of the family who tried to understand Blanche and to forgive her. No doubt a priest helped him with this. And a private detective he hired as well. The detective found her in St. Louis or Chattanooga or some other down-at-the-heels town that could have served as the backdrop of a Tennessee Williams play, and Dad brought her to Philly, where he built a little addition to the back of the house on Hillcrest that had a bed and a sitting area and a bathroom and where he installed her so she could live out the rest of her lonely days in relative comfort and something approaching dignity.

Which wasn't long. I don't think Dad ever asked what possessed Aunt Blanche to conspire with the lawyer to make off with the remains of the family money, to ruin everything like that. I doubt it mattered much to him at that point. I think he simply couldn't bear to think of Blanche choking and gasping and dying in some decrepit rooming house and dumped in a pauper's grave, a few members of the local parish recruited to say prayers with the priest over the plain off-the-shelf casket bought by the Altar Society for just such a person as Blanche, who no one ever really knew. I think the Eleanor Rigby scenario troubled him very deeply, so he decided to bring her home to Philadelphia, where in fact she did die in that little addition a few years later, the lawyer's name on her lips. In what context I am not sure.

Which is where I come back to Sparky. His arrival came shortly after Blanche's departure, and the addition was turned into a guest room and a spot for a second TV and phone. On several occasions, we tried to induce Sparky, an otherwise bold, adventurous dog as has been documented, to enter that space, and each and every time he resisted. He would howl miserably and yelp and prostrate himself and struggle until he got away. And for as long as he was with us, Sparky never could bring himself to cross the threshold of that sad room where the tragic Blanche breathed her last.

That, I believe, is when I first had an inkling that dogs were more than just . . . dogs. They had feelings, not just the obvious mammalian imperatives but rich, complex inner emotional lives that so often we humans are blind to even when dogs are rarely blind to ours. They sense things deeply, not just instinctually but emotionally. I think dogs yearn for us to understand them, and nothing I've experienced in my relationship with the canine world has ever disabused me of that notion. Even when dogs are broken or vicious or untrusting, even when they have seemingly lost the ability to connect with human beings or even other dogs, when somehow their psyches have been shattered, even then love can change them, just as it changes us.

NEVER WAS THAT MORE evident than in a story we published in *Guideposts* about a dog who went to war and came back, like so many soldiers, broken. We called the story "A Different Kind of Hero," and we got mail about it for months. I think you'll see why.

"A Different Kind of Hero" was about a military working dog (MWD) named Ddoc, who served two tours of duty in Iraq and Afghanistan. The double D denoted that he was bred to be a MWD at Lackland Air Force Base, one of nearly seven hundred canines who served as sentries and scouts, sniffing out bombs, clearing buildings, and protecting troops. MWDs are tough and extraordinarily brave. Storming an objective, they are the first ones in. No hesitation, just single-minded commitment to the mission and the protection of their unit. Many of these amazing dogs are Belgian Malinois, long known for their ferocity in battle. Ddoc was a Malinois. A proud one.

After his discharge from the military, he somehow ended up in a shelter from which he was adopted by a family who soon discovered they couldn't handle him. Enter a behavioral health therapist stationed at Fort Bragg in North Carolina, Sgt. Chloe Wells.

Sgt. Wells wasn't a dog handler. She just loved dogs and with her husband, Jeff, had already adopted a Malinois named Ranger and a German shepherd named Sofie. Through the grapevine she heard of this homeless dog, Ddoc.

"We're not keeping him," Jeff said when she brought Ddoc back to their modest off-base house. "We can't keep up with the dogs we have."

"Just until I can find him a good home," Chloe pleaded. "He's a veteran. He needs a safe place. We owe him that much, at least."

Chloe got out food and water bowls. Jeff knew the battle was lost, so he dug through a closet for some old blankets and made a bed for Ddoc on the living room floor.

Chloe had put Ranger and Sofie in another room so Ddoc wouldn't feel too stressed meeting the other dogs. She led him into the living room after he ate to show him his bed. Ddoc grew hyperalert. He circled the living room, sniffing and searching, checking under the furniture and in corners, double-checking, triple-checking, Chloe suddenly realized, for bombs.

"It's okay, Ddoc," she said. "You're safe now." But Ddoc wouldn't stop patrolling until he was satisfied that the area was secure. Finally, he lay down on his blanket with a deep sigh. How exhausting it must be for a dog to carry such responsibility. *He still thinks he's on the front lines*, Chloe thought sadly.

BOOM. Jeff and Chloe were used to hearing practice rounds fired at Fort Bragg. Ranger and Sofie had learned to pay no mind. Ddoc snapped to attention. He leapt up and circled his bed, panting, eyes frantic. Every few minutes he'd stop dead in his tracks, cock his head, and listen intently and then go back to pacing. Nothing Chloe did arrested his intense anxiety. He was trembling, backing away from her, eyes darting, as if he were somewhere else entirely, reliving an experience so traumatic he had never completely stopped living it.

Chloe knew that look. At Bragg, she worked with a team that counseled returning soldiers with PTSD—post-traumatic stress disorder. These were soldiers who suffered extreme trauma on the battlefield, the debilitating psychological effects of which lingered long after they had returned home, long after they had left the service, often for the rest of their lives if treatment was not given or if it failed. At its essence, PTSD is an extreme insult to the mind, an assault on our very moral core, an injury to the soul. It can be as crippling as lost limbs or blindness or brain damage. It can impair a person from living normally or happily for the rest of his or her life. It is one of the greatest tragedies of war.

Chloe dropped to her knees and took Ddoc's head in her hands and whispered to Jeff, "I didn't realize he had these problems. I thought he was just having trouble adjusting."

"Chloe," Jeff said, "this guy is really hurting. What are we going to do?"

"Jeff, this dog has PTSD. I'm sure of it. Something had to cause it."

That very night Chloe tracked down Ddoc's former handler, Mike, still stationed in Afghanistan. They talked for a long time. The handler was emotional about what happened to Ddoc and was disturbed that he'd fallen through the cracks back in the States.

The incident had happened only months before. Ddoc and Mike were out on patrol in Taliban-contested territory. Mortar fire erupted and Mike and Ddoc were blown off their feet. Mike landed on top of Ddoc and tried to return fire. Their position was dreadfully exposed, deafening mortar fire exploding all around, smoke and rocks and dirt flung into the air. Ddoc took hold of Mike's combat fatigues and dragged him to the cover of a ditch, where he stood guard over Mike until the firing finally stopped. Then he led a rattled Mike safely back to base.

Ddoc spent the night trembling under Mike's bed. The next morning, he wouldn't come out. In fact, he couldn't bring himself to go out on patrol again. They brought in a trainer to work with him but to no avail. Finally, they sent him home.

"Ddoc found and alerted our unit to no less than fourteen IEDs," Mike had told Chloe. "He never backed down in a firefight or when we were searching a house. He saved many soldiers' lives." But he would never work in the military again.

What were they going to do about Ddoc? Did anyone know about treating military dogs with PTSD?

Now Jeff stroked the dog's head gently. "He's a hero, Chloe," Jeff said. "He stays here. With us." Chloe eased her cheek against Ddoc's powerful neck so as not to startle him and hoped he didn't mind the tears.

Jeff and Chloe took Ddoc into their bedroom and let him sleep next to their bed. In the dark of the night Ddoc cried out in his sleep, his muscles twitching, paws moving like he wanted to run. Repeatedly Chloe woke the dog and tried to comfort him, but she feared she alone could not fully heal Ddoc. "God," she prayed, "help Ddoc, your loyal creature. Help me help him. Ease his fear and his pain."

In the morning, she opened the back door to let Ddoc out into the yard. "Ddoc, go on. It's okay." He wouldn't leave her side. He just sat leaning heavily against Chloe's leg, staring out at the dawn. Was this when they went on patrol back in Afghanistan? As the sun rose over the Hindu Kush?

Chloe rustled up a leash and led Ddoc into the yard. He stayed within inches of her. She knelt and stroked him. "I'm here. I won't let anything bad happen to you. I promise." She left for work hoping Ddoc would be okay inside the house and that there wouldn't be any sudden noises.

All that day she dealt with soldiers struggling to re-adjust to civilian life, men and women who were tormented and confused by memories they couldn't exorcise. She fol-lowed her training, expressing empathy while staying emo-tionally detached and objective. Yet in their eyes she saw Ddoc's haunted eyes, and when she returned home that night the dog was waiting for her and her objectivity went AWOL. She had to save Ddoc from a life of misery and uncertainty. She wanted him to be a dog who greeted the dawn with joy.

Her vet put Ddoc on antidepressants and antianxiety meds. *Just like my soldiers*, thought Chloe. She gave Ddoc a pill every time she thought there would be an artillery barrage, but the drug took thirty minutes to hit the brain, and sometimes when the firing started before that, all she could do was hold Ddoc close and tell him over and over that he was safe and loved and protected. Sometimes she told Ddoc that God stood guard over him.

At Bragg, she was learning things from treating returning troops with PTSD that were amazingly applicable to Ddoc's situation. Indeed, she was seeing PTSD as a completely shared experience between human and dog. It wasn't as if a dog had some lesser manifestation of it. It was every bit the injury to a dog's psyche as it was to a human's. A dog was every bit as appalled by the carnage and madness of war.

Exercise was often helpful for her patients, so Chloe took Ddoc on long runs. He was like Forrest Gump, running as if he could never catch up to what he was chasing. Ddoc slept better at night after running all day and cried less, but Chloe was exhausted.

One night after a particularly trying shift at work, Chloe came home beaten down by the strain of helping people navigate their way through the psychic labyrinth of PTSD. She was met with the sight of Ddoc and Jeff curled up on the floor together, Ranger and Sofie looking on. Chloe could scarcely contain herself. She held her breath for what seemed like forever. Then she got Ddoc's leash and took him outside. "This is your home. No one will ever hurt you here."

Ddoc raised his eyes and met Chloe's. His tail wagged, just a little. He inclined his head and slowly, tentatively, licked her hand. In an instant, she was on her knees, hugging him. "You understand, don't you? You understand!" Ddoc wagged his tail more than Chloe had ever seen.

Progress was slow and steady. Chloe took Ddoc to the park, the pet store, never trying to push him through his fear. She let him take it on his own terms. She knew he was working things out in his mind, sorting his traumatic memories from reality. He was working through his PTSD memory by memory, just like the soldiers at Bragg. The more she worked with Ddoc, the more she learned that what helped him was the same as what helped her soldiers, that same unchanging message of reassurance: you are safe, don't give up hope, you are not alone, not ever, you are going to be okay, you are loved by a universal force more powerful than any harm that can befall us.

Bragg is one of the facilities used to train combat dogs, and one day Chloe heard that a memorial sculpture of a Malinois honoring the MWDs killed in action in Iraq and Afghanistan was to be unveiled. Was Ddoc up for that? There would be a ceremony and dignitaries and speeches. A pretty large crowd, for sure. "Want to give it a try, boy?" she asked him.

The minute Chloe arrived with Ddoc, she knew she'd totally messed up. There were hundreds of people, a long line of handlers with their dogs, vets in the black vests of the Rolling Thunder motorcycle chapter. Motorcycles! Chloe groped for Ddoc's meds in her purse. She wanted them at the ready if he went into a panic attack.

She led him slowly to the edge of the crowd, both of them tentative. They stopped. Ddoc sat. His eyes scanned the crowd, checking for danger. A speaker had taken the stage. "Dogs have been used by the US military in every conflict since the Revolutionary War. In Iraq and Afghanistan, they cleared thousands of miles of roads. Had it not been for their bravery many of us would not be here today."

Chloe glanced down at Ddoc, who appeared for all the world to be standing at attention, head high, shoulders erect. A hero, just as Jeff said. She felt herself flush with pride, with love.

"Special Forces dogs are loyal, reliable, and brave. They consider their team to be their pack. And they will do anything to protect their pack."

Chloe thought of Ddoc standing guard over Mike in the wake of the mortar attack. Suddenly, Ddoc tugged at his leash and eased a few feet into the crowd. There was an explosion of applause as the speaker finished. Ddoc tensed and Chloe eased him back, but Ddoc quickly regained himself and moved forward, all the way to the front. No fear. No dread. He was home. He was with his pack.

Dogs and handlers milled about, veterans who would not be alive if their dogs hadn't saved them. Soldiers told stories of incredible heroism, of dogs who did not return and were mourned as deeply as comrades, equal in arms.

Chloe and Ddoc made their way to the memorial statue. It was surrounded by fifty-eight inscribed concrete squares of dogs who had given their lives. Ddoc sat next to the statue and Chloe snapped his picture. He bore an uncanny resemblance to the statue. People stopped. They stared. Soon everyone was taking Ddoc's picture. "Is he the one the statue is modeled after?" folks wanted to know. "Is that really him?" Chloe just smiled.

Today Ddoc is back in training. But not for war. Never again for war. He is training to become a therapy dog for soldiers suffering from PTSD. Chloe discovered that Ddoc had an incredible effect on her team's patients. A gift. Ddoc understood what they were going through. He'd been there. The soldiers were at ease around him. In Ddoc they felt a comforting presence, a dog who knew what it was like to suffer as they had, and who miraculously helped them open up about their pain. They understood Ddoc, and he understood them. He knew they were warriors, like him. He could provide them with the assurance that there was indeed light beyond the darkness if they only believed it was possible to feel safe again.

THAT TRUST BETWEEN CHLOE and Ddoc, between Ddoc and soldiers with PTSD, is the foundation of any relationship with a dog. No one knows for sure exactly what brought our two species together so intimately as long as fifteen thousand years ago, around the end of the last ice age when the glaciers were unshrouding the earth, but it started with a tentative bond of trust. Our planet was poised for an unprecedented proliferation of warm-blooded life. Certainly, we humans domesticated wolves to help us hunt, herd, and guard. To perform tasks at which they are better than we are. How we figured out that wolves had greater talents than we did, and how to turn those talented wild creatures into domesticated dogs is lost to time. Perhaps, as some anthropologists have suggested, a brave and innovative wolf, dissatisfied with scavenging behind a lumbering group of prehistoric hunters and gatherers, took matters into her own hands (or paws) and summarily led the humans to their prey (come on, guys, follow us!). The wolves then did not have to worry about the dangerous business of subduing the quarry. Man did their bidding, and they got the leftovers. This may be slightly more fanciful than plausible, but something tells me it was the wolf that made the first move.

These were the initial human-canine interactions. Call it a strategic alliance. Both parties benefited: wolf led man to food source, man shared scraps with wolf. The wolf-dog's hunting prowess was extraordinary. In fact, some researchers have hypothesized that it was this alliance with the wolf-dog that gave modern man a decisive advantage over the predecessor he eventually vanquished, the Neanderthals. We envision our immediate cousins on the evolutionary timeline as knuckle-dragging brutes. It may just be that their greatest disadvantage and their ultimate fate was sealed by not having dogs. Our wolf-dogs made us better hunters and therefore better nourished, more able to seize territory. This nourishment may have even enhanced brain development in modern man. Could it be possible that dogs made us smarter?

Our dogs soon demonstrated other talents that could aid us. We shared more than food. We gave them shelter. We bred them for selected strengths. We nursed them when they were sick and injured. They rewarded us with loyalty and devotion commensurate with the ferocity of their core instincts. From that shared alchemy of needs arose something startling, something transformative for both species and based in absolute trust: Love.

CHAPTER 2

After we brought Millie home, it was a few weeks before her vaccinations kicked in and we could walk her outside on the Manhattan streets. I was looking forward to it. Nothing attracts an adoring, cooing crowd in New York like a puppy, especially a golden retriever pup. You think New Yorkers are tough? Just watch them make fools of themselves when a golden puppy comes trundling down the street. Kids squeal, doormen bow, cool cats whip off their shades and shout.

Except none of that happened with Millie because she declined to trundle down the street. She refused to go anywhere beyond the sidewalk immediately in front of our building. She'd politely do her business, I'd praise her effusively, then try to walk her down the block. Immediately she'd come to a crouching halt, digging in her nails, nipping at her leash, like she had encountered a force field. All efforts to entreat her to venture farther failed. I followed the tried-and-true strategies. I tempted her with her favorite toys, enticed her with high-value treats like sirloin beef chunks, which I gave to the garage guys next door to wave in the air. Real sirloin.

Early one morning I bent down in exasperation and looked into Millie's eyes, stubborn with fright. Across the street a garbage truck raucously hoisted an industrial-sized Dumpster high in the air, like a monster in a Japanese horror film lifting a car with an earthshaking bellow, the garbage Godzilla. The clamor set off car alarms. Drivers honked at the traffic stoppage occasioned by the groaning, grinding garbage truck. There were rolled down windows and angry exchanges.

Millie cringed and drooped her ears, as if she was trying to deafen herself to the cacophony most urbanites are perfectly inured to. An annoyance most city dogs learn to put up with. She was from sleepy, backwoods Florida, bred by a family who was not in it for the money but for the satisfaction of producing a few fine dogs. *What am I doing in this madness?* I could see her thinking. *I want to go back inside with my toys and my bed and my people.* She wanted to be where she knew it was safe, and I couldn't blame her. So I complied, just as the terrifying Dumpster was slammed back to earth and Millie made a beeline for our door.

Things didn't improve. Sometimes I would lift Millie up, carry her halfway down the block, and release her only to have her immediately jerk me back in the direction of the apartment. She was already powerful at twenty pounds or so. I'd find myself brooding about her time in the airplane up from Florida and cursing the lout who smashed the luggage cart she was a passenger on into practically anything he could find. I berated myself: We should have driven down and gotten her!

We should have borrowed from our retirement savings and rented a private plane! "The whole ordeal traumatized her, poor thing," Julee concluded.

Lord, I prayed one night, *this isn't working. I can't have a dog in the city who won't go outside.* Especially a dog who was going to be very large, if her parents, Petey and Maggie, were any indication.

Up at our house in the Berkshire Hills it was different story. A great story. Millie loved the woods and yard. She was bold and fearless, a different dog. At dusk, she would stand on a little bluff above the driveway, on tippy paws as it were, raise her head, and shout to the emerging stars, a mighty bark even for a youngster, a bark that echoed off the hills like a cannon shot and silenced all the other neighboring dogs, who would pause respectfully for a spell until they answered back from their own little hilltops. She loved the house in the Berkshires. She loved the country.

Which is where we decided to retreat that Fourth of July weekend. Julee was overseas again for a few weeks, and I decided that rather than continue the failing effort to get Millie acclimated to Manhattan street life we'd spend the holiday hiking and grilling in the country, just the two of us. Still, I was feeling despondent upon our arrival even as Millie shot out of the Jeep and tore across the lawn, ears and tail flying. I felt like I had let our dog down. She just didn't trust me. She didn't believe in me; I was convinced she simply could not accept that I would keep her safe amid all that noise and chaos and confusion. "She's just a little old country girl," Julee, a little old country girl herself, had said, climbing into the car for the airport, waving and wiping away a tear as the car drove off, me holding Millie in my arms and looking, I'm sure, rather at a loss.

It was on the Saturday, I think, of that long weekend while Millie and I were hiking a buggy trail around Fountain Pond Park, that inspiration struck. At this point in time I'm satisfied to say it was divine inspiration, for I never could have conjured up the solution to my problem that came to me that day as I was slapping gnats off the back of my sweaty neck. We were sitting on a squat rock sharing some water when I suddenly thought: Winky.

Winky belonged to Amy Wong, a colleague and friend of ours, and a wonderful dog owner. Winky was her russet, sixty-five-pound, six-year-old Carolina dog mix rescue, wise and worldly, a dog who was completely of the city. Whip-smart, just like her owner. Little fazed the confident Winky. She strode the streets like she owned them. Amy would say Winky was like a cop walking her beat. Maybe another dog could teach Millie to walk outside. An experienced dog. A dog like Winky. "What do you think, Millie?" I said, filling her pink porta-bowl. She gave me a happy look and wagged her tail. I don't think she knew what I was talking about. I wasn't even sure what I was doing. What if Winky didn't like Millie? Then what?

I prayed Amy was in town. She picked up her phone when I called from that rock in the woods and said she was and she'd be willing to meet up with Millie and me at our apartment the next day. That night Millie and I packed up and headed back to New York. I think Millie was a little disappointed. There is nothing sadder than a disappointed dog, all sighs and discouraged body language and questioning looks.

The next afternoon a napping Millie raised her ears when the apartment buzzer went off. "It's Winky," Amy's voice announced through the intercom. Millie cocked her head and rose to her feet. She knew something was up.

A minute later, Winky burst into the apartment and greeted me happily, wagging and wiggling.

"Hello, Dingo," I said, using my nickname for her. She calmed down, then sniffed Millie perfunctorily, vaguely indifferent to the puppy, who was in turn ecstatic at having a real canine visitor. This had never happened before. This was a first. This was something else!

Winky let out a quick, bossy bark intended, I surmised, to put Millie in her place, which worked because my puppy retreated slightly, taking up a toy in her mouth and sitting politely, her tail pounding against the carpet, expectation in her eyes: *Okay, what's next?*

We leashed up the dogs and took them down in the elevator. Millie stayed on her best behavior until we got to the lobby, where she drew herself up and put on the brakes, slipping and sliding on the polished tile. Winky paused, gave her a curious glance, and continued toward the door to the dreaded outside. Reluctantly Millie followed, glancing at me for reassurance.

"Good girl, Mil," I said. Amy held the door, and out we went into the shining July Fourth afternoon.

Once outside the building, though, Millie reverted to her fearful ways. She dropped onto her belly, paws splayed, ears back, her tongue lolling out. *Noooooo* her body language screamed. Again, Winky paused, this time looking a bit more concerned than curious. Amy and I stood back.

Winky took a step or two toward the prostrate puppy, lowering her head. She was assessing the situation, that was quite clear. Then she turned and started up the street, Amy in tow. I stayed with Millie, who stood up and then posed like a statue watching her new friend go. She shot me a quick, frantic look but didn't move.

And that's when it happened. Winky slowed her gait, stopped, and turned to look back at Millie. Their eyes locked. It was a moment I will never forget. I could feel Millie's vibrations rippling up the leash as she moved tentatively forward, both straining and holding herself back, Winky's gaze boring into her. It said, *Trust me.*

All at once Millie was on the move, bursting through the force field, then galloping a bit until she caught up to Winky and glued her snout to the older dog's flank as they continued on their way, me catching up. I was speechless with relief, but the garage guys cheered and random people on the street applauded, happy for an excuse to celebrate something, especially on Independence Day.

From that day on, Millie navigated the streets of New York with increasing confidence—like a real New Yorker—and Winky became her best friend for life, her mentor and protector. Years later, on a bleak December morning when Winky was old and blind and cancer-ridden, Millie let out a sigh and a whine at the very moment of her passing fifteen blocks across town.

But on that glorious night as fireworks exploded over the Hudson River, a spectacle Millie and I viewed from the roof of our building, I called Julee in Budapest and reported the extraordinary events of the day. After a long pause, she said, "All she had to do was find someone she could really believe." And that someone had to be another dog, because there are things they do better than us when it comes to their own kind.

NOW THAT THEY WERE best buddies, it was only natural that Millie would invite Winky to spend a weekend in the country. What friend wouldn't? So later that summer Julee, me, Amy, Winky, and Millie all piled into the Jeep and drove up to western Massachusetts. It was a good thing Amy was small because she had to share the backseat with the dogs.

There was one activity I had my heart set on that weekend. I wanted the dogs to scale Monument Mountain. All my dogs had and I was anxious for Millie to make the trek earlier than any of them, to make her mark in the world. I was bound and determined to get a dramatic summit shot of her to send back to her breeder in Florida: Look what she can do! What a dog!

We started out early. Julee stayed back at the house to finish some work on a song and do a phone interview for an upcoming show at Joe's Pub in New York. She took a dim view of my plans. She often does. "Millie is too young, Edward, for something like this. Her joints aren't even fully formed. And I don't care how smart Winky is. She's a city dog. What does she know about the woods? You should try something less ambitious. You're being reckless."

It was a frequent accusation. This time I should have listened.

We made the summit in good time. Millie was an absolute champion, scampering over boulders with only an occasional boost, following the trail right behind her mentor, Winky, who glanced back frequently to check on the pup. On one level, Winky knew Millie belonged to me and Julee, but on another level entirely, on a dog-only level, she fully accepted that Millie was her responsibility.

Thanks to our early start, there was only one other person on the summit. We had snacks and water, then I pulled my camera out of my pack, asking Amy to try to get wiggly Millie to stay still on the topmost rock so I could get my shot. I was changing positions. I wanted an angle that would make it look like she'd climbed Everest. Out of the corner of my eye I saw Winky. She was moving toward the edge of the summit cliff. I watched in horror as she simply vanished over the side.

For a second my voice was trapped in my throat. Amy was still fussing with Millie when I finally said, "Your dog just fell off the mountain."

No one is calmer in an emergency than Amy Wong. She pulled out her cell immediately to see if she could get a signal. I crawled on my belly to the cliff edge and peered over. I could see the tops of the pine trees several hundred feet below. No sign of a russet dog in all that sticky green. I called her name. Nothing. Unsurvivable, I thought. And not just for poor Winky. My conscience would never survive this.

Amy couldn't get a signal on her cell, but the other guy on the summit could and called 911. The Great Barrington rescue team was on its way. Meanwhile, Amy was calling Winky's name. Still no response. "Sometimes incapacitated animals keep silent so as not to attract predators," she said. A fount of information, even in a crisis. I could hardly swallow. But Amy was talking at a normal speed. That was a little unsettling. Normally Harvard grad Amy Wong talks as fast as she thinks. People are amazed at how many words a minute come out of her mouth. Now she was talking like a normal person. That only worried me more.

I was praying silently, frantically. *Lord, I'm such a total jerk for bringing the dogs all the way up here. Please save Winky, and if she can't be saved, please don't let her suffer.* The thought of her alone and in pain was unbearable.

Sooner than I expected a strapping young fellow came up the summit trail with ropes and rappelling gear. When he got to the top we explained the situation and helped him secure his ropes. "She went over right there," I said, pointing. Then I crawled out to the edge and pointed down to where I thought she might be. The guy nodded.

"She's not the first dog to fall off this mountain. A few of them have survived. You folks head down. You can't do much up here." With that he swung out over the void and disappeared. I was tempted to carry Millie every step of the way down, but she was having none of it so I put her on the leash and held on tight, my knuckles whitening after a few steps. Descending a steep trail with a leashed dog is awkward and I fell hard a few times, but I figured I deserved it.

Halfway down Amy got a signal and called Julee. She was waiting for us at the bottom when we got there, glaring at me while trying to console Amy. She snatched Millie's leash. "You really did it this time, Edward," she whispered.

I had nothing to say in my wretched defense. Why hadn't I listened to her? Why had I listened to my ego instead?

Julee and Millie got a ride back to the house. Millie, ever the distracted, exuberant puppy, didn't seem to think anything was particularly amiss, though she was confused that Amy and I weren't coming back with her and I dreaded how she would react when she realized Winky was never coming back. I hoped she was too young to understand. Sadness and joy are both fleeting things for a puppy. But dogs form bonds, deeper in some ways than even humans, an atavistic need for solidarity that goes back to the time before they joined with humans, instinctual as much as social.

By now the parking lot was crowded with emergency vehicles from several surrounding towns. People pulled off Route 7 to see what all the excitement was about. A newspaper reporter showed up. I paced around for what felt like forever. Then two things happened. The rappelling man called down from the trees and said he'd located Winky. Moments later a sturdy orange ATV arrived on the scene carrying none other than Dr. Barbara Phillips of All Caring Animal Hospital, black medical bag in hand. Dr. Barbara was Millie's Berkshire vet and had seen her just the week before for a routine well-puppy checkup. She waved as she and the ATV disappeared into the woods, the engine straining up the steep grade.

God had sent Dr. Barbara. That meant Winky was alive.

"She survived the fall," I told Amy in utter disbelief.

Amy nodded. "She's a tough dog, that's for sure. If any dog can survive a fall like that, it's Winky."

I tried to discern doubt in Amy's voice. It was there some-where, I knew, just out of my reach. She was as tough as her dog.

Less than a half hour later, the ATV returned to the park-ing area, emerging from the trees like an orange angel. Winky was curled in back with Dr. Barbara, her ears perked high, alert. She caught sight of Amy walking toward her and stood up. Tears stung my eyes. I felt rubbery with relief and grati-tude. It was a matter of alpha-dog pride that Winky wanted to stand to greet her person. Amy hugged her gently. *Thank you, God. I owe you big time.*

"She's a little banged up, especially her left hind leg, but I don't think anything is broken," Dr. Barbara said. "You'll have to take her up to Pittsfield to get her X-rayed and cleaned up. She'll probably need that wound sutured. Tell them her I gave her a little Valium to keep her calm."

The little monster in me said it deserved a little Valium too and maybe something stronger. I acknowledged it, then silenced it.

I drove the Jeep to Pittsfield, about forty minutes away. Amy sat in back with her dog. Winky was a bit dazed but was struggling to stay alert and vigilant. Ah, the obligations of an alpha. We spent a few hours at the Pittsfield vet hospi-tal while they sedated Winky and stitched up the nasty gash. Miraculously, she had no other injuries. No fractures, no inter-nal bleeding, after falling several hundred feet off Monument Mountain. "Maybe the trees broke her fall," the vet opined. Maybe they didn't, I said to myself.

It was late by the time we got on the Taconic Parkway back to Manhattan. Amy, Winky, and Millie were all asleep in the backseat, Millie resting her chin on Winky's chest. Even in her puppy brain, all pinwheels and carousels, she knew how close Winky came to death. She wanted to be close now. It is truly extraordinary the rich and complex relationships dogs form, and Millie was already developing a lifelong devotion to her friend Winky. Julee stared out the passenger window, silent. About halfway back to the city, she reached over and squeezed my arm gently, kindly, forgivingly. "I promise," I said without her having to ask. It was a promise I was to keep for eight more years.

I DON'T THINK I ever felt as protective of a dog as I did Millie, and that near-nightmare on Monument Mountain only increased that sense. Somewhere deep inside me was the conviction that I was put here on this earth to keep her safe so she could play whatever role heaven had deemed for her. So it was shocking when I nearly got us both killed the following summer.

It was the familiar drive up to the Berks. Millie was a little over a year old by then. It started out as a postcard-perfect May day, though there were warnings about stray spring storms. I wanted to beat the showers, which was probably why I was guilty of rushing Julee in her packing, the inevitable effect of which is to slow her down. Not that Julee doesn't pack for a long weekend like she's going on a world tour. But all my hectoring apparently became unbearable. Julee threw up her hands and told Millie and me to go on by ourselves. "I'll take the train up first thing in the morning. You can meet me at the station. It'll be much more relaxing for me that way."

I didn't argue. I just wanted to get going and at this rate we wouldn't get up to the house until the next morning anyway. So Millie and I gladly took off.

We followed the clouds up the Hudson and were on the northern reaches of the Taconic Parkway when the fugitive sun disappeared completely. We drove straight into a bank of scowling thunderheads. Millie snoozed on her bed in the back load space of the Jeep. It was full of blankets and pillows and stuffed toys, thanks to Julee. Millie wouldn't stir until we got within a mile or so of the house when her head would pop up, she'd yawn, shake off, and peer at me impatiently. *What's taking us so long?*

I turned off the Taconic onto Route 23 East toward the Massachusetts line and Catamount Ski Resort. Hail peppered the roof and a scimitar of lightning slashed the sky followed by a crack of thunder that seemed to come from all directions at once, almost as if it were coming up through the ground, from the bowels of the earth. More lightning, more thunder. Millie's head shot up.

"It's okay. We're fine. Good girl."

The rain grew so thick and wild that it might as well have been night. I dropped my speed as we entered a series of graded turns. Maybe I didn't drop it enough.

We were passing a swamp marsh on our left that was beginning to overflow the road when we hit a massive puddle. The Jeep hydroplaned, twisted. I tried to steer with it, but there was no traction. We were airborne. Your mind really does slow down in a life-or-death moment, the result of the adrenal glands pumping rapid response chemicals to your frontal lobes, giving a little extra edge to your reaction time. The gift of a million years of evolution at work. I found myself thinking about the Gold Cup hydroplane races on the Detroit River my dad used to take me to every summer. From the terrace of a restaurant called the Rooster Tail we'd watch the hydroplane racing boats hit speeds of 100 miles per hour, skipping and slamming off the water. Sometimes going airborne.

That's what the Jeep did. We went airborne. We flipped over once, twice, bouncing, careening down an embankment toward the water. I tried to fix in my mind what I would do if we landed wheels up in the swamp. It was like a coin flip. Heads or tails. Wheels up or down. Up and I'd have to get the door open fast before the cab filled with water. I'd have to get Millie out fast or she'd drown. If she survived the impact. I had my seatbelt on. She didn't have one.

A tiny eternity later we bounced and came to rest in about three feet of water twenty yards or so from shore, *wheels down*. I forced open the door with my shoulder and waded around the back, my heart hammering, my breath coming in gulps, the rain lashing my face. I yanked open the hatch.

Millie was sitting on her waterlogged bed, pillows and blankets strewn about—thank God she had them—looking at me as if to say, *What happened?* Her bodily functions were working just fine, the evidence of which was bobbing around inside the back of the Jeep. I took it as a good sign—everything was still functioning in good order—and it was the first time I ever thanked God for something like that. It remains one of the most grateful instants of my life. Funny what makes an impression like that, a detail that becomes its own story. Millie was safe.

Behind me I heard cars pulling over and people getting out, shouts of "Are you all right?" between giant claps of thunder. I put one arm under Millie's belly and the other under her chest. "Time to learn how to swim, sweetheart." Not quite the way I envisioned it, not a peaceful summer afternoon on the Green River.

I lifted her out of the Jeep and put her in the water. She looked up at me, panicky. "Just swim, Millie. You can do it." I gave her a little nudge. Dogs don't really swim, at least not like people. They mostly run in the water, the same motion as if they're on land. Millie had the advantage of webbed paws, common in water dogs, and a big buoyant chest that was just beginning to fill out at fourteen months.

She started to paddle, scrupulously keeping her snout above the surface, occasionally snorting and spouting water, casting me a glance now and then. On shore people were shouting, urging her on. "Come on! You can do it! Yeah!"

Thunder and lightning exploded above, and the rain nearly blinded me. It felt like the storm was jumping up and down on us, each burst of thunder like a shotgun blast and the rain hitting the water like buckshot. Millie kept on, undeterred, paddling, snorting. She was a dog who suddenly knew what she was about, a dog on a mission. She risked a look behind to see if I was okay. In a few minutes, we were clawing our way on shore and climbing up the embankment to the road where hands helped us the rest of the way. There was clapping and cheering for Millie and concerned looks for me, some of which I took to be more dubious than sympathetic. Millie shook herself off and went around greeting her fans, swamp water flying off her whipping tail. We were wrapped in blankets and towels. The cops arrived. I was ushered to the back of a patrol car to give my account, and Millie ended up in somebody's van, getting warm and sharing a turkey sandwich with the driver. A woman came forward with an extra collar and leash she excavated from her trunk. She was a *Guideposts* reader, as it turned out.

A tow truck came to drag the totaled Jeep from the swamp, all dripping and oozing with mud and muck, like *The Creature from the Black Lagoon*, a movie that scared me as a kid, but not as much as this. This *really* scared me. By now the adrenaline had completely fried my nerves and a creeping sense of guilt began to supersede the elation of being alive. The rain had eased and I got a good look at the wreck. The front passenger side was completely crushed. Anyone sitting there would not have survived. It was exactly where Julee would have been sitting if I hadn't been such a pest.

That night Millie and I sat in front of the woodstove, trying to get warm. I'd borrowed a car from a friend so we could get around for a couple of days. Tonight, we were content to stay inside and watch out the front window as the sunset bruised the westward hills, the kind of moody sunset you get in the wake of violent weather when the atmosphere is recovering. The storms that had swept through brought a cold front behind them. I threw more wood on the fire.

Millie was curled up at my feet. We'd been shivering since we emerged from the swamp, but now warmth seeped into us.

She was breathing deeply, peacefully. I wondered if she was dreaming (in fact she would have nightmares for the rest of her life, something I have never forgiven myself for and hope I never do). For the first time since we left the road and went airborne my heartbeat slowed from a gallop to a canter. With the warmth came a peace, an easing of guilt and fear, a peace that I and my dog had been watched over. I didn't pray once during the accident. I had no time to even think. Only react. Now I let my mind drift into a prayerful state. No words, just a spiritual focus. I tried to open my soul so that God could gaze into it and discern my incredible gratitude for keeping us all safe. Maybe I didn't deserve it, but Millie and Julee did. Finally, I managed to say, "Thank you for the bravest dog ever." And somehow, even if I had almost killed her, I felt closer to Millie than ever, a deeper friendship born of adversity. We'd been through it, all right.

Of course, the cops could not let such a dramatic accident as ours go without an official response. I hadn't been speeding, but they wrote me a summons for driving too fast for conditions anyway, kind of a catchall violation. I certainly wasn't going to argue. I just wanted to go home.

I'd tossed the ticket on a low ledge near where we hang Millie's leash without giving it a second thought. The next morning, I discovered its soggy remains shredded on the floor. Millie was going through a paper-chewing phase, but I couldn't help thinking she just might be trying to make me feel better.

But sitting there that night of the accident with Millie, warming my still sodden feet and staring at the fire crackling and snapping in the woodstove, I thought of those early humans gathered around the communal fire, their dogs at their sides, a hard day of the hunt behind them, or maybe ahead of them. The men and the dogs resting, allowing their strength and courage to build. Dogs must have impressed those ancients with the depth and selflessness of their bravery, a courage that would travel through time down to the dog that slept beside me now.

The day after the accident in the storm, Millie and I decided to head back to the city. Julee was anxious to see us in one piece and we had to surrender the loaner car anyway. I had the Berkshire pet taxi take us to the Metro-North train station in Wassaic, a little more than an hour away. Dogs were allowed on Metro-North trains.

Millie took the window seat, sitting up straight, almost regally, and watching the northern Dutchess County farmland roll by. Fortunately, we didn't see any horses (more on that later), but she woofed a few times at some dairy cows. Apparently, she was reserving judgment. Eventually the conductor entered the car to collect tickets. I handed him mine. He did a classic double take when he saw Millie.

"Dogs have to be on the floor," he said. His voice was clipped and officious, no apparent daylight for compromise. Millie spared him a brief glance.

"She likes to look out the window," I said.

"Those are the rules. Dogs ride on the floor."

An older woman, the kind that still dressed up for a trip to the city, chimed in. "Don't be ridiculous. She isn't bothering anyone."

"Those are the rules, ma'am."

A male voice farther back in the car joined in. "Come on, man. Let her sit there. She's better behaved than a lot of people I see on these trains."

Laughter broke out. "And cleaner, too," someone else said. More laughter. I caught the conductor suppressing a smile. Maybe he was thinking of his own dog.

"All right. She can stay. But she goes on the floor if the car gets crowded. I'm probably gonna hear about this!"

I thanked him and put my arm around my golden. We rode like that all the way into the city, like we were made for each other, truly best friends, perfectly comfortable to just sit together in silence, watching the farmland transform into small towns, small towns into suburbs, suburbs into an urban tangle, and finally the subterranean run into Grand Central, where we disembarked, strolled through the magnificent Beaux Arts concourse with the universe on the ceiling, and caught a cab home.

Within a week we had a new Jeep. I'd put the accident behind me, or so I thought, until it was time to head back up to the house. Millie refused to get into the Jeep. She looked at me like I was crazy.

"Come on, Mil!" I used my happy voice, clapping my hands and slapping my thighs. "Come on!" After you've had a few dogs you tend to lose the kind of inhibitions normal adults retain.

No deal. There was no way she was going to get back in that death trap. I placed a treat strategically on the backseat so she would have to climb in to get it. She wouldn't budge. I added a second. She turned her head away. *Oh my God, what have I done to her?* I told Julee what was going on and she gave me a dark, accusing look. I hated those looks. I felt my metaphorical tail slip between my legs. "Call Jane," she said. Jane was a trainer who had worked with Millie not long after we got her.

Jane came right over and was eventually able to coax Millie into the backseat, but it was clear Millie wasn't happy about it no matter how much we practiced and praised her. Even just driving around the block Millie would pant anxiously. Jane worked with her a few more times with only marginal improvement. "She is the most stubborn dog I ever met," Jane said, shaking her head.

We recruited Winky again, who loved riding in cars. Julee and I thought Winky might be able to allay Millie's traumatic fears. Winky's presence helped, but Millie still wasn't comfortable. Her best friend couldn't help with this. How could I help my dog?

We bought her an herbal collar that, we were promised by the purveyor, would create a kind of temporary nirvana. All it did was make her itch. And the anxious panting did not abate. It broke my heart to say nothing of what it did to my conscience. It wore on me. This was all my fault. Millie loved going to the country and now I'd ruined it for her.

Eventually, I poured my heart out to Dr. Barbara, her Berkshire vet. Millie was sitting next to me in the examining room. I half expected her to be nodding in agreement: *Yes, that's correct, he crashed the Jeep into the swamp in the middle of a thunderstorm. I was trapped in back and got wet.*

I went over everything we had tried with Millie. "She still pants all the way up here. It's three hours. I'm afraid she's going to have a heart attack. I'm just sick about this."

"No," Dr. Barbara said, "she won't have a heart attack. She's just nervous, like someone who is afraid of flying. She's a dog so she pants instead of sweats. What she does have is a classic case of PTSD. Post-traumatic stress disorder. The accident happened at an incredibly impressionable age. Their brains are like soft clay—they're absorbing everything. The experience imprinted deep on Millie's psyche. I'm not sure we can change that very much." Dr. Barbara gave Millie a pat and a treat, which is one reason Millie loved going to the vet's.

"But we can try giving her a sedative before long car trips. Alprazolam works well," Dr. Barbara said.

"Alprazolam?"

"Yes, Xanax."

"Xanax? You want to give my dog Xanax?"

"They respond well and metabolize it very quickly, so it's quite short acting. It probably won't knock her out—she's way too anxious in the car—but it will calm her."

At that moment, I absolutely hated myself. And that self-loathing was only compounded by my own long, ugly battle with drugs and alcohol years earlier. By the grace of God, I had been sober for a good long time a day at a time and now I was giving dope to my dog? It felt so wrong!

After that, it always terrified Millie to get into the car for the long ride up to western Massachusetts (though she was okay with short trips). And yet she always did it, and rode stoically in the backseat, panting heavily most of the way up. But once she was there, she was as happy a dog as I have ever known. When her time came, one of the last things I said to her was how sorry I was about the accident all those years before. We were sitting in the yard, Millie at my feet, a late summer breeze riffling her fur. I started to unburden myself of my guilt, then realized how absurd it must seem and caught myself, though not before I started to cry. Millie looked up at me and rolled on her back for a belly scratch. I'm pretty sure that's how dogs say, "I forgive you."

CHAPTER 3

Maybe you've noticed that Julee and I are crazy about our dogs. You might suppose that it's because we don't have children. I don't think that correlates. I don't believe dogs or pets are substitutes for children any more than I think children are substitutes for dogs (though I could be persuaded). Julee and I decided not to have children for various and complicated reasons. It was a difficult and very, very personal decision. But we always knew we'd have dogs.

We love across species in such a profoundly different way than we love our own. The two forms of love are not the same. Our hearts give us no choice but to love our children. At the very least we are obligated by nature and society to try, even if some parents love imperfectly or not at all. Even the best parental love can be tinged with conflicted feelings and insecurities.

Loving a dog is a choice. We can survive quite nicely without each other. A dog does not propagate my genes or carry on my family name, does not try to be like me or live up to my so-called accomplishments. Rarely do parents pressure their adult children relentlessly to produce a dog before they die. A dog will not support me in my old age. But she will love me deeply and unconditionally from the moment she enters my life. I will be the most important thing in her universe. Neither of us will ever hold a grudge against the other for more than a few minutes. No festering family feuds. She will sleep with me even when I snore like a drunken sailor and forgive me when I tromp on her tail even though she cannot comprehend how I could be such an oaf. She will spend all her life trying to figure me out, and she will sometimes succeed at it to such an unnerving degree that I believe she knows me better than I know myself. And if that doesn't keep me honest, I don't know what will.

All she wants in return is to be loved, and not necessarily in equal measure. We are not expected to dance around crazily when our dogs return from a long walk or roll over on our backs in ecstasy. I don't go running to the door with a ratty old toy in my mouth. No, we are expected to make their lives safe and secure. Dogs surviving in the madness of our civilization don't always possess the keenest coping mechanisms. Our neuroses are communicable. We can cause our dogs to be highstrung and edgy. All they want to know is that they are protected in a world dominated by humans, the most dangerous animal of all but the ones to whom they are ineluctably wed.

Or maybe the real reason I love dogs is because one introduced me to Julee, with a little bit of divine intervention. In fact, I never would have met my future wife if her dog Rudy hadn't intervened in the most remarkable and prescient way at what turned out to be the right moment but felt so wrong at first.

I was walking aimlessly (or so I thought) down West Seventy-Second Street in Manhattan, a few blocks south from where I dwelt at the time, on a seemingly ordinary May evening. I glanced at the building I was passing just to see if Tiny Tim was around. Everyone said that personification of sixties' craziness lived there, and once I thought I saw him disappearing into the lobby with a bag of groceries, a small-ish dog on a glittery leash slipping in behind him. Across the street was an incomprehensibly named building, the Oliver Cromwell, the sight of which almost always made my Irish blood simmer a bit. What would possess someone to name an apartment building after that English fiend? Why not call a building the Attila the Hun?

But I digress.

Further down the side of the street I was traveling was a building of both architectural and cultural significance that had loomed bastion-like over Central Park for more than a century. Funded from the coffers of the Singer family, they of the sewing machine fortune, the storied Dakota had seen and made history. Roman Polanski filmed the demonic *Rosemary's Baby* there, and twelve years later, a true demon holding a copy of the J. D. Salinger novel *Catcher in the Rye* in one hand and a gun in the other shot and killed John Lennon just inside the entryway to the building as Lennon was returning from a recording session. We all know where we were when that happened. I was trying to wait tables in this la-di-da French restaurant in New Haven, Connecticut, after getting kicked out of the playwriting program at the Yale School of Drama, banished for a year.

I often looked for Yoko when I was near the Dakota. Once I met her dog walker picking up after her beautiful Labs and struck up a conversation, which I kept brief because he had his hands full. Folks who walk and pick up after dogs to the stars can be a bit snooty, by dint of their tangential propinquity to fame, I assume. But he was perfectly congenial, though I didn't pry too much about Yoko and I never saw her, except once, perhaps, in the fog, black-clad, being helped out of a sleek black sedan just a few yards from where her husband was assassinated.

It was in the region between Tiny Tim and Yoko Ono, a sidewalk crowded with purposeful pedestrians, that I espied Rudy, a corpulent, buff-colored cocker spaniel, trundling at a measured but determined pace, completely undeterred in his tempered progress along the busy sidewalk by his fellow New Yorkers, who were using their two legs to get past him on his four. Attached to the other end of his braided leather leash with matching collar was a dazzling blonde with massive clover-green eyes. I could almost feel a kind of zephyr when she batted her thickly mascaraed lashes.

"That's the fattest cocker spaniel I've ever seen," I couldn't help myself from blurting out, instantly hoping against hope that this might by some miracle prove to be a good conversation starter. I was met with a dismissive glare. Julee kept moving, but Rudy suddenly grew obstinate. He stopped, looked up at me, woofed matter-of-factly, and bulldozed his way over, dragging a scowling Julee behind him and nearly toppling her off her skyscraper Valentino pumps. She was an actress and singer, I was soon to learn, rushing home from an audition to walk her dog. I would say she was not in the greatest mood, and I was doing little to improve it.

We walked around the block together while I tried to smooth-talk my way out of my opening conversational salvo, and the more I gabbled, the more I sensed Julee was trying to keep the corners of her mouth from drifting upward.

"Rudy has the most magnificent ears I've ever seen," I said, and it was true.

"Thank you." That got me another turn around the block.

"And his tail is very expressive for being so . . . stubby."

"It's called docking. I wish they didn't do it."

"Do you ever see Yoko?"

"No, but I know her dog walker."

"So do I!"

That gave me a way to direct the conversation away from my comment about Rudy's weight, though he really was a porker if the truth be told and he kept lunging at anything remotely edible.

"Sometimes in the morning I see Mary Tyler Moore walking her young golden, Dash. She lives in the San Remo. She did something really nice for me."

Julee had a beautiful sixteen-year-old-niece named Jenny back in Iowa with whom she was especially close, almost like sisters. "Jenny wants to be an actress, too," she said. But that probably wasn't going to happen. Jenny was also a severe type 1 diabetic and had recently lapsed into an irreversible coma brought on by diabetic shock. She was officially diagnosed as vegetative by her neurological team, but Julee held out hope that somewhere deep inside Jenny there was a metaphysical spark that no damage to the brain could ever douse, like solar flares pluming off the soul. "When I hold her hand I feel something more than warmth and flesh," she told me. "There's someone still there. I read to her."

Jenny's favorite book was *The Velveteen Rabbit*, so one day while Rudy and Dash were doing their dog greeting thing, Julee asked Mary if she would record the story for Julee to play for Jenny. Mary, a type 1 diabetic herself, agreed. *Man*, I thought, *this woman has guts*.

"And the reason Rudy is overweight is because he's coming off a couple of years of prednisone. It's steroid bloat."

"What's wrong with him?"

"He has hemolytic anemia and possibly a complement deficiency. Doctors are studying us because I have lupus and they think it's unusual both of us would have these similar conditions."

Lupus. A disease named for the wolf . . .

Suddenly, as if to impress me with his canine virility, lest I think age and illness and corpulence had diminished him, Rudy provoked a squabble with a larger, younger dog that was all growling and slobbering and leash entanglement from which I eventually extricated him without harm to either combatant. I walked Julee and Rudy to their building on Seventy-Second Street.

"Do you ever see Tiny Tim?"

"Sure. I was behind him in line the other day at the store. He was buying paper towels. He pet Rudy."

Rudy looked up at me all smiles about his brush with fame, apparently.

I'd run out of conversation at that point but believed I was coming close to redeeming myself, clawing my way out of that conversational abyss. Julee showed lukewarm interest in my offer of Chinese food later that week, scribbled her number on a taxi receipt excavated from the depths of her bag almost as an afterthought, and disappeared into the elevator, Rudy giving me a final look over his shoulder as he slipped past the closing door. Upstairs on the twelfth floor, unbeknownst to me of course, Julee let herself into her apartment, tossed Rudy a treat (prednisone wasn't the only reason he was so portly), and called her mom back in Iowa. "Mom," she said, "I just met the man I'm going to marry."

Rudy vibrated his stubby tail and demanded another treat. He thought he deserved it. And he did.

Me? I was hoping just to see her again. On the way back to my place eleven blocks uptown, I ducked into a pet store on Columbus Avenue. Usually you get the girl a little something. I got Rudy a toy, Mr. Fancy Ball, planning to drop it off with Julee's doorman in the morning. An inner voice told me it would be a good idea. And as I climbed the steps to my own apartment building, it occurred to me that sometimes God shouts, sometimes he whispers, and sometimes he sends a woof.

OUR RELATIONSHIP TOOK OFF from there—Julee, Rudy, and me. And I'm not sure we would have made it without Rudy in the mix. Rudy had that gift for defusing a situation, especially those situations that arise early in a relationship. Julee and I could be having a strained discussion over where to go to eat or what movie to see or what friends to meet for coffee. Of course, the discussion really had little to do with eating or going to the movies or what friends to favor. It had to do with testing limits and defining the dynamics of a new relationship. And whenever things got a little too strained, Rudy would intervene. His favorite strategy was to bring us one of his toys. Not just any toy. He usually appeared carrying the aforementioned Mr. Fancy Ball in his mouth. And usually it worked.

Julee called home to Iowa periodically to see how everyone was doing. But I knew she really wanted to talk to Jenny. Her sister, Kate, would hold the phone to Jenny's ear (Jenny lived in an addition Kate and her husband, Mike, built onto their house so they could care for her at home) and Julee would tell her all about her work, New York, Rudy, me. I would watch Julee, sitting cross-legged on the couch, laughing, singing, hyper-animated, talking to Jenny for about as long as she talked to the rest of her family combined. She'd finally, reluctantly, hang up with a cheery good-bye that faded into a hollow echo as soon as the phone hit the cradle and her smile would disappear, like a wisp of smoke blown away by a breeze. Her body would fall in on itself slightly. I didn't know Jenny. I barely knew Julee, really. I didn't know what to do or, more to the point, what to say, because someone like me thinks words are always the answer. Without words, I am lost. So I would just sit there in a fixed state, not knowing quite what to do.

Rudy knew. He would trot over, lift his bulk onto the

couch, and put a paw on Julee. And he would keep it on her. Once he looked over at me as if to say, *This is how you do it.* And so I did. No words, no words.

But it was another time with Rudy, an episode that would bind us immutably, that I have come to know as one of the deepest moments of connection I have ever had with a dog, a moment profound and transfiguring, refluent to the very beginnings of our joined history, man and dog.

Julee was appearing in a musical revue at the Village Gate playing, among other singing legends, Janis Joplin, which was really doing a number on her vocal cords. On this particular weekend, they'd added an extra midnight show on Friday followed by a VIP meet-and-greet for special guests of the producers, including an up-and-coming singer who claimed to be quite the material girl.

Julee asked if I would mind letting Rudy sleep over at my apartment since she would be engaged until quite late. It was no problem at all. I was dogless at the time, so this was a rare and exciting opportunity for canine companionship and bonding. One important way dogs form attachments is through sleep-bonding. Why do you think they always want to jump into bed with you? So they can feel secure and attached, so they can solidify their connection to (and possession of) you, and so they can hog the sheets and drool on the pillows.

"Are you sure he'll want to stay in a strange apartment away from you?"

"He loves you, Edward. Don't worry."

"How often does he have to go out? He's getting up there in years. Can he make it through the night?"

Julee scoffed. "Of course, he can. He'll only get you up if he's having a real problem, only if it's an emergency. He's a good dog. He'll let you know."

That night on my way home from work I dropped by Julee's apartment to collect Rudy (and Mr. Fancy Ball, of course). We went for a long walk in Central Park. We visited Frederick Roth's famous sculpture of the sled dog Balto, hero of an early twentieth-century diphtheria outbreak in Alaska. Rudy gave stony Balto a sniff and a woof and pretended not to be impressed. Then we walked east until we came upon the statue of Hans Christian Andersen near Fifth Avenue. I thought Rudy might go after the sculpted Ugly Duckling figure situated near the great author's feet. I pointed and made quacking noises and flapped my arms. Rudy looked at me like I was a fool. Besides, it was time for his dinner.

So I took him home and fed him, but not before stopping at my corner deli for a few things, including a sandwich I wanted to have at the ready while watching the Yanks play Boston on TV that night. The owner, my friend Hassan, took a real shine to my loaner dog and sliced off a generous piece of bologna, which Rudy devoured like I imagined a Tasmanian devil might devour bologna.

Rudy and I watched the game, which the Yanks won in extras and through which Rudy mostly snored, and we turned in. He seemed tired from our long walk in the park.

At some point in the absolute dead of night I felt something wet and cold and rough on my cheek, then my nose, then my forehead accompanied by licking and slobber. I awoke with a start and a garbled cry.

"Rudy?"

He was sitting at the end of the bed, panting, shifting his weight from side to side, his eyes bright and urgent in the gloom. Immediately I remembered Julee's words: "He'll get you up if it's an emergency."

I leapt from bed, grabbed a pair of jeans, which I tried to don while lurching toward the closet, occasioning a kind of hopping, pirouetting process of pulling the pants on. I snatched a T-shirt from the dirty laundry because it was the closest at hand, kicked my feet into some shoes, and grabbed the leash, all the while saying, "Good boy, what a good boy to let me know, such a good boy. Hang on, I'm hurrying. Hang on. Good boy. Don't pee on anything . . ."

I got the leash on him, wondering if maybe the bologna wasn't the culinary culprit. *That was dumb*. I upbraided myself all the way down the stairs to the street. I didn't want to chance the elevator. That could be a disaster. I didn't even want to contemplate it, Rudy having an accident in the elevator car and it getting away from us before we could clean up, some poor person on an upper floor walking into that situation.

The air was warm and electric, the way only Manhattan is in summer at three thirty in the morning. Rudy immediately pulled me toward Columbus Avenue and around the corner . . . to Hassan's deli. Did I mention it was open 24/7? Oh, I didn't.

Rudy bulled past the guy dropping off bundles of the *Daily News* and made a beeline for the deli counter where Hassan was prepping for the morning rush. The back of my neck flushed hot at the canine scam I had just fallen victim to.

"Ah! You are back for more meat!" Hassan laughed, pulling the bologna out from the cooler. Rudy grinned appreciatively and activated his tail-stub. He sat patiently and looked back at me.

"You sneak!" I hissed.

Rudy gobbled the bologna. Hassan gave him another and me a slice and took one for himself, whereupon the three of us stood in a little circle like any three males at three thirty in the morning anywhere in the world, chewing our meat thoughtfully, nodding appreciatively, as if having a cocker spaniel–instigated midnight bologna bash was the most natural, manly thing in the world.

And somehow, suddenly, it was. Why not run down to the deli for bologna in the middle of the night? Nothing could have made more sense to Rudy or made him happier. After all, this was guy bonding. He acted like it was the most amazing thing ever, to be able to do that. When we finally got back into bed, I gave him a big hug and said, "But no more." To God I said, "Don't ever let me forget what this moment feels like." And I haven't.

JULEE AND I GOT married a couple of years later, semi-eloping to the Bahamas (we announced the elopement; Julee said she dressed up in a costume for a living and didn't want to do it for her wedding).

I don't think we ever would have made it to that little aquamarine church in Nassau if it wasn't for Rudy. The two of us loving something equally and passionately, the way we both loved Rudy, only brought Julee and me closer. And of course, there was the time I saved Rudy's life. I suppose that really sealed the deal.

I was walking him one evening right after his dinner. You'd be wrong if you thought his appetite might have been sated at least partially. Rudy's appetite, like most dogs', was on constant overdrive, like some famished demon was at the controls. You could feed him a whole bag of dog food and he'd still look at you like he was on the verge of starvation, eyes pleading for one more measly morsel before he fainted. So on this night, like on most of our nightly ambles, Rudy's nose was sweeping the street, like olfactory sonar, for something, anything remotely edible— soggy pizza crust, a renegade French fry, a grease-soaked napkin. On this particular night, he really scored.

He got a broken hunk of bone. It could have been part of a cow's femur. I couldn't tell. I made a desperate pull on the leash, but for a fat old dog Rudy was quick, quicker than me. The bone was in his mouth and halfway down his gullet before I fully reacted. I jerked hard, really hard because my temper had gotten a bit of the better of me, and that was probably my mistake. I noticed Rudy stop dead still. His sides were heaving, but he didn't seem to getting any air. He looked at me, panicked. *What have I done?* I thought desperately. Rudy was lurching around near some garbage cans, trying to dislodge the bone from his throat. *God, I think I've killed this dog. I've only got a minute or two. You have to help me. Julee will never forgive me. I'll never forgive me. I don't know what to do.*

Yet suddenly, miraculously, I did. I remembered an article I had helped edit by a man named Heimlich. It was about how to save a person from choking. Would it work on a dog? Well, it had to.

I lifted Rudy (no small feat), put my arm under his chest where I guessed his diaphragm was, and attempted an exploratory squeeze. Nothing. I remembered Dr. Heimlich telling us the compression had to be applied with considerable force, even if you risked bruising or possibly cracking a rib. I gave Rudy a hard squeeze. And again. Harder.

Out popped the hunk of bone—a slimy, arcing projectile. It flew a few feet and smacked a passing woman on her bare leg. She looked appalled.

"I'm sorry," I said. By now I was laughing with relief and at the fact that Rudy was actually trying to retrieve the bone to have another go at it. "I just saved his life . . ." I said, leaning into the leash two-handed, but I was laughing too hard at her horrified expression to complete a sentence. "I'm . . . sorry . . ." It was some kind of hysterical reaction to stress that only eased after she stalked off and I had kicked the offending bone down a storm drain. By then Rudy was back to sniffing.

What woman wouldn't marry the man who saved her dog's life?

The first year of marriage, as any honest couple will admit, is touch and go at best. You need all your emotional and spiritual reserves to survive it. And your wits about you at all times. It is a period of enormous adjustment and growth, and growth is hard, it is painful. But you emerge better and stronger and more loving for it. If you make it.

Rudy helped us make it. He made us take the focus off ourselves at exactly the right moment. He was a master of comic relief. And an objective referee. If either one of us raised our voice one decibel above what he had somehow determined was the acceptable acoustic limit he would march around barking: *Time out! Time out!*

What I remember him most for that year was our first dinner party on a crisp fall night, a night when winter is trying to get its foot in the door. We lived in a walk-up box that could have easily passed as a medium-sized storage unit in most other parts of the country. Yes, it had a kitchen and an area where a table could be put up. A bedroom that was only a few square feet bigger than the queen-sized bed that occupied it.

We cooked coq au vin, one of my few gastronomic specialties. Julee did the baking, the salad, and the dessert. And the *gougères*. Julee is a serious cook. Nevertheless, we were tense, sniping here and there. Julee was worried about all the things that could go wrong. Basically, I was oblivious to them. I just wondered if we could actually fit these people in our diminutive, subletted space, and what the heck we would do with their coats.

Our guests arrived more or less on time, just as I was finishing the coq au vin and sweeping the bones into the trash. I received the coats and scarves and threw them on the bed. What else to do with them? The closets were all packed with stuff. I risked an ironing board decapitating me every time I opened one. The place was so crowded I could barely find my own foot.

Timing is everything when serving. We had a few tight minutes. Julee broke a mild sweat, and I muttered a few fragmentary oaths and prayers under my breath. I guess the most remarkable thing about the evening was Rudy's surprisingly exemplary behavior. I'd talked to him earlier about no begging, no bullying, no harassing. He seemed to understand and had not made a nuisance of himself the whole time. In fact, we'd barely seen him.

The night was shaping up to have been a great success, much to our relief, when I went to retrieve our guests' coats. I carried them out in a big heap. "Help yourselves," I said, my arms starting to buckle.

People did. And as they extracted their wraps from the pile I held, things began dropping out, dripping out. The coats were raining chicken bones.

"Oh my goodness!" one woman exclaimed.

Rudy! I gave Julee an urgent look. Rudy had invaded the garbage—stealthily, I should add—retrieved all of the chicken bones left from the coq au vin preparation and systematically buried them in our guests' coats. Don't ask me what he was thinking. I will never know. Only God knows. And I think he was probably scratching his head. Don't think I don't plan to ask for an explanation someday, though.

There was a moment of shocked silence, then a lone snicker, then an aw-shucks guffaw, and finally a burst of laughter. Soon everyone was doubled over at Rudy's dog madness. He stood there, paws planted stubbornly on the foyer floor, looking as if he didn't understand our reaction. As if he would never completely understand human beings. The guests all gave him a pat on the head as they squeezed out of our place.

Now the night really was a success. Julee and I cleaned up cheerily and Rudy got a little leftover chicken. But no bones.

Rudy lived a long life that was inextricably entwined with the life I would live with Julee for many years after he went to his reward. His mark was indelible. He was an unforgettable presence, our divinely dispatched matchmaker. I still talk to Rudy in my head, mostly about the dogs we have had since. I ask him for advice. He usually tells me to chill out. Dogs know how to take care of themselves.

There came a day around age fifteen when poor Rudy could no longer take care of himself. It wasn't one specific ailment or misery, but a conspiracy of symptoms and woes that were simply getting the better of him. We'd spent many, many hours in the emergency room at the famed Animal Medical Center on Manhattan's East Side. AMC is the Bellevue of animal hospitals. The ER is basically, well, a zoo. I guess I shouldn't be surprised at the strange and wondrous variety of creatures New Yorkers harbor because this is, after all, New York. I swear I saw an ocelot, which was rushed to a treatment room probably because it was illegal to have one, the scraggly owner following furtively. But the good doctors at AMC will treat any sick or suffering creature, and they are the best in the world. Julee, Rudy, and I saw snakes, goats, vultures, an electric eel in a fish tank, among the usual array of dogs and cats in the ER. It's a 24/7 show.

That's where we took Rudy one fall morning when we knew it was time for the saddest decision we could make, and maybe the first really important decision we had made as a married couple. We'd tried to feed him some prime rib the night before, but he refused. He hadn't been eating regularly for a while, a sure sign that life is losing its meaning for a cocker spaniel.

A nice vet from South Africa met us in a treatment room. She'd seen Rudy before and warned us he didn't have much time left, but she was very kind and understanding about it. She never tried to push us into a decision and seemed quietly pleased we had arrived at this point on our own.

"If you're ready, I can take him back now." We nodded and took off his leash and collar. We hugged him and told him we loved him and that he was going someplace where there was no more pain. The last thing I whispered to him was thank you, and then he was gone.

It seemed strange that we wouldn't be with him. We really hadn't thought about the process. We just surrendered him. It felt like a betrayal. We dropped the leash and collar in the waiting room. Maybe somebody could use them. The whole thing just seemed so wrong. "We're never going to do it that way again," Julee said. I nodded. We walked up First Avenue.

"Should we get a cab?"

"No," she said. "I can't go back to an apartment without a dog in it."

So off we went. By then Julee was doing a show at the Variety Arts Theatre, a mash-up of Shakespeare's *The Tempest*, peppered with vintage pop and rock songs (her big show-stopping second act number was "Go Now," originally recorded by the Moody Blues) and a cheesy old sci-fi movie called *Forbidden Planet*. The show had been a huge hit in London and snatched the coveted Olivier Award from *The Phantom of the Opera*, which I wrote off to the ennui of the Brits for having bestowed endless honors on Andrew Lloyd Webber. That night for the first time ever, Julee called in sick for a performance and let her understudy go on.

I didn't cry that day. I was numb. Frozen. It had been years since I lost a dog. Then coming home from work one night I saw our trash sitting out on the curb. With a new dog on premises (Sally, whom you will meet soon enough), we finally agreed to dispose of Rudy's old things. Peeking out from under the lid was shredded and chewed Mr. Fancy Ball. I sat down on a stoop and wept.

I should explain those tears. Earlier in this book I mentioned that I had been sober for a number of years. But not for very long when I met Rudy. The night when Rudy first found me on West Seventy-Second Street, I was sorely in need of finding. I was a few weeks out of a drug and alcohol detox unit, where I had been rushed after suffering alcoholic withdrawal seizures, flopping around on upper Broadway on a hot Saturday morning like a beached game fish, some well-meaning but misguided soul rushing out of a coffee shop to jam a spoon between my jaws, which only resulted in a bunch of cracked fillings. In fact, when I first spoke to Julee I still had thick slabby scabs on various extremities from slamming myself into the pavement in the throes of those convulsions. I was scabbed over in other ways, I'm sure.

Maybe that's why my first attempt at conversation was a bit disordered. I'm not sure my neurons had completely unscrambled themselves, or ever would, because brain damage was definitely in my immediate future if not already the case. You can't unscramble scrambled eggs, as they say. My neurons and I had been through the wringer. I'd been an alcoholic since my late teens at least and probably since my virgin lips kissed that first revelatory drop of whiskey, a brand, ironically, called Old Grand-Dad, when I was maybe thirteen, on a chilly autumn night in the apple orchard behind my parents' house in Birmingham, Michigan, the light from a nearly full moon making the label look as if it were aglow. My paternal grandfather was my alcoholic progenitor, from what I know. And when I poured that first shaft of liquid light down my throat, I felt it pierce a place in my soul that had always been shrouded by hidden doubts and fear. It burned like a demon and warmed me like the sun itself. I didn't just think I liked this new feeling. I thought, I want to feel like this *all the time*.

And I tried. With fervor. Perhaps the world enabled me because I did well in school and put my talents to use. But it was my own driven will that propelled me at Mach speed down the Jellinek Chart, the famous clinical roadmap to alcoholic recovery or ruin. By my twenties I was suffering the delirium tremens and using all sorts of drugs to replace or supplement the drinking, which only made things worse . . . and I always came back to alcohol anyway, day or night, first thing in the morning and last thing at end of the day. Brutal, relentless, solitary, suicidal blackout drinking. My thirst, as the Irish say, could have cast a shadow. Was I drinking myself to death? Only by default. Actually, I was living only for the next drink. Death was just a clinical side effect, a contraindication.

I finally wrested my MFA from Yale Drama after being constrained to take a year off (a year from which many probably never expected me to return), but there were a few people, true angels, who still believed in me and to whom I am still hopelessly grateful to this very day, immortal fixtures on my lengthy gratitude list. I more or less lived in the psychiatric wing of the Yale Student Health Service in my final semester, being turned loose to go to classes, work-study, and the library, usually lightly tranquilized and full of Antabuse, an unspoken condition of my readmittance to the MFA program.

Within months of graduation, free of the kind of institutional supervision and structure an education imposes, I'd lost what few jobs I could get, landed on the streets of Manhattan and Hoboken, New Jersey (and in hospitals and rehabs and ERs and the back of patrol cars), begged for change in Lower Manhattan, smoked discarded cigarette butts I snatched out of the gutters, choked down the cheapest forms of alcohol I could lay hands on and . . . and . . . got sober.

Through no fault of my own, I might add. A confluence of people, forces, and sneaky little miracles swirled together to transport me into the AA rooms. I was drinking rubbing alcohol cut with grenadine and sniffing airplane glue in between bouts of vomiting blood when an old friend from Ann Arbor was shocked to find me in her apartment half-dead. I remember her pouring the dregs of a tall boy of Olde English 800 malt liquor over my head and then firing the empty at me in disgust. But she got me to a twelve-step room on Perry Street in the Village by marching me through a torrential rainstorm (where is a cab when you really need one?) and beating me about the head and shoulders with her umbrella to keep me from veering into a liquor store. My friend was not in recovery herself, but she knew people who were, and they swooped in to take me under their wings.

I'd tried AA and twelve-step rehabs before—like I tried Brussels sprouts when I was a kid—and didn't develop a taste for it or for the God stuff either. I was raised in the church and the church was still in me, but I'd long since doused those embers and could see no part God might play in my troubles. If I had a god, it was alcohol. And in that sense, I knew quite intimately and fundamentally the power and omnipotence of God. Alcohol had created my universe.

Two men in particular came to my rescue. They appointed themselves my sponsors and they told me not to worry too much about the God stuff and just let God worry about me. One was a restaurant manager and the other a playwright-waiter. Both were gay, not that it mattered. Not that I cared. How could I? I was in no position to judge. I was in no position, period.

I did everything they suggested. I went to meetings daily, often a dozen a week, and helped clean up afterward, putting away chairs and sweeping the floors. I called my sponsors when I felt the slightest itch to get high. I read the Big Book, AA's bible, and I prayed. Prayed?

"I can't pray," I'd protested vehemently. Prayer, I thought, was for weaklings. "I don't believe in it."

"Pretend," they said. "And stay humble. You really need to do that, Edward."

So I said pretend prayers to a pretend God. A week or so into my newfound sobriety, I turned thirty, an age more than a few people would have put money on that I'd never make it to. Some of my friends in the fellowship said they were worried about me. I assured them I planned to spend a quiet night in the SRO where I was staying on the West Side, adjacent to the old railroad yards and with a peekaboo view of the Hudson. Ever since my days as a sailor on the Great Lakes ore boats, I liked to be within sight of the water whenever possible.

I was summarily overruled. I would instead attend a sober party, which sounded like the most absurd contradiction to me, but what the heck? I'd already signed on to be a teetotaling square. Which was how I found myself sitting in a chair against the wall at Gay Men's Health Crisis, sipping a Diet Coke with lemon. Apparently, it was the only place they could keep an eye on me.

It was the beginning days of the AIDS crisis in New York, the grim vanguard of the sick and dying having appeared over the medical and social horizons a year or so earlier. There is no way to convey the fear and irrationality that ran through the city and the country unless you were there at the epicenter. And I was there. Turning thirty on December 11, 1983. I guess it was a kind of Forrest Gump moment.

GMHC was ground zero in the fight against AIDS in New York. I had certainly heard of it, but I had never been inside until now. I was decidedly straight and busy killing myself in a far more self-directed and less contagious way. Was this my so-called Higher Power's idea of a joke?

I tilted my chair back. I was not a dancer. Too self-conscious. And who would I dance with here? Well, why not these people? The gay men and women in that room were all sober, many of them with a death sentence hanging over their heads, and they still chose to reach out to God, to life itself. They lived to die sober. Would I have been that brave? Or would I simply have hastened my own end?

Whatever the room had been used for during the day, everything had been shoved in the corners to accommodate a dance floor that was already slick with sweat and liberally spilled nonalcoholic drinks. The place was packed. Somebody had brought in a serious sound system with an absolutely prehistoric bottom range. The whole place reverberated with bass lines. I expected to see the walls going in and out like in an old Popeye cartoon. Prince and David Bowie and Culture Club, Duran Duran and the Clash, Donna Summer and Men at Work, Eddy Grant and the Pretenders: they threatened to pulverize the speakers. My hearing was shot after ten minutes. The room must have been ninety degrees even with the wide-open windows letting in the freezing December air.

So much of my life recently had pointed the way toward death, dusty or otherwise. I thought about dying more than I thought about anything, except maybe the next drink. Now, improbably, I found myself in a room where the emerging statistics said that as many half of these men could be dead in two years (many of them would be, as it turned out, some who had become my friends). Yet all around me there was life and love and belief. Faith and humility. All the things I suddenly realized I actually wanted and needed but thought were denied to me by some juxtaposition of fate and atavistic bad luck. Something I left behind way back when in that apple orchard tilting the whiskey bottle up into the moonlight.

I didn't dance, but I sat there all night feeling very much at home . . . and strangely at peace.

*　　*　　*

I HAD STAYED SOBER for almost three years, the proudest and happiest years of my life to date. I'd become treasurer of a popular Upper West Side meeting. I met and sponsored many wonderful sober people and found a serious job, which in the spring of 1986 had taken me to Europe and eventually to Copenhagen, Denmark, where I was only prevented from throwing myself from a high hotel window by the mysterious and completely unbidden intervention of a couple of Interpol agents whom no one could ever remember having sent to my room that night and no one was ever able to locate or identify afterward.

It's harrowing ground I covered in that earlier book, *The Promise of Hope*. Suffice to say that my sobriety dissipated with one long willful pull on a schooner of Carlsberg at a table on the Copenhagen waterfront one otherwise fine spring evening and ended almost a month later flopping around on upper Broadway. The one thing I learned is that you are never cured.

In the blackout terror of those mostly unaccounted for weeks in Denmark I did discover what probably saved my life at last, a startling connection to a Higher Power and the beginnings of faith, a mystery that was still being revealed in many amazing ways. So when that big burly cocker spaniel woofed at me on West Seventy-Second Street it felt like something preordained, something in a form God knew I could accept and trust.

Those early weeks of my rocky reentry into sobriety I spent a lot of time with Rudy. He'd look at me with those big wet eyes, and I felt things would be okay, even when the pan-

ics came, like breakers in a midnight tide pounding me down.
I was afraid I had lost my soul, that those three magical years
of sobriety were all I was allotted, that the connection between
me and something in the universe great and all-loving had
been severed for good. I had severed it. Me, at age thirty-two.
With my own hand wrapping itself around a drink and putting it to my doomed lips. I thought of altars and cathedrals,
vestments and liturgy, incense and penance, and I'd walk with
Rudy through the fertile smells of spring in Central Park and
feel weightless with relief, knowing that all that was asked
of me was a simple daily surrender to a power greater than
myself, that anything more complicated was unmanageable.
In the life of a dog I saw that simplicity in its most distilled
and unvexed form. A dog knows what it wants and needs, and
stays focused to those ends. My sole task was to stay focused on
being sober a day at a time.

In those days, you usually couldn't bring your dog into a
twelve-step meeting, though I managed on occasion to smug-
gle Rudy into the Hargrave House, which was large enough
that we could sit incognito in the back. Meetings were almost
always held in church basements, and there was often a con-
tingent of canines-in-waiting tied up out front, which always
goosed my spirits. Sometimes Rudy and I would just sit there
with the dogs and I would smoke and read the Big Book. Rudy
and I got a little career going, too. I snagged a freelance gig for
Seventeen magazine, ghostwriting an advice column under his
name. Rudy would test out new products like doggie ice cream
and squeaky toys and report to the readership, with my assistance, of course. The column ran with a picture of Rudy at my

old IBM Selectric (Rudy was old school) with a lovingly framed autographed picture of a stunning white standard poodle with a rhinestone collar next to it. And it was right around this time that I got a surprising call from a headhunter to whom I'd long forgotten I'd once given my resume, asking if I would be interested in interviewing at a publication called *Guideposts,* which I naturally assumed was a travel magazine.

No matter how old you are, early sobriety is just like adolescence. It can be as awkward and as painful and as thrilling as a middle school dance. My sponsors told me to take a job, any job, which is how I ended up at *Guideposts*, even after I learned it was not a travel magazine. A journey, perhaps, but that is another story. Anyway, it was like getting a first job all over again, and I fully intended to spend no more than one year there. Possibly less, depending on how much after-hours access I had to the copier for running off my new and improved resume.

Rudy's death a few years later felt like I had lost a big piece of my life, like a part of me had just fallen away. I'd lost a companion in my sobriety, a dog who had helped me find my way back to something I thought was lost forever and to Julee and marriage and work and life. He was a healer. Would I have gotten sober again without Rudy? Would Julee and I have stayed together? I ask these questions not necessarily to find an answer but to remind myself of the mysteries God lays before us to guide us in his steps.

OF COURSE, I AM not the only one who got sober with a kind of canine sponsor. Not long ago we published "Master of the

Hounds," a story by Los Angeles–based dog trainer Matt Beisner that spoke to me in an especially convincing way.

By his mid-twenties Matt Beisner had managed to make most of the wrong choices a young man can make. His life was a mess, a mess that nearly turned tragic late one night after closing time in Los Angeles.

He barely remembers leaving the club and climbing into his car. After that he remembers nothing at all until he came to in the back of a police car, handcuffed behind a steel mesh partition. Squinting in the spastic light cast by the whirling strobes atop various police and emergency vehicles, Matt could make out a mangled motorcycle on the side of the road and a man and a woman being loaded into ambulances. Sirens shattered the night as the ambulances roared off, a sound that tore deep into his conscience. "It was one thing to destroy my own life with alcohol," Matt remembers thinking. "To destroy the lives of these two strangers was another thing altogether."

Matt stared down at his shackled wrists. He'd never been so afraid, not since he was a little boy. He was not a praying man. "I knew about God," Matt says, "but I wasn't so sure he knew about me." Nevertheless, the urge to pray overpowered his fear, an urge that he was too weak to resist and too desperate to ignore. He bowed his head and asked—no, begged—God to spare the lives of that couple. "Whatever you want me to do I'll do. They didn't deserve this. Please don't take them, Lord. This is my fault. Take me!"

It was a prayer more sincere than courageous. Yet the guilt he felt was like a pain signal from the soul, a kind of spiritual ache every bit as real as its physical counterpart. Doctors say that feeling pain is a message from the body that you are still alive and kicking. Can remorse be a pain message from the soul?

By the grace of God, says Matt, the couple survived. Matt avoided jail by agreeing to enter a rehab facility. After he got out, he joined a twelve-step group. He came to believe that God did know about him and cared about him. A day at a time life got a little better. But early in his sobriety Matt broke a cardinal suggestion of the twelve-step program. "I started a new relationship in my first year, a definite no-no. You can't risk putting anything ahead of your program. But I met a girl and the girl had a dog."

I can totally understand that. Falling in love is a kind of high, a very powerful high even for the non-addict.

The dog was another issue completely. At the end of their first date Matt took the woman back to her house. She invited him in for a minute. Matt was feeling good about the date and the possibility of something more when the woman dropped a bombshell. "I hope you like my dog," she said, turning the key in the lock.

It was like the door to hell had been opened and out charged a demon. Well, actually it was a Tibetan terrier, all fifteen pounds of him. For all Matt cared it could have been a Tibetan *mastiff*.

Funny how our childhood traumas follow us through life. For Matt, it was Halloween night when he was seven. "I had just opened our neighbor's gate when a massive shape came hurtling out at me from the dark." A German shepherd. Snarling, teeth bared, fur up. "He was bigger than me, way bigger."

Before Matt could slam the gate and turn tail, the big dog sank his teeth into his scrawny right forearm. It took a minute for the pain to register through the panic. "Eventually the physical wounds healed but the emotional scars . . . not so much," admits Matt. "They became a part of me."

Now Matt fought the urge to jump back from his date's terrier. "I knew if I was to have any chance with this girl, I'd have to man up and face her fifteen-pound ball of fluff."

"Meet Kingston," the girl said cheerily. "He's only seven months." She sounded just like a proud mom.

"Hey, little guy," Matt said in what he hoped was a dog-friendly voice and not a fearful croak. He reached down to pet the little guy. *Grrrrr* . . . Kingston took a step forward. Matt flinched. He couldn't help himself. His date laughed. It must be funny, Matt thought, to see a ball of fluff make a grown man cower. The girl tugged him past the dog and through the door. Kingston lunged and snarled.

"Don't worry," Matt's date said. "He's a real sweetheart when you get to know him." Matt wasn't sure if she was talking to him or the dog.

The rest of the night was uneventful. Matt didn't even try to kiss her, fearing it might provoke a frenzied attack from the protective terrier. That's all he needed, to be taken down by a fluff ball while trying to make a move. *This dog hates me*, Matt thought as he slipped into his coat and took his leave, probably never to return.

And yet he liked the girl's laugh when Kingston had growled. She had a nice house, much cooler than his. So they had a few more dates. Matt started spending most days at the girl's house, trying to get his life together. Like her. The girl, now technically his girlfriend, had a life. She went to work, to the gym, to the grocery store. Ran errands and connected with friends. Matt used this time to halfheartedly search for jobs online. He tried to meditate and pray, as he had learned in rehab. Kingston came to tolerate his presence, barely.

The good thing about a girlfriend with a house is that the house usually has a refrigerator, which usually has food. One day Matt tore himself away from his desultory job search, in quest of a turkey sandwich. The fixings were all there. Then he sat down to enjoy his repast. He was about to take that first bite when . . .

Grrrrrrr . . .

It came from his feet. Kingston. Matt shooed him away gently. Kingston must have interpreted this as fainthearted-ness. He pressed his advantage.

Grrrrrrr . . .

Don't flinch, Matt warned himself. *Don't show weakness whatever you do. Or else this will never end.*

Matt totally ignored Kingston's display and carried on eat-ing his sandwich.

All at once there was another sound emanating from the vicinity of his feet, a new sound. It was a plaintive little whine, as sweet as it was pathetic. Matt stole a peek down at the dog. He was met with Kingston's imploring eyes. *Oh please*, they said, *share just a little bite. Then we could be friends.*

Yes, the eternal pact between dog and human.

Matt thought, *Maybe this dog isn't so tough. Maybe it's just an act and he's really just as scared as I am.*

Matt tugged a piece of turkey from between the bread and tentatively offered it to Kingston, the back of his mind swirling with images of a German shepherd hurtling out of the night, wondering if Kingston could leap up and seize the whole sandwich in one bite, tear it out of his hand, or just tear his hand off altogether?

Kingston surprised him. He took the offering ever so gently, no, politely. Matt could have sworn there was real gratitude in the dog's eyes. This wasn't begging. This was sharing. Lunch between the two became a routine. Soon they were going for long walks around the girlfriend's neighborhood.

It became clear to Matt that Kingston craved interaction, so Matt taught him a few tricks—sit, down, stay. Then Matt tried some more complicated moves. Kingston yearned to learn! Soon the two were completely in sync, communicating in a way Matt often had trouble with when it came to his fellow humans.

One night they had to show off. "Check this out," Matt told his girlfriend. "Kingston, come." Kingston trotted over. "Stay." Kingston stood stock still, eyes riveted on Matt. Matt pointed his finger at him. "Bang." Kingston flopped to the ground, rolled on his side motionless. One one thousand, two one thousand, three one thousand, four one thousand, five one thousand . . .

Finally, Matt said, "Good boy," and Kingston sprang up ready for his next feat. "This is an amazing transformation," the girlfriend said. "I thought you were going to faint when Kingston barked at you that first night."

It was not to last. The relationship with the woman, that is. She and Matt went their separate ways. But there was a parting gift. Matt got Kingston.

Matt volunteered at an LA animal shelter, helping to take care of abandoned pets. One day someone mentioned that the most frequently cited reason for giving up a pet was that the animal didn't behave in the home.

"Of course, they don't behave," Matt said. "They're animals. They have to be taught."

A whole bunch of lightbulbs went on. He asked one of the senior trainers to mentor him. "I'd worked with him just a few weeks when he told me, 'You have a gift with dogs, Matt. A calling.'" That seemed a bit over the top to Matt. Still he believed that if there were more good, compassionate trainers to help people properly acclimate their dogs to home and family life, to life with humans who themselves are sometimes pretty difficult to get along with, we wouldn't have to endure this cruel spectacle of man's best friend caged and subjugated, lonely for a human to bond with.

Then came a revelation, so strange it took Matt some time to accept. He was meditating one night when he heard a voice, as clear and emphatic as a wolf's midnight howl. It said, "This is your dog."

What was his dog? Suddenly an image came to his mind. A dog. An amazing dog. A good-sized animal with a thick golden coat and ears that stood up. An image so clear it was as if it was being revealed to him in some form of super HD.

Matt didn't know what to think. Maybe he was putting in too many hours at the shelter. Maybe he was letting this dog business get to him. Except the next morning Matt encountered that very same dog, a new resident of the shelter. Not a similar dog. *The very same one.* The recognition was unmistakable, what Aristotle called *anagnorisis,* the moment when a character in a drama finally perceives his destiny.

Except that once again Matt recoiled. "He was a Jindo," Matt says, "a fierce and ancient breed of Korean guard dog. The label on his cage said 'Aggressive' in bold red lettering. I said, no way! I wasn't ready for a dog like that. I'd stick with fluff balls."

Then that night during his evening meditation it happened again. The voice. Clear as could be. "Go get that dog."

Okay, this was scary. Matt had never experienced voices and visions. He wasn't sure what to do with the big dog in the cage but now it felt like that dog was living in his head. The next day he played fetch with the Jindo. "When I tried to get the ball out of his mouth, he lunged at me, jaws snapping." Back the dog went into his cage with the warning sign. Matt went home that night more confused than ever, and even more so when he sensed the voice again: "That dog is meant for you. I want you to bring him home."

Matt Beisner was the furthest thing from a religious fanatic. He had just begun to grasp the meaning of a relationship with a Higher Power. So the voice intruding on his meditations was completely alien. *Whatever you want me to do, I'll do.* That's what he'd prayed in that terrifying moment, cuffed in the back of a police car when he was convinced he was responsible for killing two people.

"God gave me a second chance," says Matt. "Didn't this dog deserve one, too?"

Matt adopted the Jindo, whom he named Renge. He worked with him tirelessly. Beneath Renge's ferocity Matt discovered fear rather than fierceness, the fear an animal cloaks himself in when he has been mistreated and abused. Only compassion could heal that kind of fear. Compassion, such a seemingly human state of awareness, the awareness of another creature's pain, was written deep into the nature of dogs. They respond to love. And Renge came to love Matt and Kingston and the other members of their pack, especially Brooklin, the spirited woman Matt married.

Word got around the LA dog community about the miracle Matt had worked with the aggressive Jindo. People brought their problem dogs to Matt and asked for a miracle, too. The real miracle, Matt would tell you, was the one that took place in him, the one it took a fluff dog and a turkey sandwich to facilitate. How else could a man who was deathly afraid of dogs find a wonderful new life as a professional dog trainer?

How is it that dogs can enter the realm of our souls? Is it simply the cold calculus of evolution that has shaped this survival behavior? Or is there a greater hand at work in the relationship between dogs and their humans, more metaphysical than mechanistic, more holy than we often realize?

CHAPTER 4

— 🐾 —

Sometimes the heart breaks slowly.

A couple of weeks after the startling encounter with Buzz that I recounted in the introduction, I came home on a Friday night to find Millie lying in the hallway, staring balefully at a full bowl of kibble.

"She won't eat her dinner," Julee said. Her voice could not mask her worry, though I know she was trying.

In her nearly eight years on the planet Millie had never skipped a meal. Not ever. I knelt down beside her.

"What's wrong, Mil?" I asked. She turned her head away, like she might be ashamed of her lost appetite.

"It's okay," I said, running my fingers through the thick furrows of her neck. "You don't have to eat if you don't feel good." I cupped her head in my hands and looked into her eyes.

"She's confused," I said to Julee.

"I think she's scared," Julee said and told me why.

Millie had been on a walk with her walker, Rich, and a few other dogs late that afternoon. On their way back up Eighth

Avenue about ten blocks from our apartment, Millie suddenly sat down. Not unusual for her. Sometimes she would sit stubbornly as a protest that she wasn't ready to conclude her walk. She could walk for hours and didn't like to be short-changed. Occasionally heading back to the apartment, she would actually flop down in the middle of a busy sidewalk, pedestrians veering around her, until you got her up and moved in a direction opposite from home. Then she would pause, with a grateful look over her shoulder. So Rich urged her on, hoping the prospect of dinner would motivate her. That's when Millie lowered herself gingerly to the sidewalk. And that's when Rich knew Millie wasn't just acting bratty. Something was wrong.

Rich and the other dogs gathered around Millie, and Rich poured her some water. He was about to call Julee when Millie rose unsteadily to her feet, determined to keep going. But it was slow going. It took them a half hour to cover the ten blocks.

"Maybe it's just a stomach bug or something," I said. "She scarfs up everything she can find on the street. She got a hold of a nasty hunk of pizza crust last night. I had to wrestle it from her. I think I was able to extract about half of it from her mouth."

"She's not having any of those types of symptoms," Julee said, getting down on the floor with Millie and me. "Rich said it was like she fainted."

"We shouldn't force her to eat," I said. "She knows what's best. I'm sure she'll be fine."

I cringed inside at the sound of my voice. It's always a shock to hear yourself lie, even just to yourself. But sometimes that's what we do when we are too frightened to contemplate what could be true.

A little while later I offered Millie a slice of fresh turkey. She was still lying in the hall near her bowl, as if she couldn't bear to leave it even if she couldn't bring herself to eat. She sniffed the turkey, gave it a lick, then took it from my hand. She swallowed and looked up at me expectantly. I got her another piece. This one she snatched eagerly. I tossed a third slice on top of her kibble. Millie studied its floppy trajectory, stood, shuffled to her bowl, and devoured its contents.

"Good girl!" Julee said.

I breathed a sigh of relief wrapped in a prayer of gratitude. Maybe it was just a bug. You never know with a dog. Later, though, when I took her for her bedtime walk she was tentative, unsure of herself on the smooth lobby steps. She wouldn't go far and wanted to come inside as soon as she was through with business. There she curled up on her bed and closed her eyes.

"Let's see how she is in the morning," Julee said. "We'll take her to the vet if she isn't better."

That night I lay awake, my mind awash with worry. Millie had always been a hearty animal, a big strong country girl who learned to love the city. I tried to remember if she had ever acted like this before but came up blank. A sick dog is such a sad thing. There is so much guesswork. They can't really tell you what's wrong or how you can help them, but you know they need you. They're counting on you. They let you know. So you fuss and you fret and you pray that they aren't suffering.

And this was Millie, my Millie. Julee and I bonded deeply with all our dogs. But to me Millie was special, my soul dog, as a friend called her. Maybe it was because she seemed so vulnerable as that puppy who was afraid to venture down the block and then so brave to overcome that fear, thanks to Winky. Isn't that what courage is? Not the absence of fear but the willingness to confront it? I remember in the first few days that we had Millie, all fourteen pounds of her, we had a vet come to the apartment to check her over. Millie had fleas and worms and required a shot. I held her as it was administered. She cried and burrowed into my chest as if to say *Protect me!* I think it was that instant when she pressed against me, her heart racing, that I felt a closeness to her, an obligation to see that no harm would ever come to her, that I would rather die than let that happen. "I'll always protect you," I whispered as the vet put her equipment away.

"She's going to be big," the vet said. "Look at those paws!"

I remember taking one in my hand and examining it and thinking it was the most beautiful paw I ever saw.

I finally drifted to sleep around dawn and immediately fell into a dream that Millie and I were hiking one of our favorite mountain trails in the Berkshires, steep and winding, the sunlight fractured by the trees. We emerged breathless onto the rocky summit ridge where improbably we came upon a patch of wildflowers, preternaturally vivid in their color, reeling in the breeze. Millie tried to eat the flowers. I didn't know if they were poisonous. I told her to stop. But she wouldn't.

I was awoken a couple hours later by a dirty sock being shoved in my face compliments of a hungry golden retriever. It was Millie's favorite way of rousting me from bed to get the day started, especially a Saturday. And I have no doubt whatsoever that dogs know what day it is.

"Look who's feeling better," I said to Julee.

Millie jumped up on the bed, wagging her tail, the mattress listing to one side.

"Come on, let's go out," I said.

She was pretty much back to her cheerful self, though she still seemed a little hesitant with the lobby steps. Maybe just a precaution from the night before. She ate breakfast with her usual gusto and then took up her station by the kitchen window, monitoring the street five stories below. Her eyes moved with the traffic, both pedestrian and automotive. She seemed to glare at a tow truck in the process of impounding some poor soul's car. She spotted a matched set of Cavalier King Charles spaniels being walked by a neighbor and erupted with a little woof of recognition.

"I think she wants to go to the dog park," I said, reaching for her leash.

"That's too much for her," insisted Julee, shooting me a warning with her eyes. I was not fool enough to argue with her, not after the scare we had the night before.

"All right," I said. "I'm sure it was just a bug. But we'll take it easy anyway."

Instead of the dog park we headed for the tailored grounds of a sprawling apartment complex a few blocks away and found a nice bench to sit on. Millie liked to sit upright on benches, tall and erect, like a person. She leapt up and tucked her tail demurely. Situated side by side we were roughly the same height. Like we were made for each other. I put my arm around her. An overdressed older couple strolled by and smiled. There was a soft breeze with a hint of spring in it, like a whispered promise, and a few buds were on the branches of the trees.

"What was up with you last night?" I asked her. It's funny how we talk to our dogs. It's perfectly illogical, yet we all do it. (Admit it, you do.) I could never imagine not talking to them. A trainer once told me that they like the sound of our voices, that they need to hear us, like the classic RCA dog listening intently to his master's voice on the Victrola. They may not understand full sentences or grammar, the trainer explained, but they know words (some dogs are reputed to have a vocabulary of up to 150 words, though I suspect at least half of them are words for food). And more crucially they understand tenor and inflection to a degree our human ears could never detect. When we talk, they understand more than we imagine, not by our words but by the feelings betrayed in our voices, feelings we can't hide from them. Don't even try.

Millie looked at me out of the corner of her eye. I felt her body shift. The she leaned into me. Her weight on my chest, almost burrowing, just like when she was a puppy and she needed to know that I would always be by her side.

THERE IS TRUTH IN illness, a kind of definitive acceptance of physical reality, the biology of destiny. No organism of any kind on the face of the earth escapes sickness and disease. Nobody dies of good health.

Yet there may be no form of denial more tenacious than our efforts to minimize disease in ourselves or in those we love. To reject the reality of being sick or that a disease may actually be central to our very identity. We fight the notion that our bodies have turned against us. But there is nothing more natural than being sick.

At least that's what I tell myself, and I've noticed that dogs, like some people (my mother used to insist until her dying day that she had never been sick a day in her life), will sometimes carry on despite being ill, as if they, too, fall into the denial trap. When Millie's BFF, Winky, was undergoing cancer treatments late in life, she had to wear a cumbersome protective cone, or e-collar, around her neck so she would not disturb the radiation site. The minute she was left alone, however, Winky devised a way to release herself from the hated cone. It wasn't good enough to be liberated from the thing. No, Winky would take great pains to hide the cone under the bed or in the back of the closet.

"Out of sight, out of mind," Amy said later, laughing at her explanation.

I sometimes forget, or try to forget, that I was severely asthmatic as a kid. Asthma defined me as much as anything did. It sometimes crippled me. I came to believe that the natural coloring of my fingertips was blue.

It was worse at night, after everyone had to gone to bed. I would take a variety of medications and potions depending on my condition that day, including an inhalant and a pill quietly laced with a barbiturate that was turning me into a full-blown junkie before the age of ten. The air in my bedroom would be vaporized and mentholated. I'd fall asleep on propped up pillows, like I was leaning against a soft, steep mountainside. The hope was I'd sleep until morning.

On many nights, though, that was a pointless hope. I would wake up gasping for air, my chest constricting like some unseen force was crushing it, as if the air had been sucked out of my room. I'd swing my legs over the side of the bed, plant my palms on the mattress, and hunch my shoulders. There I would sit in the suffocating dark, fighting for every miserly breath, the wheezing sounding to me like a thousand tiny demons screaming inside my chest. Sometimes I would pretend I was adrift in outer space, trying to get back to my capsule before I died of hypoxia, a word I'd heard the pediatrician use. Sometimes my asthma would relent. I'd fall back to sleep all sweaty and headachy. But usually not, and I would sit on the edge of that bed like it was the edge of the world, measuring out the time till dawn in drawn breaths.

There was another struggle that went with the desperate breathing, maybe even a deeper more profound struggle—to restrain myself from gathering enough air to call out a single word: Mom.

What boy wants to be pathetic and dependent? It didn't help matters that my older brother would ridicule me in the morning if I woke him up with my mom calls. Or that I knew that my mother needed her rest and felt guilty depriving her of it, especially during the years when she needed her energy to care for Bobby. What could she do for me anyway? Any more medicine would probably stop my heart, and for some reason, we rarely went to the emergency room, a lapse that would be unthinkable today and ultimately became part of my life in college. But back then I'm not sure why an ambulance was rarely called. Maybe it was a cost thing.

In my bedroom, it was as much a battle against calling for my mother as it was capturing another breath. But I was weak and scared and lonely and afraid of dying alone so as often as not, after an hour or two or three, I'd surrender to a half gasp and a half cry: "Mom!" And she would appear, carelessly knotting the sash on her robe, prettier than ever in the dimness, her prematurely gray hair, completely white really, seeming to illuminate the way to my room, where she would pace, and wring her hands, and sit with me on the edge of the world, and pace and wring her hands until morning came. I hated scaring her and bothering her and even disappointing her. Some blustering relative once advanced the half-baked theory that I was just seeking attention because of the care Bobby required. I wished the worst on that man, terrible things that I regretted and confessed to a priest later, but I really wanted him to know what it was like to sit alone in the dark, wondering if each breath was your last. In the depths of those long nights, hundreds and hundreds of them, I couldn't help asking why God would do this to a little boy. I never got an answer.

Then a presence entered my life, a wonderful unexpected presence, an angel of sorts. Pete.

Or Pierre, as he was officially christened, a poodle purchased in the aftermath of Bobby's death, when I was probably acting even sadder and weirder than I realized. Plus, my father had fallen in love with a poodle somewhere in his business travels and became intent on acquiring one. So one day he drove me out to the country to a sagging old house with a chicken-wire pen in back, which he led me to without stopping at the house. The pen was full of leaping, twirling poodle pups.

"Pick out any one you like," my father said.

Dogs are curious in their choices of places to sleep. Sometimes it's at the foot of the bed, like a good, traditional Norman Rockwell dog. Sometimes they commandeer the bed, like Marty and Sally (whom you'll hear about later) did to Julee and me for years, occasioning a nightly battle for sleeping space. Pete, for reasons known only to him, always slept on the second-from-top step of the carpeted stairs leading to the second floor of our prototypical suburban dwelling. That put him closer to my bedroom than any other inhabited space.

On those nights when I would swing my legs over the edge of the bed and take up my breathing position, Pete would soon poke his head into my room. Maybe he was alerted by the demonic wheezing. He was hard to see. He was as black as the dark, but his eyes glistened and there were little crescents of white rimming them. He'd curl up at my feet and there he would stay for the duration. Sometimes I'd invite him up on the bed, technically verboten. He'd stretch out with his head in my lap. With some effort, I'd run my hand through his curly coat. At least I wouldn't die alone. I don't think he helped me with my breathing, but if there was anything that calmed me on those interminable breathless nights, it was Pete, as if he had been sent. He would never leave my side if I was wheezing, like that dog and the Victrola. Maybe God wasn't so heartless after all. No wonder that years later it seemed so wrong, so perverse, almost medically sadistic, that the doctors treating me at the University of Michigan in Ann Arbor pronounced Pete as a major part of my problem and said that something would have to be done about him. But before anything could be done, one rainy winter night Pete escaped from my parents' yard and was hit by a car. At least that was what I was told.

GUIDEPOSTS HAS HAD MANY stories about dogs helping people through a difficult illness or condition but none more amazing or inspiring than the tale of Gabrielle Ford and Izzy.

Gabrielle Ford was a beautiful young woman with her whole life ahead of her. Just not the life she once dreamed of. At age twelve her speech became slurred. Worse, her sense of balance deserted her. In high school, other students would snap when Gabrielle blundered into them, "Hey, watch it!" If she slammed into a bank of lockers, kids would sneer and demand to know "What's wrong with you?"

Doctors didn't know until tests finally revealed her diagnosis: Friedreich's ataxia, a progressive condition of the central nervous system, a cruel disease about which little could be done except to prepare the patient for life in a wheelchair. Imagine that future for a teenager. So Gabrielle sank deeper into herself. After graduation, she rarely left the house. Why subject herself to the stares and comments? "If I couldn't hide my disease, I figured I'd just hide, period," she told us. She had her mom and dad and her two sisters. What else did she need?

"A friend," said Gabrielle.

So she badgered her parents for a dog and finally her mom, Rhonda, relented. Gabrielle got busy researching breeds. "Coonhounds are known for their beauty, strength, and courage. Those were the things I wished people could see in me," she told us.

Into her life bounded Izzy, a beautiful black and tan female coonhound pup. A special dog, more special than Gabrielle knew. Izzy was never far from her side. At night Izzy slept in her room. Gabrielle liked to sing her lullabies at bedtime. In the morning Izzy woke her up as reliably as an alarm clock.

Gabrielle's parents were insistent that their daughter take full responsibility for the coonhound, including walking her. Which was scary at first. Gabrielle didn't like leaving the house. Besides, walking a big dog like Izzy from a wheelchair and with impaired coordination was no small thing.

Yet Izzy sensed Gabrielle's fears. She'd rest her head in Gabrielle's lap when she knew she was tense. She'd look deep into Gabrielle's eyes as if to say that everything would be all right, that she understood Gabrielle somehow in a way that went deep. Soon the walks weren't so scary. Not with Izzy by her side.

One morning she woke up to find that Izzy wasn't in her room ready with her usual greeting. Gabrielle was so alarmed she crawled into the hallway. She found Izzy lying on the carpet. Her breathing was shallow; her wise brown eyes were open but unblinking. "Mom!" Gabrielle yelled. "Come quick! There's something wrong with Izzy."

Gabrielle collapsed next to her beloved companion and begged God with all her heart to please save her dog. "Lord, I don't know how I will live without Izzy. You sent her to me, you can save her."

They got Izzy to the vet, fast. The diagnosis: Izzy had swallowed a rock and would need fairly routine surgery. She was going to be all right. Rhonda and Gabrielle couldn't have been more relieved. Izzy had probably found the rock in the garden. They'd watch her more closely from now on.

Except the surgery turned out not to be so routine. Izzy had difficulty coming out of the anesthesia. The vet ran some tests, the results of which would be available in a few days. Izzy was released. Back home she paced and whimpered, walking in circles, lying down, and then getting up again.

The test results came in. Izzy needed a complicated and expensive surgery—thousands of dollars—to fix a liver condition that could kill her. Gabrielle was inconsolable. They didn't have the money. Was she going to have to say good-bye to her only friend, the best friend she had ever had?

Gabrielle's uncle knew a reporter at the local paper who might be able to get the word out. Maybe they could start a "save Izzy" fundraiser. It was a long shot, but what else could they do? Gabrielle didn't think it would make any difference. Nobody cared about her in high school. Why would anyone care about her and her dog now?

A few weeks later, a man came to the house to see Gabrielle. A teacher, Rhonda said. Gabrielle and Izzy struggled downstairs where they saw a man holding a poster in one hand and a brightly decorated can in the other. The poster said, "We're all praying for you!" The words on the can said "For Gabe & Izzy." And it was full of money, collected from the teacher's classes. "My kids read the article in the paper. We hope this helps," he told Gabrielle. "Izzy is in everyone's prayers."

"I don't know how I can thank you," Gabrielle stammered, wiping the tears from her eyes.

"You could bring Izzy to meet the kids."

Gabrielle froze. School held such traumatic memories for her. It was the start of everything that had made her turn away from the world. Her mom squeezed her arm. Izzy licked her hand. *All right, I'll do it*, she promised herself. *For Izzy*.

It was the scariest thing yet. The hallways. The lockers. Even some of the kids staring at her. By the time she got to the teacher's room and rolled her wheelchair to the front of the class she was convinced she wouldn't be able to get a single word out. She just stared at the students. They stared back, expectantly. Silence. This was a disaster. And then . . .

"Whooooof!" Izzy let out a half bark, half howl. The kids cracked up and Gabrielle relaxed. Inside her something unclenched.

Izzy got her operation and the liver problem was resolved. Except she still had periods of lethargy and, increasingly, unsteadiness. Gabrielle couldn't stop worrying. There were more tests and more guesswork. The veterinary neurologist made sure Gabrielle was sitting down when he told her Izzy's diagnosis. "Izzy has a progressive muscle disease. It is extremely rare. The closest thing I can compare it to is Friedreich's ataxia."

The doctor's words took Gabrielle's breath away. No wonder Izzy had understood her so well! No wonder she felt so God-sent. Gabrielle was almost too busy hugging her best friend to hear the vet say that Izzy's condition was not curable but it was treatable.

Soon Izzy and Gabrielle were a team, telling people around the country about Friedreich's ataxia, even when Izzy had to travel in a little wagon, making friends wherever they went.

"Beauty, strength, and courage. That's what coonhounds are known for," Gabrielle told *Guideposts*. "That's Izzy." A dog who shared those qualities with the young woman who was so in need of them.

AFTER THAT ALARMING FRIDAY night, even though Millie didn't have any more "fainting" episodes, a sense of unease stayed with me and Julee. We watched our golden girl like a hawk. She would be eight in a few days, on April 1 (yes, she was an April Fools' dog), and due for her first senior dog checkup at the end of the month up in the Berkshires where Dr. Barbara, Dr. June, Dr. Maddie, and the rest of the All Caring Animal Hospital staff had treated Millie since she was a wee pup. They loved her almost as much as we did. I'd already been feeling wistful about that, even a little blue. Why were their lives so short? Why did we have to watch them grow old and die? Why were our hearts broken over and over again? I could almost understand some people never wanting to get another dog after losing just one. It's too painful. Yet for some of us living without a dog to love and be loved by is more painful, a void we have to fill over and over again.

One night on her walk Millie sat down. My mouth went dry.

"Mil?"

She looked at me and eased herself down on the sidewalk.

"Up!"

She stared at me. Playful defiance or a plea for help? I couldn't tell. It was a standoff. Maybe she was just enjoying the early spring night. *Please, God, let that be the case. Don't do this to me.* Then soon enough she was back on her feet headed for home, eager for the treats she knew awaited her, sashaying her hips in that distinctive way goldens do. I always thought she walked a little like that old movie star Kim Novak in the film *Picnic*. The one where William Holden has his shirt off for half the movie, which was adapted from the stage play by poor William Inge.

But the mini-scare was enough for me. I'd broken out in a cold sweat and a foreboding seemed to grip me, like a dissonant chord, a note of dread reverberating through me. I tried to deny it. I told myself it was nothing, just my own neurosis. Maybe I'd lived in New York for too long. Dogs are dogs, I told myself. They deal with stuff all the time, and a lot more stoically than most humans. But Millie was more than a dog to me. So as I hung up her leash, I asked Julee if she thought we should move up Millie's vet appointment to this coming weekend, even though Julee would be on the West Coast for a concert. "The sooner the better," she said. We both knew we wouldn't rest easy until we got to the bottom of this.

"Want to see Dr. Barbara?" I asked Millie.

She wagged her tail, looking as happy as I had ever seen her.

AT ITS HAPPIEST, A dog is joy personified. Maybe that is not quite the right word, but you get what I mean. There is nothing happier than a happy dog. How they melt our hearts with those big sloppy smiles!

And that's all we dog lovers want—to make our dogs happy. I've tried to make people happy . . . with mixed results. I have always managed to make my dogs happy. Their happiness quotient is fairly simple. They want to play. They want to run through the woods and hurl themselves into a pond. They want to fetch a ball, until your arm is practically hanging by a tendon. They want a bone or a branch to gnaw on and a comfortable spot to nap. They thrive on affection and praise. They want you to respect their dog ways. They want love and more love and to love you even more. Most of all, they just want to hang out with you. That's what makes them happiest.

The Jeep did not make Millie remotely happy that day driving up to the Berks to see the vet following her episodes of "fainting." The four milligrams of Xanax helped but only by degrees. She would never really settle down until we reached the hills, climbing the grade on Route 23 past the Catamount ski area and across the Massachusetts line toward South Egremont, a classic New England speed trap. As I slowed the Jeep to a law-abiding crawl, her panting would ease. As we neared Great Barrington it would all but abate. She'd rouse herself and peer out the window with a discerning gaze, as if assuring herself that her kingdom was in order. Dogs have an incredible sense of the familiar.

By the time we would pull into the driveway, Millie was standing up on the backseat, all but blocking my rearview. She didn't care. I'd turn off the engine, jump out, and fling open the Jeep's passenger door. Out like a missile my golden would shoot, a galloping white blur tearing down a hill and across the lawn, kicking up the turf, tail aloft, ears flying. She'd turn a big circle and come hurtling back at me, tongue out, bright, grateful eyes: *Thank you, thank you, thank you!* Happy, happy, happy.

That day when we came up from the city, my golden girl was true to form. She flew out the car. Millie weighed ninety pounds, almost all of it muscle and bone. She was incredibly strong, and I could feel the pounding of her paws through the ground as she parted the dusk. She ran with abandon, as if she were trying to take flight. She came to a skidding stop at the far edge of the lawn and peered into the darkening woods and up the hill that rises above the house.

For a minute, she stood as still as the statue of Balto in Central Park. Then she erupted like a cannon, a huge bellowing bark that banged off the trees and the hillside, her front paws leaving the ground with each fusillade. For a good five minutes, she said her piece to the woods, a joyous, exuberant, undeniable bark. Whatever wildlife was in there didn't stay there. I could hear deer crashing through the underbrush, owls taking flight. Distant dogs responded, paying homage I liked to think, their barks echoing off the old green hills. Finally, with a satisfied swagger she turned and trotted up the hill toward where I was standing. *Nothing wrong with that dog,* I told myself.

I fired up the Weber and cooked burgers—two for me and a mini for Millie. We ate in front of the woodstove and watched the Yankees drop an early season game to the Angels. It was an early night to bed for her appointment in the morning.

In the middle of the night I was awakened by a presence in the bed. Millie. Which was strange, very strange, because Millie wasn't a bed dog. Julee and I assumed that beds were too hot for Millie. She had a heavy double coat characteristic of

Devon cream goldens. Julee was forever ordering orthopedic beds with magical cooling properties and Millie would reject them all. Her preferred sleeping situation was a cool hard floor, which she would take to with a contented half groan, half sigh. That sound always pulled the curtain down on my day. I love that sound. I still listen for it some nights.

She rested her head on the pillow. Her eyes were locked on mine. Sometimes she looked at me in a certain way and I knew she was saying *I love you.* There was no doubt about that look. Dogs are creatures of love. They love deeply, sometimes uncontrollably, and always completely. They want you to know how much they love you. They need you to know. I've often wished I could love as well as a dog.

"You okay, Mil?"

Her tongue flicked out to give me a lick on the chin. That was strange, too. Millie wasn't much of a kisser.

"Let's go back to sleep. Big day tomorrow."

She stretched, yawned, and settled in.

But I lay on my back staring at the ceiling beams, smiling in the dark, recalling a particularly amazing night, the last time she joined me in bed.

CHRISTMAS UP IN THE hills is magical, a muffler of snow wrapping the hilltops, the air so cold it seems to freeze sound, the stars like celestial tinsel arrayed across the sky. On this particular Christmas, Julee and I were going to have a guest—Winky, Millie's uncontested BFF. In the years since Winky taught Millie to walk on the streets of Manhattan that hot Fourth of July weekend when she was still a skittish pup straight off the plane from Florida, they had become devoted friends. I had never seen two dogs develop such a deep relationship. For instance, I know they communicated about me. I could see it in their eyes sometimes, glancing first at me and then at each other. What are you saying about me? I wanted to ask. Ah, but there are secrets dogs will never reveal. They'd hang together at the dog run on weekends in the city or Winky would be Millie's house guest in the country, hiking the trails with us, playing in the yard, having a cookout. They'd sit shoulder to shoulder and watch me grill with the same intensity of interest most folks watch a major sporting event.

That Christmas, Amy, Winky's owner, was spending the holidays with her family in Philadelphia and decided to leave Winky with us.

"There's so many kids running around down there," she said. "It'll be chaos."

"You sure she shouldn't go?" I asked, trying to sound sincere. Truth was, I was looking forward to having Winky with us. I loved that dog almost as much as I loved Millie. And nothing would make Millie happier at Christmas than to have her best friend on hand. I imagined the frenzy of shredding wrapping paper on Christmas morning, the dogs still shaking off the snow, little ice balls flying everywhere. Total wonderful canine chaos. My kind of Christmas.

"Remember, she's not allowed to sleep on the bed," Amy said. "That's the rule. So don't let her con you."

Amy spent a couple of days with us before heading to Philly. Winky and I drove her about an hour down Route 22 through the petrified world of winter farmlands, to the train station in Wassaic, the farthest outpost of Metro-North, on the evening of the twenty-first. I thought Winky should see Amy off at the station instead of just seeing her disappear in the night. I had a pocketful of sirloin chunks that I conjured up just as Amy climbed aboard the train, crouching in its terminus spewing steam, warming up for the long trip back into the city. For a second I was reminded of the David Lean epic *Dr. Zhivago*, which has endless scenes of trains plowing through the frozen tundra. I waved to Amy and rewarded Winky. Winky didn't even turn back. We drove north back toward the mountains, the moonlight plucking the occasional stray strand of straw sticking up out of the snow cover.

By the time we got to the house, I was ready for bed. I said good night to Julee who, as was her habit, occupied the den and was fully under the spell of a *Law & Order* rerun that she'd no doubt seen a half-dozen times by her own admittance. The ubiquitous cop drama has that habituating effect on people. I believe that at any given moment a significant portion of the US population is engrossed in an episode of *Law & Order*. No wonder so many surveyed Americans believe a quarter of their fellow citizens are involved in law enforcement. (It's more like 2 percent.)

Nevertheless, it was time for bed. Millie would be up shortly. As I shut off lights and banked the woodstove I heard Winky's paws lightly on the stairs. I followed a few minutes later. I was about to crawl under the covers when I noticed I had a bed mate: Winky.

She was curled up next to me, a pleading but determined look in her eye.

"What's up with you, Wink?"

She blinked, yawned, stretched. Her tail slapped the mattress once.

I knew what she was up to. To heck with the rules. Her owner had disappeared and now she needed some bonding time with a new leader. Winky was a rescue. She'd spent months in the canine version of the joint. Amy suspected she might be a recidivist, as hard as that was for me to imagine about a dog as wonderful as Winky. She knew what it meant to be abandoned and displaced. She knew how to survive in a way a dog like Millie would never have to.

I stretched my hand out to reassure her when a large white head appeared at the foot of the bed. You-know-who. There was a look of astonishment in Millie's eyes, of sheer disbelief at this shocking development. Winky in bed with me? Winky didn't budge.

Millie must have stared at us for a good minute or two before turning a few circles and arranging herself on the floor with a half groan, half sigh. There was no doubt in my mind that she understood Winky's insecurity and was happy to tolerate it. What a dog!

The next day we hiked a pretty but deserted section of the Appalachian Trail through deep snow, the tree branches sheathed in ice that glinted in the low sun. The dogs dodged and cavorted, churning up clouds of crystallized powder. Millie would excavate a stick from the snow and taunt Winky with it until she gave chase. At one point, we had to cross a stream on a succession of half-submerged rocks. No problem for Millie with her giant bear paws or me with my technical footwear, but Winky faltered halfway across, not trusting the icy rocks under her slender feet. Her eyesight was somewhat compromised at this point in her life. She stood helplessly, the rushing water all around her. I crawled back out on the rocks to get her, Millie behind me leading with her nose, smelling Winky's fear.

Millie was perfectly magnanimous. After that bedroom stunt of Winky's the night before, you might have expected her to maybe butt-check Winky into the fast-moving frigid water. Instead she let out an encouraging woof as I put a leash on Winky and led her to shore. Later, on the return crossing, Millie made sure Winky was safely situated between us.

I was proud of my girl because, frankly, dogs can be petty and vindictive when they feel wronged (perhaps we humans infected them with one of our more unsavory traits). We all got extra rations for dinner. Julee made a fantastic winter stew, and the dogs got a little with their kibble, and before we knew it, it was time for bed. I made my way up the stairs. There was a commotion behind me. I was practically knocked off my feet by Millie, making a dash for the bedroom. By the time I got there, she was ensconced on the very spot Winky had commandeered the previous night, giving me a look that said, *This is how it has to be, I'm afraid, though I am sure I am going to get very warm and uncomfortable.*

Winky arrived a moment later, putting her front paws up on the mattress. Millie shot her a look: *Back off!* And Winky did, slowly, and settled herself on a rug at the foot of the bed. I stifled a laugh that turned into a yawn, and I cracked a window, despite the sub-zero temps. I fell asleep thinking I would never fully grasp the complexities of the way dogs live and think and interact, that it was a miracle of understanding that was just beyond my grasp. After that night both dogs slept on the floor curled up one against the other, as if by agreement.

Now, years later, Millie had returned to the bed for the first time. "Do you miss Winky?" I whispered. Millie opened her eyes. She knew Winky's name almost as well as her own. "She's in a better place now," I said, "where there's no more pain." Millie looked at me for a long time, then breathed out, shifted her weight, and went back to sleep.

FOR YEARS WE'VE TAKEN our dogs to VCA All Caring Animal Hospital in Great Barrington, where they practice an exceptional level of veterinary care. I've never seen a dog more eager to see the vet than Millie.

Dr. June was on duty that gray morning of Millie's inaugural elder care checkup. I was still having trouble coming to grips with it. I didn't want to think of Millie getting old or, worse yet, *being* old. There is nothing in the world sweeter than an old dog, but to me Millie would always be the strong young dog who never met a steep rocky trail she couldn't beat me up, the scrawny worm-ridden puppy who leaned her weight all the way into me, all the way into my heart, when she got her shot. There was nothing geriatric about her, not a stiff joint in her body. She had only just turned eight and we'd taken such good care of her.

Millie was happy to see Dr. June, who got right down on the floor with her and slipped her some treats while she looked in her ears and eyes and took her temperature. I always thought it was funny that Dr. June would warn us about watching Millie's weight while plying her with chicken tenders.

"Anything unusual with Millie?" Dr. June asked. "Changes in her behavior?"

I almost didn't tell her about the episodes. Deep inside I resisted; I felt I was opening a door I would never be able to shut. Maybe it was better just not to mention it. Maybe it would resolve on its own. Maybe it had all been a fluke. Or maybe I was in denial.

"Well, there's been a couple of times recently when she suddenly got weak, almost like fainting." Dr. June paused in her examination. "Once she wouldn't eat. We thought she had a virus or something. But it cleared up."

Immediately, Dr. June palpated Millie's abdomen almost like she knew what she was going to find. Millie wagged her tail at the fun of it all. She must have figured this was worth at least another couple of treats.

"Her spleen is enlarged. You can actually see it when she is on her side. There is probably a mass causing small ruptures. When that occurs Millie's blood pressure drops until she can reabsorb the blood, a capacity dogs have. That's what causing the episodes."

"A mass?"

"I think we should take an X-ray."

Dr. June summoned a tech and they took Millie away, causing me a fit of anxiety. I didn't like them taking her away. I didn't like the idea of X-rays. It seemed like another step, another door. It felt like the beginning of something, of some process that would take our dog farther and farther away from Julee and me.

I tried to shove my angst aside and say a sensible, polite prayer but already I felt the stirrings of anger within me. Who could I blame for this other than God? And I didn't want to hear any of that stuff about how God needed her back in heaven with the angels. I needed her right here. The angels had all the dogs they needed, including several of mine. Forget the angels.

I waited, fidgeting and pacing, no small feat in an eight-by-eight examining room. I remember once, when Millie was about two, they took her in back to shave out a stubborn knot behind her ear that she had been obsessively scratching. I waited in this same room, hardly concerned. It was just a knot. They returned her twenty minutes later. "So she developed a hot spot from all that scratching," the young tech said, turning her so I could see. The room began to spin. I had to grab the examining table so I wouldn't collapse. The right side of Millie's neck was shaved, revealing a raw angry patch of shredded epidermis, about six inches by four inches. The skin was inflamed and oozing. It looked like something out of *The Walking Dead*.

I am by no means squeamish. Ask anyone. I am the opposite of squeamish. I gawk when others avert their eyes. But this . . . this grotesque disfigurement of our beautiful golden girl shocked me to the point of swooning. And I have never fainted, not once in my entire life. Passed out, maybe, blacked out certainly, but never fainted. Now I felt my knees buckling. How had I let this happen to her?

"It looks a lot worse than it is," the tech said, taking my arm. "We'll give you medicine to put on it and some antibiotics and she'll be fine in no time. Millie's such a good dog we don't think she'll even need a cone—an e-collar—though we'll send you home with one just in case."

"No! No cone!"

"Really, it's no big deal. Some dogs get these hot spots all the time."

"Not my dog," I stammered.

"So just make sure she doesn't get another knot. Use a brush occasionally."

I hung my head, feeling like a criminal.

Something told me this X-ray was going to be a lot worse. Dr. June and Millie were back sooner than I expected, Millie practically bounced into the room. Dr. June slipped the X-ray onto a light box. I saw the problem before she finished pointing to it. The spleen looked like an overcooked hardboiled egg with solid pieces of albumen protruding from cracks in it, like something trying to get out, like an incubating demon. Once again hatred boiled up within me, hatred for what might be, for what I might be told. For that thing.

"That's the mass," Dr. June said. "We'll need to do a splenectomy almost certainly. We'll do an ultrasound to confirm the findings, but I don't think there is any doubt we'll have to take the spleen out."

"Cancer?" I said, my voice cracking. There, I said it, the demon's name.

"We won't know until it's biopsied. These things are usually about fifty-fifty. So don't worry yet. It could just as likely be benign and she can live quite happily without her spleen."

"When?"

"The sooner the better."

That didn't sound encouraging. We set up the ultrasound for the day after next, when the radiologist was in. Then Millie and I were off. I didn't know where to. I thought we might drive up to Stockbridge, a quintessentially quaint village that's a must stop on any New England bus tour. I thought maybe Millie and I could sit in the corner of the historic front porch of the Red Lion Inn and have coffee and scones. Every candidate for governor in modern Massachusetts political history announced his or her candidacy from that storied porch. I first sat on it when I was a freshman at Michigan visiting my girlfriend who went to school nearby. I'd hitchhiked all the way from Ann Arbor after promising my parents I'd take a bus. Something was drawing me back to it now. Millie loved to people watch. And I needed something comforting and familiar, a place I could drift into a simpler past.

Halfway to Stockbridge on Route 7, Monument Mountain reared up on the left, a craggy, striated shoulder of quartzite rising above the tree line. Monument Mountain was just about Millie's favorite spot in the world—and, by extension, mine, too—a steep gorgeous hike up to a glorious view, though we'd only been to the very top once and never again, not since her friend Winky fell off the summit cliff.

"Want to hike?" I asked her. Dr. June said there was no reason to limit her activities until we knew more.

I pulled into the parking lot. Millie jumped out and off we headed up the Indian Monument Trail, the southern approach. Millie bounded ahead, waiting from time to time for me to catch up, occasionally crashing off into the trees where technically she wasn't supposed to be but who can say no to a dog who is only obeying the very instincts with which God Almighty endowed her? Not an argument I expected would sway a park ranger, but I was sticking with it if necessary.

William Cullen Bryant wrote an ode to Monument Mountain in the early nineteenth century that's not very good. Later, Herman Melville and Nathaniel Hawthorne orchestrated their first meeting at the summit of the mountain, one of the great writers ascending the Hickey Trail on the north side and the other the Indian Monument Trail (which is lost to time), where they discussed the great ideas of the day, a thunderstorm-shortened conversation that nevertheless gave Melville the idea to write a massive book about an obsessive quest for a Great White Whale. It always amused me that Moby Dick was born on Monument Mountain.

A ways in, we stopped for water, then turned onto the Squaw Peak Trail, which ascends a steep, knife edge route to the eponymous summit. Legend has it that a brokenhearted squaw threw herself from the top of the mountain. Yet another romantically despondent squaw threw herself off Bash Bish Mountain into the onomatopoeic falls, one of my other favorite spots in the Berkshires, just a relatively few miles away. Everywhere you go there is some legend about an "Indian princess" flinging her tragic self to her death from some mountaintop or another. You never hear about Puritan women doing this. Or men, for that matter. What's with all these suicidal Indian princesses? Not to get all PC about it, but I don't think much of these legends, which I suspect were the product of a lot of white male fantasies and ample measures of colonial ale.

Millie and I were headed to a high, exposed outcrop called the Devil's Pulpit. It offered a spectacular vista. And there was always a friendly breeze to cool you off from the climb. If there was something wrong with Millie, she certainly wasn't showing it. She'd always been an exceptionally strong hiker, and today she was climbing well. I wondered if it was just bravery. At one point, I had to tell her to wait up. She sat patiently, casting me a sympathetic look.

"Hey, you're older than me in dog years," I said. Not by much, I didn't add.

We made it to the top, finishing the route, ascending some neat rock steps carved out of a small cliff that led to a rocky perch some 1,600 feet above sea level. There were expansive views to the east—the Berkshires, the Housatonic River Valley, small dairy farms cut out of the hillsides, their grazing fields seemingly perfectly geometric from this height and distance, like the squares in a fine quilt.

Millie and I sat down at the point of the pulpit, my legs stretching over the edge. We watched a pair of hawks wheeling below us, banking off the updraft. I put my arm around my dog and said, "Remember how I used to keep you on the leash because I thought you might jump off this cliff and try to catch one?"

It was an irrational fear to be sure. But as you know I'd had a traumatic experience with a cliff jumping dog that had stoked my irrationality for a period. Never again had I taken Millie to the summit of Monument Mountain. Devil's Pulpit was our spot.

The day had become so blue and clear it seemed like a still life. I poured her some water in her pink portable bowl, drank the rest of the bottle myself, and shared some jerky with her. Then I held her close. "If you're sick, you don't have to hold on for us. We'll be okay. You can fight, but I don't want you to suffer. Not for us. You can be with Winky if you want." Her ears perked up at her friend's name and she looked around. Winky had died four months earlier after battling two types of cancer for more than a year.

I tapped my head with the empty plastic Poland Spring bottle. *You're way jumping the gun, dude. We don't know anything yet. It could be nothing.*

But something told me it wasn't.

CHAPTER 5

·🐾·

What is more human than to comfort? To show compassion to the suffering instead of turning our backs? And yet turn our backs we do, or at least I have, more times than I care to admit. It's the safer choice because to comfort, to show compassion, we make ourselves vulnerable to the feelings of others. Sometimes I have protected myself with indifference, not because I don't care but because I'll care too much.

Dogs have taught me to care because they seem to care about everything, from the poor ball stuck under the couch to the toddler crying in his stroller. Millie, for one, could never ignore a crying child. Millie helped teach me not to be afraid of my feelings.

First, though, there was Sally Browne, our sweet little cocker spaniel, who over the course of fifteen years on this earth taught me many things, things I often learned in spite of myself, compassion chief among them.

Of all the thousands of walks we went on together, one has stayed with me, a permanent reminder of something I have no business forgetting. It was a winter day, an obstreperous wind blasting up Thirtieth Street from the half-frozen Hudson. I'd rushed home on my lunch hour to attend to Sally. I was in an impatient mood, even for me. Julee was in England doing a TV show called *Top of the Pops* and we didn't have a dog walker at the time (or the finances for one except in emergencies). She'd left a message saying the weather in England was balmy and her hotel room was bigger than our apartment, which did nothing to improve my mood. Being a junior editor then, I wasn't granted extended lunch breaks, though my editor-in-chief, Van Varner, was a dog person to his very soul, and if there was ever anyone who would grant absolution for a seventy-five-minute lunch hour to walk the dog it was him. Still, I was busy with all the important things I thought I had to get done. I was in a hurry.

Sally could be as obstinate as she was sweet. That day she seemed to have forgotten—or more likely decided to ignore—the concept of heel, a word I kept saying through clenched teeth accompanied by a sharp tug on the leash, equally ignored. So I was more or less dragging her rather than walking her while she attempted to sniff every rank inch of sidewalk. The nose of a cocker spaniel is relentless, which is probably why the French favor them as bomb- and dope-sniffing dogs.

I wasn't interested in dope or bombs. I was interested in Sally getting her business done and me getting back to work without getting blown all the way over to the East Side.

Around the corner came a man—I'm tempted to say an old man, but really there was no telling—dressed in a soiled and ragged overcoat, grubby strands of dark hair half-tucked up under a frayed watch cap, his eyes sagging and sad, his overall demeanor rough and a little forbidding. Naturally, I glanced away. *Don't make eye contact, for goodness' sake. Don't engage.* I didn't have any money or cigarettes or anything else he might want and I was in a hurry after all. I wasn't so much ignoring him personally as I was ignoring the whole social problem of him.

Not Sally. She made a kind of scurrying beeline to the man, her stubby remnant of a tail vibrating in delight. Why had she picked this sorry soul to suddenly be her best friend? What was she thinking inside that curious little brain? My hand tightened on the leash. My instinct was to pull her back, but self-consciousness got the better of me and I slackened my grip. No reason to embarrass the poor man. No reason to embarrass myself might be more like it. And no reason at all to dampen my dog's spirit.

Sally sat obligingly, allowing herself to be adored and stroked by the grimy hands, her eyes soft and welcoming. She gazed up at her admirer, as if no one had ever been this nice to her before. His weathered features relaxed and he smiled. "You *beeaauutiful* girl you," he murmured. "Thanks for saying hello."

He never even looked at me. Quickly, he straightened up and was off. I watched him disappear down the block, and couldn't help but wonder what it would have been like if I had been the one to stop and say hello. It is a question I still think about.

Sally was motivated by a kind of pure compassion so many dogs possess, though not necessarily purely instinctual. I think it is a choice, a decision. I think they know. We got her the day we lost Rudy, the day Julee couldn't return to a dogless apartment. As I said, Sally wasn't all sweetness and light. She had a touch of Caliban in her, if you recall the musical Julee was doing at the time, based in part on Shakespeare's *The Tempest*. Sally could be sassy and, frankly, egotistical. If you don't think dogs have egos, you never met Miss Sally Browne. She was an unabashed Daddy's girl and had a complicated relationship with Julee when it came to who was the queen of the roost. But if Julee was having a bad day, especially if she was anxious about a show or an audition, Sally wouldn't leave her side. She had this dear habit of putting her paw on your arm when you were upset and looking right at you as if to say, *Don't worry, I'm here for you.* And she always was.

I suspect I know how Sally developed such a strong ego. It was my fault entirely. As I mentioned, Julee was doing this crazy rock 'n' roll Shakespeare sci-fi musical. Our apartment was close to the theater, so I would often walk Sally down to meet Julee after the performance. We'd wait out in the lobby just as the show was letting out. You can imagine the effect a cocker spaniel puppy had on a New York theater audience. The house sat about three hundred patrons, and it seemed as if every one of them stopped to coo over Sally. She in turn loved saying hello and giving kisses to the kids. The show was cultishly popular and fans came to see it multiple times. I think Sally thought they came to see her multiple times. She became the official mascot of *Return to the Forbidden Planet*. The producers said she was good for business.

One night walking home from work, I stopped at the theater during intermission to poke my head into Julee's dressing room. I started to ask if there was anything I could pick up for dinner later, but she interrupted me. "Edward, there's this strange guy in the audience. He's sitting right in the second row, center stage, kind of big, just staring. I don't think he blinked once during the whole first act. He's freaking us out a little bit."

Erin, the actress sharing the dressing room, nodded. "There's something not right with him."

"Okay, I'll check him out when the show is over," I said. "I'm sure he's harmless."

"I hope so," Julee said.

I returned later with Sally in tow, of course. She needed her nightly fix of adoration. There were so many new friends to meet and greet!

We got there just as the last notes of the finale were fading, a great up-tempo Byrds number called "Mr. Spaceman," Erin's big showstopper. Minutes later the audience streamed out. Sally attracted her usual cooing throng. I spotted the big staring guy pulling up the rear of the crowd, though there was something diminished about him. And familiar.

It was Brian Wilson, the lead Beach Boy himself, and arguably one of the few true geniuses pop music has produced. One of his later hits, "Good Vibrations," was the big opening number for the show, which I assumed was the reason he was there. It wasn't long after he wrote that song in 1966 that Brian began a long descent into drug addiction and madness. His genius deserted him. He became a Malibu recluse, exploited by charlatans and opportunists. Eventually he was diagnosed with a mental illness, though even then there was controversy over the diagnosis and the doctor. It was a tragic, heartbreaking demise of perhaps the greatest musical talent of his generation. Even the Beatles stood in awe of his groundbreaking LP, *Pet Sounds.* John Lennon said it beat anything the Fab Four had ever done.

And here he was, just a few feet away, maneuvered cautiously through the lobby by two handlers, his eyes wide open, just as Julee had said, with the opening act of a smile that seemed to have gotten stuck before the curtain was completely raised. I didn't know what to do. I'd listened to the Beach Boys when I was a little kid. I remember the first time I heard "Good Vibrations," my transistor radio concealed under my pillow when I was supposed to be sleeping, Pete at the foot of the bed, his ears twitching at the high-pitched theremin riff that lent an otherworldly touch to the song. How difficult it was to see Brian Wilson like this, a broken genius.

Sally, however, was unburdened by such memories, by the collective regret of a generation for one of its saddest casualties. She trotted right over to him. Her leash had slipped out of my hand so there was no stopping her. I followed, mortified. "I'm sorry," I started to say.

Sally sat right at Brian Wilson's sandaled feet. He peered down at her, apparently curious. She met his gaze with that eager, imploring expression of hers. *I'm here for you.* His half-smile suddenly became unstuck and spread slowly across his face and he knelt to stroke her long, luscious ears and scratch her Champagne-colored head. He didn't say anything, and I could think of nothing to say either, not to the great Brian Wilson. Brian didn't seem to want to go anywhere. I started to get a little nervous wondering what the Lord had in mind here, but Sally appeared to have the situation well in hand.

Finally, his handlers eased him up and got him on his way. There was a long black limousine parked at the curb, into which he uneventfully disappeared. I hoped the prayer I said went with him. I'm sure God heard my prayer of thanks for giving us such a kind little dog who sensed vibrations beyond my perception.

"YOU TWO ARE QUITE the couple," Julee would frequently tease us, even though Julee actually spent more hours of the day with Sally. She liked to take her shopping, and women would do double takes when they saw four paws and sometimes a black nose poking from beneath the curtain of a changing room at Barneys. Somehow Julee always managed for Sally to gain admittance to the restaurant on the top floor for lunch.

All of that was to change. Julee got an offer to replace one of the lead singers of the band the B-52's, Cindy Wilson, who retired after their big hit "Love Shack" to raise a family back in Georgia. Julee was joining the group for a worldwide tour, getting back to New York only intermittently over the next two years. It was, as anyone in that business will tell you, an offer she couldn't refuse. And as someone who had been waiting tables in an Upper East Side Chinese restaurant called Pig Heaven just a couple years before, it was a miracle, a rock 'n' roll answer to prayer.

The Bees rehearsed for the tour upstate in Lake Placid at the Olympic hockey arena. I took some time off work with Van's amused blessing, and Sally and I drove up and spent a week with Julee before the Bees started the tour.

I wanted to do it right so I rented a shiny Cadillac, as black as eyeliner, and Sally and I hit the road on one of those genius days that straddles spring and summer, her sitting in front next to me in the big Caddy, giving me appreciative glances between looking out the window and woofing at motorcycles. It was perfect conditions for a drive to the mountains and it was on that long, memorable journey that Sally experienced a moment of ecstasy that she would remember the rest of her life.

I decided the best lunch option was a McDonald's drive-through, since it was unlikely that I, unlike the unflappable Julee, would be allowed to bring a dog inside a restaurant, a prohibition I disagree with strongly, by the way. Dogs do quite well in Europe, hanging out in restaurants with their owners.

We eased the Caddy up to the intercom to place our order. It was like navigating a small yacht, and I almost plowed into the menu board. The metallic voice coming through the speaker provoked Sally into a small fit of barking until I shushed her. "I can't hear," I said. Finally, I was able to order a Quarter Pounder and fries and rolled on to the pickup window. The procedure fascinated Sally. You talk to a box with a voice but no person, you hand over money, and you get food. It was a kind of epiphany. Her eyes were popping out of her head. She concentrated intensely on me receiving the food. The car instantly became suffused with that universal fast food aroma.

Sally's nose went into overdrive and she inched closer to me, the way they do, the incremental incursion.

"Off," I said but eventually took pity on the poor drooling dear. I withdrew a French fry from its red half-box, blotted the grease and salt with a napkin, and fed it to her. Her eyes rolled back in her head. I'm not kidding. She had never tasted anything so wonderful, so otherworldly. I gave her one more fry and then we were on our way. Sally must have licked her chops for a full five miles up the Thruway, glancing over at me as if to say, *Did that really happen? Was that a dream?* I'd always suspected McDonald's put something addictive in their product, a way to hook kids on the stuff. Now I knew it worked on dogs.

The night before the Bees were to embark on the first leg of the tour, there was a celebratory dinner, definitely not fast-food fare since the band was vegan before vegan was popular or trendy. In fact, Julee had warned me not to mention that I'd stopped to consume McDonald's, let alone that I had corrupted our dog.

We'd have to leave Sally at the lakeside inn where we were staying. The accommodations were rustic luxury, and we were worried about leaving her alone in the suite. She was still young and she could still do damage, especially to furniture and books and rugs. So we arranged to have a sitter, the elderly mother of one of the inn's owners.

"You know, this might be just the thing for her," he said. "She's never really bounced back from my father's death and she's gone downhill lately. A cute puppy might just make her smile." When he introduced his mother, I saw what he meant about her being depressed. She was one of the saddest looking ladies I'd ever seen. Her whole body seemed to be collapsing on itself, as if her grief bore down on her like the gravity of a large planet. But it was the eyes, dark and retracted, that betrayed her state most acutely.

So Sally had a sitter and I had vegan, which wasn't so bad even for a committed carnivore (at the time, at least) like me. The band traveled with its own chef, Jan, and she could make anything taste delicious, even if a bottle of Beano was as much a requirement on the table as salt and pepper.

It was a wonderful evening, the band and their crew like adventurers preparing for an expedition. The tour would put them in front of huge audiences across five continents. "Where *is* Montevideo?" Julee asked, laughing. "Paraguay or Uruguay? I get them mixed up!" Everyone was having a great time. How odd was it, I thought, that an inspirational magazine editor would be breaking bread (and whatever else apparently) with rock stars?

Julee and I returned to the inn sated and sleepy, though she hadn't even begun to pack and the tour manager had dictated an early departure, with pointed looks at both Julee and fellow lead singer Kate Pierson, who was notorious for always being the last one on the bus.

We were worried that Sally might have run riot over the owner's depressed mother. We opened the door with a degree of trepidation. But there was Sally sound asleep in the woman's lap. She ran a hand gently through Sally's downy fur. There was a beautiful expression on her face. Her eyes were bright as new pennies.

"What a kind creature," she said. Sally stretched and gave me a languorous look, yawning so her tongue curled out like a little gargoyle's. "I wish I could have her." A minor part of me was tempted by the inconceivable—to give Sally to her. I was sure the woman hadn't smiled like that in years. I knew Sally had orchestrated the transformation. But Sally, I believed, was meant for me and Julee. We were convinced that Rudy had picked her out for us, with a little help from heaven.

In the morning, the inn's owner sidled over as I watched the band load the buses with people and equipment. "You know," he said, "that dog of yours did wonders. We're going to go out with Mom today and pick out one just like her." Just like her? I didn't think so. Not quite. I'm a little too dog proud to concede anything like that. There was no doubt, though, no doubt at all, that they would find exactly the dog that was intended for them. That's how I think we are brought together with our dogs. It's not happenstance. It is ordained.

Late that summer, during a short break in the tour, Julee, Sally, and I went to Michigan to visit my mother, her introduction to her new granddog. They hit it off. They were both tough and proud and independent. They'd sit out in the yard together next to Mom's statue of Saint Francis, her favorite saint for his love of animals. Rudy, appallingly, used to lift his leg on Saint Francis, but Mom always laughed and said Francis didn't mind. It was all holy water to him. Mom and Sally became inseparable.

It was a bittersweet visit. My mother, still living tenaciously on her own in a house next door to my brother and his wife, was in the early stages of Alzheimer's, the disease that would eventually kill her after a long, heartbreaking journey. I was in the early stages of denial.

We brought an ample supply of Sally's food, and when we would go out, we'd leave clear, simple instructions on how Mom was to feed Sally. A couple of days passed and I noticed the dog food was disappearing at an alarming rate. And I had an idea why.

"What are you trying to pull?" I asked Sally. Sally just turned her back.

I told Julee what I suspected. "Mom can't remember if she fed Sally so she just dumps more kibble in her bowl. I'm sure Sally has caught on. She's being conniving. She probably goes to her every five minutes and acts like it's her feeding time, gives Mom that can't-you-see-I'm-starving look. Of course, Mom falls for it because she can't remember if she fed her or not and she doesn't want us to know she forgot."

We put a stop to it right away by measuring out Sally's meals into carefully marked sandwich bags and hiding the rest, all of which Mom definitely noticed and curtly dismissed as silly and unnecessary. "I know how to feed a dog," she snapped, and I remembered all the times she fed Pete when I should have, all those years ago. How unnerving it is when you first reach that point in life when you overrule a parent, when you first doubt their capacities. I stared into Mom's grass-green eyes, the ones I had inherited, and saw both defiance and fear, and more relief than anything else, as if she too had secretly questioned her capacity to do something as straightforward as feed a dog. Until that moment I had thought Mom's lapses were dismissible as the vagaries of age. I'd more than thought it. I'd clung to it. Because my mother had always been a smart, faith-filled woman, who had endured things in her life that no mother should, including the death of one child and the near death of another, things she never could have survived without her trust in God. She was proud of her Irish heritage and used to brag about how when she was young she would walk right into a business even though the sign on the door said "No Irish." When JFK won the presidency, she wept. Now I wanted to because I knew Mom was in the grip of something that would never let go. Not until it was over. Both of her sisters had died of Alzheimer's, as had her father, and everyone was pretty sure it ran in that side of our family, probably all the way back through the generations to County Wicklow.

I worried Sally might lose interest in her new best friend once the bonus food supply got shut down. But you know something? That didn't dampen Sally's devotion and affection for Mom at all. They became closer than ever. Sally even chose to sleep in Mom's room, which is one of the greatest honors a dog can bestow. And when it was time for Julee to return to the tour and me to New York and we had to say good-bye, Mom pulled Sally close and cried. It was the last time they would see each other.

SALLY LIVED A LONG and fruitful life, full of adventure and love and friendship, not so different than what we wish for our own lives. More than fifteen years after I first held her in the palm of my hand, Julee convinced that Rudy had picked her for us, Sally was reaching the end of her time on this earth.

That Saturday morning in May, the first day of the year that had managed to fulfill the promise of spring, Sally wouldn't eat. She had been declining all week, ever since Julee had left for Germany for a series of concerts she couldn't contractually reschedule and which she had promised the film director David Lynch, with whom she had collaborated on the music, she would absolutely do. We'd talked about what to do if Sally worsened. "Do what's best for her," Julee said, climbing into the car that would take her to JFK and trying not to start crying again. "I trust you. I don't want her to suffer."

Actually, Sally had been declining for some time, more than a year, refusing anything but Gerber baby food spoon-fed to her by Julee and needing to be carried outside by me. She walked like that old man character of Arte Johnson's on the old *Laugh-In* show, shuffling obstinately at her own pace amid the pitched pedestrian battle that is a New York City sidewalk. But you do those things for an old dog because there is nothing sweeter in the world.

I'd spent the last couple of days with Sally up in the Berkshires. Once Sally had loved to hike and climb and swim in these hills, and chase toads and butterflies in the yard. Now she spent almost all her time in her dog bed, which I positioned in a transient patch of sunlight, then nudged across the living room as the day progressed, the solar warmth being good for her elderly bones. I sat on the couch trying to read and write. But mostly I just watched her breathe.

That last morning, I got down on the floor, lifted her head, and looked into her eyes. "Are you ready? Is that what you're trying to tell me?" It was time to do what was best for Sally, even if I wasn't sure I was ready to let her go. Sally and me, we'd been together for a long time and through a lot together. It was almost impossible to imagine life without her.

I reached Julee at rehearsal in Cologne and held the phone to Sally's magnificent golden ear. Her eyes seemed to brighten though she must have known that Julee was sobbing. Then I lifted her up, carried her out to the Jeep, and brought her to her vet's. Dr. Barbara said Sally's kidneys were shutting down and there was nothing much more to be done. Except the kindest—and hardest—thing of all. Dr. Barbara gave me a few minutes alone with my girl.

I counted her slow, shallow breaths, each one precious. Almost as if it had risen up from her old body, an image of a younger Sally came vividly to mind, sitting on a heap of rocks at the top of our driveway, patient and alert, awaiting my return home. She knew my comings and goings intimately and was always in position, watching, waiting, even when I was late. It never felt like I was home until I spotted Sally standing sentry like that. I once talked my way out of a speeding ticket by telling the trooper I didn't want my cocker spaniel to worry about me.

Why is it that we humans form such intense bonds with our animals? What makes us reach across the boundaries of species in search of something that, perhaps, we can't get from one another? Are we struggling to fill some primal loneliness, an estrangement from our natural origins? How lonely this planet would be if we were the only creatures on it! How lonely it would seem without Sally.

"You are a good girl," I whispered.

The shot was simple, almost routine, like so many other shots and vaccinations I'd held her for through the years. I felt the weight and warmth of her as she let out a long last breath, a final sigh. And even in her old tired body I could immediately feel the manifest difference between living and not living, a kind of palpable lightness, as if the essence of who our dog was had left and gone somewhere else.

Where? I think heaven. If you are a doubter that animals go to heaven, I feel sorry for you. Either animals go there or no one goes there, because I cannot imagine a God who could contrive paradise without animals and the love and joy they bring us. What kind of a cruel heaven would that be? The fact that we can share the deepest and most complex emotions with our pets is proof. Only through the alchemy of two souls meeting can this kind of love take hold. And a soul lives beyond its mortal mantle. A soul belongs in heaven.

She was in a better place now, a higher plane, Julee would say. For a shining moment, I saw our girl running among the flowers, chasing butterflies and toads, no more pain. There is nothing sweeter in the world.

BUT IF SALLY HAD helped teach me to be a more compassionate human being, someone who was not so quick to judge and rationalize the sufferings of others, then what I was to learn from Millie was an amplification, on a level that touched the spiritual. Millie changed my soul. And I will reveal a prejudice here that I am sure most readers of this book have long suspected: I hold the deep belief that there is something quite extraordinary about golden retrievers. I think they are anointed. They are the archangels of the dog world.

How do I justify such a conviction? Only in the most personal and subjective terms. How do you explain a favorite color or a favorite taste? How do you explain love? It is something so innate and deeply held that it defies explanation. And yet I believe it in my very soul because Millie changed my life and broke my heart. The latter was the price I paid for the former and it is a price I would unhesitatingly pay again and again until God says, Enough!

I've recounted some of Millie's fears: her fear of the car (totally my doing), her fear of walking in the city (vanquished with the help of Winky). Then there was her equinophobia. Did I mention her reaction to horses? Millie would become completely unstrung at the sight of a horse, of which there are a surprising number on the streets of Manhattan, between the tourist carriages, our mounted cops, and the occasional urban cowboy. I never knew what set my otherwise placid golden off, but she would try to launch herself at them in full fury, fur raised, teeth bared. It took all my strength to restrain her. And still I was in danger of being dragged out into the street. Pedestrians would scatter, bug-eyed at the display. Grown men would back away. What Millie would have done with a horse once she got a hold of one is anyone's guess, but it would take her at least a half-hour to regain her composure. She would keep woofing and snorting as if she were talking to herself. I tried not to laugh, but it was one of the most remarkable things about her.

You might assume Millie was a fearful dog. Not in the least. I watched her grow into an incredibly brave and wise dog. Remember, bravery isn't the absence of fear. It's the overcoming of fear. She did amazing things in her life, like stand down a bear. But the first inkling that she was a truly special dog was the Thanksgiving when she was two.

Julee and I were having my family out from Michigan to the Berkshires for the holiday, an event that required the planning and logistics required for visiting heads of state. That's because Julee wants everything to be better than perfect, which is an issue right there. Still, the pursuit of perfection can be a lot of fun—especially when it's for your family—in addition to being a lot of work, and we were having a good time running around like crazy people the weekend before. Millie knew something was up but couldn't quite figure it out except for the fact that it apparently involved large amounts of food, which was a promising sign indeed.

I took the train down to the city Sunday night, intending to come back up Tuesday to complete the assignments Julee had given me, which consisted mostly of deciphering with one hand endless hand-scrawled, food-stained lists of things like fresh cardoon and jarred barberry while driving with the other.

Then came the call Monday morning, just as dawn was yawning over the skyline. Julee's voice seemed far away to my sleep-besotted brain.

"Ed, I broke my collarbone."

"You what? How? Where are you?"

"Home."

"I'll be right up."

"Don't worry. Millie's fine. She saved me."

Minutes later I was getting a new ticket for the next train up to Hudson, New York, and then a cab to Monterey, Massachusetts, another hour on top of the two stuck on Amtrak, by which time I'd begged God for help every conceivable way I knew how and was beginning to repeat myself. I was a nervous wreck when I jumped out of the cab and heard Millie barking from inside the house.

Julee was sitting in our recliner, her right arm in a fearsome medical device that looked like a cross between a sling and a cast. She seemed both relaxed and uncomfortable, which I figured was par for the course for a broken bone and strong pain relief. Tylenol with a number after it for sure, and probably something more. That arm situation looked painful. I'd broken my arm a few years earlier playing softball and it was not fun those first few hours in the ER. I was opting for amputation if it stopped the pain and pleading for morphine.

Millie was beside herself. She was trying to tell me the whole story. There was no doubt about that. She was circling me and woofing and darting back and forth between me and Julee and bouncing up and down on her forepaws and pulling me to the stairs: *I'm relieved you're finally here. What took you so long? She fell down the stairs in the middle of the night. I heard her . . .*

"Make me a cup of coffee and I'll tell you the whole story," Julee said.

I made us both coffee and Julee filled me in. She'd gotten up in the middle of the night to get something to drink, no doubt a Diet Coke, which always struck me as a crazy thing to grab a sip of at that hour. But that's Julee. Coming down the stairs in the dark she'd stumbled over an errant dog toy, lost her balance, and gone head over teakettle to the bottom.

"I knew something was broken right away, even though there wasn't any pain at first. But your whole body is shaking, like all sorts of messages are flying around: This is bad."

And it was. The pain came soon enough. So did Millie, who trotted down the stairs to see what the commotion was all about.

"She knew it was serious," Julee said. "She had this super-concerned look on her face, sniffing and checking me out. She sat on the landing with me. She wouldn't leave my side."

Julee managed to sit up, grab the phone, and call 911. Then she lay back down thinking about how she would tell the EMTs where the spare key was hidden so they wouldn't bust down the door.

"That's when Millie did the most amazing thing. She lay down on top of me very, very gently. She avoided putting any of her weight on my upper right side. By then I figured out I'd probably broken the right collarbone. Also by then I was feeling cold and really shaky. Her warmth was incredible. Not just her normal body heat. It was like she made herself warmer than usual. She was like this big, living blanket. She slowed her breathing. I felt her heartbeat slow. Then my breathing slowed and my heart, which had been absolutely hammering out of my chest, slowed, too. This dog was actually treating me until help came. She knew exactly what to do. Edward, she's only two. How did she know all this?"

Millie sat quietly taking it all in, her silence seeming to confirm the facts of the matter. She absolutely knew we were talking about her. I'm sure of that. Dogs know when they are being discussed.

"Then the EMTs got here, banging on the door until I told them where the key was." Julee continued. "Millie wouldn't let them near me. All these big guys in big coats and big shoes banging on the door, stomping around. She must have thought they were space invaders or terrorists. She stood over me barking. Pretty ferociously, too, for her. I'd never seen her so alarmed. And I couldn't believe these guys. They were scared to death of her, a two-year-old golden retriever. Not much more than a big puppy! They were shaking in their boots. I thought they were going to Tase her. 'Come on, guys. She's just a pup, a golden retriever, for crying out loud! Get over it.' Finally, I coaxed her into the study and closed the door. It broke my heart to do that to the poor thing, and I said some stuff to the EMTs that I won't repeat. But they deserved it, making me lock Millie in a room like that! She was worried to death about me."

I gave Millie a pet and a squeeze.

"They wanted to put me on a stretcher, but I told them no way. I'd walk, thank you. By this point I had serious reservations about this crew. I warned them they needed to be more afraid of me than Millie, and I made them promise to let Millie out of the study before I would get into the ambulance. The last thing I remember is her face at the window, looking all fraught and concerned."

Julee called a couple of friends to run over and sit with Millie while doctors X-rayed and evaluated her shoulder. Yes, the collarbone was broken, which was a good thing, the doctor said, because it's like a circuit breaker that helps protect you from breaking your shoulder or neck.

"Evolution in action," he said. I reminded myself to say a prayer of thanks for collarbones.

But there was nothing much to be done except to keep Julee's right arm in a sling and take another look in a week or two to see if the bone was healing on its own or if surgery was required.

It was quite a Thanksgiving that year, with Julee trying to do everything with her left arm (she's a righty) and everyone trying to get her to sit down and relax. She insisted on doing the mashed potatoes though, left-handed, and some of it ended up on the ceiling under which Millie sat patiently waiting for its inevitable return to earth. Gravity in action. Finally, it came time to go around the table and say what we were thankful for. Of course, Julee's answer was not unexpected: Millie. "Do you know what the doctor said?" she added. "He said Millie kept me from going into shock, which made all the difference. He said he never heard of a dog doing that."

Neither had I. I reached under the table down by my feet and found a soft, furry neck to pat. Somebody had trained her to do what she did that morning and it wasn't me.

THE SHOOTING RAMPAGE AT Sandy Hook Elementary on Friday, December 14, 2012, that took the lives of twenty children and six adults, struck close to *Guideposts*, geographically and emotionally. Our corporate headquarters is in Danbury, Connecticut, adjacent to Newtown, where the senseless mayhem occurred. Many of our employees had children in that school system. A former employee's daughter was a victim.

So this just wasn't another nightmarish mass shooting. This wasn't something you made go away by turning off CNN. This hit home. Big-time.

Julee could hardly bear to watch the coverage, but I was glued to the TV. How could this happen in our country? What sort of people had we become? No one had any answers. Just shock and pain and parents and families who would never find an answer.

I watched that outpouring of grief for hours on end. To this day it is the saddest thing I ever saw. Every minute was painful to watch, and I felt duty-bound to feel that pain, to share in it as if that would somehow help ameliorate all the suffering. At one point, there was a camera shot of a little girl hugging a golden retriever. I briefly thought about putting Millie in the Jeep and driving up to Newtown. I knew what she would do. I knew she would give comfort. Then CNN anchor Don Lemon came on to say that a group had arrived from Chicago called Comfort Dog Ministry, a team of golden retrievers and their handlers sponsored by Lutheran Church Charities. They'd been to Joplin, Missouri, after a tornado leveled the town, and to the New Jersey shore after Superstorm Sandy. These were dogs trained to deal with victims of trauma. Don Lemon had a child and a dog on camera. The little girl wouldn't let go of the dog, who sat patiently, her fur wet with the child's tears. Don tried to narrate the scene but got caught up in his own emotions. I thought, *When this terrible business is all over, I want* Guideposts *to do a story on these dogs.*

In May 2013, we published a piece by Barb Granado of Chicago, Illinois. Her golden, Hannah, had gone to Newtown, and Hannah's story itself was one of the most inspiring we've ever told about a dog.

Barb heard about the shooting when her friend Sharon called. Barb instantly thought of her own two grandchildren, only slightly younger than the twenty Sandy Hook victims. It was simply incomprehensible that children so small could be subjected to such violence.

"We'll probably be asked to go," Sharon said. Barb and Sharon were handlers for Comfort Dog Ministry. The two women talked for a bit and then hung up to wait for the call from Tim Hetzner, founder of the program. Part of Barb dreaded that call. She'd been to hospitals and nursing homes with Hannah, but they had not yet been part of a disaster response team. She was expecting to be deployed to a natural disaster when the time came, which would be difficult enough emotionally. But this was the slaughter of children, of innocent victims so much like her own grandchildren that it was hard to even permit the images to form in her mind. She didn't know if she could do it. She didn't know if she wanted the phone to ring.

And then there was Hannah. She was not even a year old, inexperienced in mass trauma situations. She'd done just fine in the nursing homes and even with terminally ill children. She was a beautiful, sensitive dog very much attuned to the emotional needs of the humans she was brought to serve. She was an angel. But she was still growing, still learning. And there was a lot to learn, especially about how cruel humans could be. This would be asking a lot of her, to travel almost a thousand miles to a scene of unimaginable sorrow.

The call came, and immediately Tim sensed Barb's doubts. "You and Hannah can do this, Barb," he said. "I've watched you. You just have to step back and let God be in charge. I only wish we had more dogs." So did Barb. Maybe that would have meant she and Hannah could sit this one out.

That night Barb lay in bed, staring at the ceiling as if she might see an answer to her dilemma miraculously appear there. How could she not respond to people in such pain? Wasn't that what she had prayed for and Hannah had trained for? Wasn't that what God asked of her?

Hannah slept serenely at the foot of the bed, that bottom-less sleep young dogs fall naturally into. As a puppy Hannah had initially been trained by prisoners at an Illinois penitentiary. Training these remarkable dogs gave prisoners a sense of purpose that many had never before had. Comfort Dogs started their work as puppies, softening these hard men. The prisoners had grown as devoted to the ministry as Tim and the handlers. They would want Hannah and the other goldens to go where the need was greatest. They were proud of their contributions. Some of the men would never again walk free, but as long as they had the Comfort Dogs to train, their lives had meaning. How could Barb turn her back on them?

Handlers themselves were trained to stay in the background and let the dogs do the work. As Tim said to Barb's Bible study when he was recruiting handlers, "These dogs are extraordinarily patient and loving. And that creates a bond, where people feel safe and unjudged. We just let the dogs do God's work."

Now Barb reached out to God asking for strength for her and Hannah to do his work. The strength to go to where the need was greatest. She awoke in the morning certain she and Hannah were being directed to Newtown.

They arrived late Sunday afternoon in what would have been a picture-postcard New England town if it weren't for the hundreds of shell-shocked people milling about and all the media satellite trucks parked haphazardly around the town square. "There was a pervasive sense of despair," Barb later wrote. It was like a Shirley Jackson story illustrated by Norman Rockwell.

Barb slipped Hannah's service vest on her. Hannah immediately became alert. She knew what the vest meant. There was important work to be done.

They made their way through the crowd, and Barb reminded herself what Tim had said: Let the dog do God's work. Still, she was unnerved by the silence. All these people too stunned to articulate their feelings, their inchoate grief, a grief that was just beginning to take form as the initial shock of the shootings wore off.

Barb and Hannah reached the town Christmas tree. Most of the residents of Newtown had taken down their decorations. They agreed they would leave the town tree lighted, as a tribute and as an act of defiance in the face of unadulterated evil.

All around the lone Christmas tree folks had left flowers and teddy bears, pictures of the victims, drawings, letters and poems, and a sea of candles. Barb felt herself coming apart. She looked into the faces of the people around her, parents and children, firefighters and police officers. A first responder came up to them. Barb didn't have to ask what he'd seen. She could tell by his eyes that he was haunted by images he would never forget. He leaned over and stroked Hannah. "Hey, gorgeous girl. Thanks for coming." Then he looked at Barb, standing back. "You have no idea what this means. Bless you."

A little girl came over, very close in age to the students at Sandy Hook. Maybe she was one of them, one who had survived and would never completely understand why or why her friends were dead. She wrapped her arms around Hannah and cried into the thick fur of her neck, wetting it with tears. A newscaster edged up, the lights from the camera following him nearly blinding Barb. His microphone said CNN on it, and he had tears in his eyes.

I KNEW THE COMPASSION Millie could have brought to the people of Newtown, but I never did take her there. The Comfort Dogs were doing God's work for her and that was good enough for me. I still say prayers for that great ministry.

Millie was a fixture in our Chelsea neighborhood, a canine celebrity, a kind and loving presence. The residents all knew her, and tourists stopped to say hi and take a picture with her. Even the Franciscans, whose New York headquarters is right down the block, looked out for her. I remember one blistering day in the midst of a heartless heat wave, walking by the Church of Saint Francis when one of the priests came down the steps.

"How's she doing in this heat?" he asked.

"Hates it," I said, which was a bit of a mystery since she hailed from swampy Florida originally.

"Give her lots of fresh water," he said.

"I do." I almost gave him the same advice. He was wearing a heavy brown cassock that looked deadly in this weather. As if on cue he tugged a handkerchief from his sleeve.

"With a little ice in it," he added, dabbing his brow.

"Absolutely."

"May I say a prayer for her?"

"That would be great."

"Father of all creatures, please keep this gentle, beautiful animal cool and comfortable today. Protect her always. Amen."

"Will you say one for her friend Winky, too?"

"I will pray for Winky."

"And one for my wife? She doesn't do well at all in this weather."

"Certainly. I know your wife. She walks Millie as well."

"Not today," I said.

It was during a heat wave like that one that Millie would pay particular attention to Maurice. Or in the depths of winter. Or any time that she saw him, for that matter. Because like Sally, Millie had a heart for the homeless.

You could detect Maurice from about a hundred feet away by the smell. Not that Millie minded. Dogs have a completely different concept of smell. In fact, all our dogs have hated scented candles and room spray. To them smell is their primary source of information. Blasting room spray is like blindfolding them.

In this case, it just meant that her friend was near and she would pick up her speed, pulling me along, tail all a-wag. Usually, Maurice occupied a particular doorway a block downtown from us on Eighth Avenue. He was set in his ways like that.

"Millie!" he would cry, arms out, speech a bit garbled, eyes just red slits even first thing in the morning, which was often when we saw him slouched in his cranny. It was well chosen, too, fairly deep and rarely used, being the secondary entrance to a more or less abandoned building.

Maurice was a wino. Not homeless. He was very particular about that, too, though he certainly had no home I knew of, and I am not sure he would have wanted one if you offered it to him. Maurice could never have managed a home even if you gave him a mansion with a butler and a staff. No, not his style. He was of the street, as he said. A proud wino.

He claimed seeing "Queen Millie" was always the high point of his day, though in a wheezy aside to me he would add, "I tell that to all the girls."

Like the man Sally stopped that winter day, there was no telling Maurice's age. The streets age you. Forty maybe? It was surprising he made it that far.

Millie didn't care about any of this. She just cared about Maurice. She would try and bull herself onto his lap, though I'm sure she weighed almost as much as he did. With the toe of my shoe I would inch his paper bag concealing an open pint of Mad Dog 20/20 out of harm's way, since Maurice certainly couldn't afford to lose a drop of his lifeblood, and I wasn't about to replace it if Millie's tail sent it skittering across the sidewalk.

In the big cities of our country, people like Maurice become part of the scenery. It makes it easier for us to ignore them. We grow to see them as commonplace, almost natural—or at least inevitable—inhabitants of the urban ecosystem. I don't think we do it out of heartlessness. It's more hopelessness. Individually and as a society we are at a loss at how to help them, how to change them, or perhaps how to change ourselves. Their problem isn't that they don't have homes. That's just the most obvious symptom. The problems go deeper, into unchecked addiction and untreated mental disorders. It is all too simple to let ourselves forget that the most prevalent cause of homelessness isn't shiftlessness or turpitude, it's brain chemistry. And we are a long way from knowing what we are doing when it comes to treating the brain.

There was nothing much Millie and I could do to help Maurice's brain, which was being slowly denuded by alcohol and whatever else he ingested. But we did what we could, and for Millie that meant complete acceptance of Maurice as a human being. She didn't differentiate between him and the deli owner or the beat cop. The only distinction I think she recognized was that Maurice needed more love. Dogs just know, don't they? And in those moments when he would let his street-loving, wino persona slip, I saw real sadness in those eyes, and a kind of desperate appreciation for Millie's affections. Which is why I would let her sit with him for a spell whenever we saw him. Sometimes people thought she was his dog, and I didn't mind a bit.

Maurice and I were clear on one thing: I did not give him money. We both knew what he'd do with it. I knew what I did with it back when I was auditioning to become Maurice. Once I bought him a pack of cigarettes—probably not very

Christian of me—but he said he was dying for a smoke and I thought, *Lord, he's dying anyway.*

I gave him a Subway sandwich when he looked particularly gaunt. He put it by his bag and said, "Maybe I'll get to it later." (Millie almost got to it first.) I was familiar with alcoholic anorexia. I used to go through it myself. I gave him a Manhattan AA meeting book, and he tossed it right back. "Got a collection of 'em."

Julee would remind me in hot weather if I saw Maurice to get him a bottle of cold water. "I don't care if he says he doesn't want it," she'd say. So I taught Millie to carry a pint bottle of spring water in her mouth and bring it to him. He couldn't refuse Millie.

He would disappear occasionally, sometimes for days, sometimes for weeks, only to reappear in his old doorway, usually with another plastic hospital band added to the collection on his wrist, which he wore with a certain sarcastic pride. Maurice didn't hang on to much, but he seemed to like his admission bracelets.

And then one time he simply didn't return from one of his mysterious hiatuses. Not in a week. Not in a month. Not in a year. Maybe he got sober. Or maybe he didn't. Millie would look for him occasionally, stopping at his doorway, sniffing the air. She stopped less and less frequently as time went on but would always surprise me when she did. She never forgot about Maurice, unlike the rest of us. Just like she never forgot about Mick, Julee's troubled brother.

*　　　*　　　*

MICK WAS NOT MAURICE. In some ways, he was worse, at least in terms of how far he had fallen. Maurice always said he was born a wino, from a whole lineage of skid row winos. Mick was born with talent to burn. He was big, gentle, intelligent, charming, and above all funny. I mean really funny, with both his tongue and his pen.

Julee looked up to Mick. He was five years older, adventurous, and a little wild, but a great student who hardly had to try and sometimes didn't. He went to the Iowa Writers' Workshop, a program that only takes the best, most promising writers. Julee could never figure out if he actually finished the program, and eventually she wasn't sure she always believed what her big brother told her. It was a painful realization, a turning point.

Mick fled Iowa for Houston after college and got a good job working for the parks department. Everyone figured he'd work days outdoors at labor that hardly taxed his intellect, and then write the great American novel at night. Some nights he might stop off at the bar, just to observe life and gather material for his book, or simply to subdue his muse. Some nights became most nights. Most nights became every night. And then mornings.

When I first met Mick, he told me he was nearly finished with his opus. He was always nearly finished with the book. Through the years I got a knot in my stomach whenever he mentioned it. I didn't ask what the book was about. What the theme was. I knew better, or at least suspected I did. But like so many people, I held on to a shred of hope for Mick, as if on the other end of that lifeline was a man who actually wanted to hang on.

Mick's drinking and drugging got worse. He ended up in a number of rehabs and detoxes. His city job had excellent benefits, which afforded him both treatment and job protection. Julee and I told ourselves addiction was a disease of relapse, though Mick was doing more than relapsing. Each time he picked up, he got worse than before, fell further away from sobriety, his hands ever looser on that tenuous lifeline. He would call and talk a good game of AA, promise to stay in touch, and then we wouldn't hear from him for a month or so.

"Ed," he'd say in the Texas drawl that had taken hold of him, "I'm fixin' to finish my book this summer on my vacation. I'm almost there."

The job went bad, as we feared it would. As we knew it would. No employer, not even the government, will tolerate habitual absenteeism and alcoholic incapacitation. Mick bounced from one job to another, a bookstore, a coffee bar, a warehouse. He didn't seem to be able to hold on to anything, including an apartment. For a while Julee sent money, which went to exactly what we thought it would. Eventually she stopped. "I'm just helping to kill him," she said. Mick would write long, frequently entertaining letters that more often than not ended in a plea for cash. More and more Julee couldn't read them. It was just too painful.

One day Julee got a call from a counselor at a halfway house Mick had been sent to after yet another stint in rehab. "Your brother took a car without authorization, and we feel we have to take action."

Mick apparently had filched the keys to one of the counselors' cars and tore off. "He didn't want to attend the AA meeting a group was bringing to the house. He insisted on going to an open meeting downtown. We said no. We warned him we'd kick him out if he went." That was like waving a red cape in front of a bull. Mick didn't like being dictated to. "That's when he took the car. We think he was interested in a girl he met at that meeting."

Mick didn't get very far. He pulled over after a few blocks. Meanwhile, the police had been called and Mick was arrested. "We think it is time to hold Mick accountable for his actions. He's always been able to talk his way out of any trouble. We think we should bring charges but decided we should call you first."

We think, we think . . .

It was a dreadful position to put Julee in—"Hey, can you authorize us to throw the book at your beloved big brother?" Julee and I talked about it and eventually we told the halfway house to do what they thought best, because Mick was just getting worse. So they had Mick charged with car theft. Mick's public defender got the case reduced to unauthorized use of a vehicle and three years' supervised probation, which meant Mick had to report to a probation officer every two weeks and fulfill certain requirements, like looking for gainful employment, not a realistic expectation under the circumstances.

Yet Mick did find gainful employment—as a paid intern for a theater company in Kansas, a move he failed to inform his probation officer of. One night his much-abused pickup truck got pulled over for a broken taillight. Kansas shared data with Texas. The cops ran Mick's Texas driver's license, and he was summarily busted and hauled back in handcuffs to Houston, where he was sentenced to prison for car theft. "In Texas law," Mick wrote us, "jumping your probation, especially across state lines, is just about the same thing as busting out of prison." The plea deal was nullified and charges reverted to the original offense. Mick got three years. All because he wanted to go to an AA meeting where he'd met a woman he was interested in and later because he thought working at a theater in Kansas would be a good move for him. This seemed to be an incredible injustice. And Julee felt responsible. "I should have told that halfway house to lighten up. I should have protected him. He always protected me when I was little. I let him down."

Except this is what happens to drunks. Their lives spin out of control. Existence becomes a series of nosedives, pulling out of one death plunge after another. You want to grab the stick from them and pull back hard, but you never can.

I sent Mick boxes of *Guideposts* material, which he gave to the chaplain, which got Mick assigned to a job in the prison library. "You're my in," he wrote me. Julee deposited a little money into his prison account so he could get cigarettes and toiletries. I would lie awake at night, wondering what it was like to be in prison. I imagined the stale smell of sweat and desperation and the sour air at night when the prisoners slept and screamed in their dreams. I wondered if Mick screamed. Or if he still had dreams. I never again asked about the book.

Mick got out early and drifted back to Iowa and homelessness and alcohol. He was in and out of shelters, emergency rooms, county jails, detoxes, and SROs. He had periods of sobriety, some of them months long, or so he told Julee. But the trust she once had in her brother was eroding. "I don't know what to believe anymore," she would say after one of his infrequent phone calls. We'd pack a box with shirts and socks and underwear, a phone card, toothpaste, shampoo, and cigarettes. And books.

Whatever else he'd become at that point in his life, Mick was always a reader. When other people in his circumstances might have hung out in the park or on a street corner, Mick would hole up in the public library. He'd read everything worth reading on the *New York Times* bestseller list. Then he'd read the entire body of work of a certain novelist he was interested in. One time he told me he'd spent a whole month reading Shelby Foote's landmark Civil War trilogy. I casually quizzed him on a few minor details concerning the Battle of Shiloh that I remembered from Foote's massive narrative. He knew the answers and then some. After Mick died, we got a letter from a librarian saying how much she would miss him. "I was always afraid we would run out of books for him."

The last job he held was as a part-time groundskeeper at a minor-league ballpark. It didn't last. He called us to say that he'd finally been able to win the disability case he'd been pursuing with a lawyer and that a big check from the US Treasury was on the way. He was going to pay us back every penny we'd ever given him. As it turned out, his lawyer got a considerable chunk of it—Mick had been fighting the government for years—but he did qualify for supportive housing and moved into a little place he could finally call home, which was kind of an empty relief for us. He sent me a note after my first book came out, the story of my own alcoholism. He said he was still working on his book. I wanted to believe him.

We heard very little from Mick after that. Hardly anything at all, in fact. And in the end, we heard nothing.

IT'S BEEN FIVE YEARS now since Mick took his life. His suicide wasn't really a surprise, not when you piece his personal narrative together, but it was a shock. Death always is. He didn't call anyone. He didn't leave a note, just an empty bottle of pills, a prescription he'd filled that very June morning, leaving little room for doubt. I've often wondered if someone had been there—Julee, me, God, anyone—if it would have made a difference. I guess that's survivor's guilt. It's a question that haunts Julee.

Death is rarely a decision. The exception is suicide. It's the one way of dying that is taboo. It frightens us because everyone at one time or another has thought about—or "ideated"— suicide. Most people have never come close to doing away with themselves, but knowing we can is a unique quality of being human. People who say they have never contemplated suicide must not contemplate much.

Some claim suicide is a supremely selfish act. I think that's a pretty selfish thing to claim. No one commits suicide because he's bored or simply in a very bad mood or to get back at people. It's because he's hit a wall of such intractable emotional and spiritual agony that he's lost all hope of getting through it. The depression is suffocating. The pain feels unsurvivable. He is killing the pain as much as he is killing himself. Imagine a despair so deep that it can defeat our most primal imperative: self-preservation.

I believe suicide is the loss of love, maybe even the failure of love. A person who kills himself must believe all love is lost, even the love of God. Most humans cannot survive the absence of love. And pain, not hate, destroys love, like a corrosive acid that consumes our soul. Dogs, I might point out, do not kill themselves. They will sacrifice themselves to save us. When it is time to die, some will go off and be by themselves. But they never consciously destroy themselves. Maybe they have a more sacred view of life.

We kept Mick's ashes in a nice box on a bookcase in our living room in New York after Julee had them blessed by our neighbors, the Franciscans, whom she turned to often in that first year or so. Millie was about four then and it was as if, Julee said, she'd been sent for this purpose—to comfort. Julee never would have survived Mick's death without her. It was the unqualified love that often only a dog can give. There were times that Millie simply refused to leave Julee's side.

I would have been fine leaving Mick nestled among his beloved books more or less permanently. It seemed right. A couple of Decembers ago, though, Julee said, "I have to let him go." Sometimes love can trap us as well as free us. So we took Mick's ashes up to the Berkshires.

One Christmas a few years before his death, Mick came to the Berkshires for a visit. Julee gave him all her air miles so he could swing the plane fare. He got to meet Millie, who was little more than a year old. Millie adored him. All dogs everywhere adored Mick. Julee used to call him "dogman." But Millie demonstrated a particularly strong affection for my brother-in-law, like he was a long-lost soul mate.

At the end of the visit, Mick said it had been the happiest week of his life. I believed him. I had to pretend to tie my boot so he wouldn't see the tears in my eyes. We hadn't done anything particularly special for Mick that week. We'd all just hung out. "Maybe I should move here," he said, half-jokingly, knowing full well the chaos an action like that would occasion. "Don't worry," he laughed. "But someday I'll come back."

It was on her birthday, a cold, wet day when the hills were wrapped in fog, that Julee stood in the middle of our yard underneath an apple tree, alone. This was something she had to do on her own. She held Mick's box in her hands while Millie and I watched through the living room window.

The apple tree belonged to Millie. In the fall, when the deer would come to feed on the fallen apples, she'd stand guard at the window. If a deer approached she would start to whine and woof, trembling with outrage and shooting me urgent looks, as if she might just launch herself through the window if I didn't let her out. I'd throw the door open and she would race down the hill just as the deer took flight, barking ferociously: *You stay away from my apples!* She never actually ate the apples. She loved to play with them, though. Their tartness excited her, I think. She'd prance in the crisp autumn air, tossing them in the air with her mouth. How could I not love a dog like that with all my heart?

Now she sat at my side, gazing pensively out that same window. Suddenly she rose up and trotted to the door and scratched once. She wanted out. I hesitated briefly before I understood and opened the door. Millie trotted down the hill until she was close but not quite next to Julee and sat down at a respectful distance. She watched Julee fling her brother into the breeze, the ashes drifting to the ground, a light cold rain soaking them into the earth. Mick had indeed come back.

CHAPTER 6

Training a dog is essential to having a dog. Everyone knows this. We have to teach them to live among us, however exasperating that can sometimes be (for both them and us). Communication between species is at once baffling and miraculous. When it happens, when you look into the eyes of a creature who is not of your kind, and there is a connection so convincing, so real, it is like looking across the vastness of time, as if there is a convergence of a shared part of our being that diverged millions of years ago. As if we are once again one.

Yet at these moments do you ever get the feeling that your dog is training you? Teaching you how to be a good human, showing you that life doesn't have to be so hard, so fraught with angst and nonsense? That the most important things in life are the simplest—love, joy, peace, play. Yes, it's true, you can't live with an untrained dog. I have a sneaking suspicion, though, that a dog can't live with an untrained human either.

All my dogs have trained me to feed them, walk them, play with them, pet them, make room on the couch for them, turn the TV down, etc. Generally, I do what I am told. They've taught me how to let them make me feel better when I am anxious or down or angry or just bored. Those are the obvious things, the easy lessons, and I'm a pretty good learner, though occasionally my dogs have expressed disappointment with me when I am slow to catch on. *Hey, don't you know my favorite ball is stuck under the couch? Wake up. What are you planning to do about it? Help me out here.*

But there are deeper lessons to be learned, lessons in trust and courage and loyalty and kindness and acceptance and relinquishment, and dogs are sensitive teachers. They are sensitive, period, sharing many of the same vulnerabilities we do.

Forty-eight hours after her elder care checkup when Dr. June discovered the suspected mass in Millie's spleen, I had her back at the clinic for a pre-op ultrasound for final confirmation. It did not go well with the itinerant radiologist who conducted the test. Not at all.

Millie, of course, was excited to be visiting the vet. She greeted the receptionists with her usual good cheer, putting her paws up on the counter and "checking in" as everyone liked to say. Then she led the way to the examining room. The radiologist, a stern woman of indeterminate years, stood by the examining table, her equipment at the ready. Maybe she was pressed for time. Or maybe she was brusque by nature.

Before we even had time to get acquainted, she bent down and tried to scoop Millie up, no small task given Millie's size and strength. Dr. June stepped in to help lift my dog onto the cold metal table. Millie, no doubt feeling ambushed, struggled. She was scared. She panicked.

I went over to help them and to calm my dog. "It's okay, Mil," I said. She looked at me as if she couldn't understand how I could let something like this happen to her. She had that pained look of betrayal dogs get.

"We can handle this," the radiologist said. "You're just upsetting her."

Me? Really? I miraculously held my tongue. But not when the radiologist whipped out an electric razor and shaved the right side of Millie's abdomen. The radiologist used a lot of body English in the process, sending Millie into another fit of thrashing, her eyes bulging.

"That's not very smart," I snapped over the buzzing. It sounded like a dozen hornets had gotten loose in the room, which made me even madder and Millie more frightened, not just by what was being done to her but how it was being done, disrespectfully and in a big rush. Millie just needed to be given a few minutes to get used to the table and the razor. She deserved at least that courtesy, that much respect, the poor dog. And dogs know respect. They give it and they receive it. It is their social currency. They expect it. Respect is everything, and Millie was thrown around like a sack of flour.

Dr. June looked at me sympathetically, maybe a bit guiltily. She loved Millie. She would never let harm come to her. The radiologist ignored me and made a few notes, then got down to business with her equipment. Thank God, the exam did not take very long. When they were done, I elbowed them aside and put Millie back on the floor myself and gave her a great big reassuring hug. Millie, being the dog she was, had already forgiven everyone in the room and moved on. She would be happy to forget the whole ordeal for a treat from Dr. June. Which she got. Immediately.

DR. JUNE WENT OVER the results with me. "No surprises," she said, showing me the scan. There it was, that demon I'd seen on the X-ray, only more delineated, more visibly my foe. "We can do the surgery Thursday," she said. "Eight a.m., unless you'd like another opinion."

I shook my head. I trusted her completely. Dr. June handed me a copy of the ultrasound findings, the grayish image of Millie's spleen looking like a picture of something from deep space, the gloved thumb of a spacewalker. Heading out to the Jeep I read the radiologist's observations of Millie, written in a thin scrawl: *robust, overweight, anxious.*

I waited until I'd climbed behind the wheel and slammed the door before I cried. It was such a remorseless description, not so much clinical as heartless. I expected more from a vet. Robust? Yes. Millie was a big powerful girl. Overweight? Only by a couple pounds, at most. She had a lot of muscle and heavy bones and a lot of fur, though she probably weighed a few pounds less after her shearing. Anxious? No, not unless you jump her, throw her on a cold metal table, and go at her with a razor. Otherwise she was calm, even serene, kind, wise, and brave, braver than this person would ever know. I wanted to grab the radiologist by the collar of her lab coat and drag her back in time with me to show her how brave, to an August day just a couple summers earlier when Millie was six.

*　　　*　　　*

AS FORETOLD BY MY trusty weather app, the Berkshires were headed for the humid 90s that day, so Millie and I hit the Appalachian Trail early in the morning before it got too hot to hike. We headed north toward East Mountain, starting from the dirt parking area off Route 23.

Millie's BFF, Winky, was with us. That summer Amy, Winky's mom, was laid up recuperating from surgery for a blown-out knee suffered at the gym. Julee and I would frequently "kidnap" Winky and take her to the hills. Winky was getting up there in years. Her eyesight was failing. It was her early lack of depth perception that had contributed to her plunge off Monument Mountain five years previous. Now it had progressed. Still, Julee and I loved Winky as if she were our own, and Winky and Millie reveled in being together as only dog best friends can, especially if there were burgers on the grill. Spiriting Winky off to the country was a help to Amy, who felt bad not exercising her dog as much as she wanted to. But really we did it for Millie and Winky.

It was a familiar part of the trail that we followed that sticky morning. I could almost do it with my eyes closed, which was more or less how Winky was managing it. Millie forged ahead, maybe twenty-five feet or so in the lead, as was her habit. Winky stayed slightly behind me. We made good progress. We planned to hike several miles to a beautiful, almost primeval spot known as the Ledges, a system of wooded ravines gouged out of the earth by glaciers a million years ago on their slow recession back to Canada.

The woods were startlingly lush at that time of year and

dense with the smell of overgrowth. You could almost sense the earth breathing. It hadn't rained for a few days, but everything felt damp and fecund in the late summer humidity. Instantly I was sweating. The dogs were panting. We'd have to take frequent water breaks, which meant fighting off the bugs when we stopped. But I wouldn't have traded a morning like that for anything, headed deep into the hills with my two favorite dogs and nothing to trouble me but a few flying pests. Besides, I'd slathered on enough DEET to clear the Everglades of all its mosquitoes.

We were not far up the trail when Millie disappeared around a slight bend ahead. Suddenly I heard bursts of furious barking. I assumed it was a deer, which Millie always got a thrill chasing off, turning to give me a self-satisfied grin when the deer got hopelessly ahead of her. *Aren't I tough?* she'd seem to say, trotting back.

There was something different about this barking, something urgent and shrill. Maybe it was another hiker taking a break in the bushes. I hoped Millie wouldn't go crashing in after them. That could be an embarrassment. As I rounded the bend and caught sight of Millie I immediately discounted the notion. I didn't detect the usual unthreatening body language she displayed when meeting up with a person on the trail. She could be cautious—especially if the person had been out in the woods for a couple weeks solid and smelled like it—but never aggressive. Now her tail was high and rigid, her head low, her fur raised. She snarled and snapped her jaws. I looked up ahead of her, saw what she saw, and thought, *What is some big dude doing out on a morning like this in a heavy hooded black sweatshirt?* Almost simultaneously some primitive, early hominid region of my brain, long buried by civilization, took over: *That's not a black sweatshirt, you idiot. That's a predator*. A bear, to be precise.

Millie threw me a fierce look before resuming her barking, a deep, chesty bellow. She was standing her ground and then some. I was afraid she was ready to charge.

"Millie! Back!"

The bear reared up on its haunches and stared at Millie. I could smell it. If it smelled foul to me, I could only imagine the stench that Millie was experiencing. It was driving her out of her mind. I'd never seen her so angry, so alarmed. She was absolutely incensed by this big smelly beast obstructing our path and was clearly determined to protect her pack. Not a good idea. She'd be no match against a powerful animal three times her size. Bravery only gets you so far.

"Millie! Come! Now!"

She backed away slightly, never taking her eyes off her adversary, moving in reverse. I'd read you should never turn your back on a bear. Millie knew this without having read it. Instinctual intelligence is an amazing thing.

"Come, Millie!"

Winky had stopped behind me. I chanced a glance at her. She was poking her nose straight up in the air, as high as she could, sniffing vigorously. I was pretty sure she couldn't see the bear but she knew it was there and no doubt she sensed Millie's alarm.

"Millie!"

Her training kicked in and slowly Millie backed off. I recalled all the bear-encounter advice I'd heard over the years. Don't run. Don't turn your back. Make noise. Millie had the latter covered.

Millie was right up against me now, still releasing volleys of ferocious barking, barking with her whole body. Somehow we had to retreat and move to safety. I inched backward. No sudden movements. Millie and Winky backed up with me. Maybe the bear was preparing to charge. Bears are incredibly fast over short distances.

We kept backing up as a unit. Sooner or later, though, we would have to turn around. The trail was too rocky and full of exposed roots. Inevitably I'd trip and that could trigger an attack. I'd be totally vulnerable. I hoped the bear was calculating the odds: one against three. Was it worth it? What was the upside for him? We weren't a threat. I said a split-second prayer. *Lord, convince this bear to let us go in peace.*

Millie sounded anything but peaceful. Her barking had subsided to a low, nasty growl. She was baring her teeth. I couldn't remember the last time I saw her bare her teeth. I don't know if I ever had. There was something almost comical about it. Sweet, benevolent Millie transformed into a snarling jackal. And poor Winky blindly sniffing the air, trying to get a grip on the situation. I had the completely inappropriate urge to laugh out loud. I'm sure it was nerves.

I thought about raising my arms and puffing out my chest, snarling and barking myself. Some woodsmen say that making yourself as formidable as possible can prompt a bear to think twice about charging. No, the bear would see right through that act, some middle-aged guy in shorts and a vintage University of Michigan T-shirt, trying to get his beast on. I wouldn't blame him for mauling me.

I had to face it. We would have to turn our backs and move deliberately up the trail away from the bear. I didn't see any other way. *Lord. It's a risk, for sure. But sooner or later I'm going to end up flat on my behind. So you're going to have to watch our backs please.*

Millie was shooting me quick looks over her shoulder. She understood this was decision time. We had to make a move. She wanted leadership. When we were a good fifty feet from our nemesis, I slowly turned around, pushing Winky ahead of me. "Go!" I said, and strode up the trail away from the bear. Not running, not strolling, just moving as confidently as I could manage. I tried to move Millie around in front of me, but she wasn't having it. She was committed to saying between us and the bear, occasionally glancing back and woofing. Once she paused stubbornly to unleash another volley of barking, and I had to grab her by the collar. "Come on," I said. "He's not after us." I kept looking back though, too, listening for the crackle of twigs and breaking branches. Nothing. I checked to see if the bear was tracking us on the parallel. No sign of it. We were getting away.

We made it back to Route 23 in a few minutes and crossed over to the parking area, where I ordered the dogs into the Jeep, jumped behind the wheel, pulled out of my spot, and aimed the truck toward the trailhead. If the bear was hot on our heels I fully intended to run him over. I'd heard bears could break into a vehicle in no time, just smash their way through a window, but I figured even a bear was no match for a V8, a blunt instrument if ever there was one. So I was ready with my foot on the accelerator, the dogs sitting upright in the backseat, staring intently out the windshield.

We waited. No bear. Finally, I let out a massive sigh of relief. It felt like I hadn't breathed in ten minutes. I praised the girls for their smarts and their bravery and then looked to the southern continuation of the trail, wondering if we should give it a shot. We could change our route and head toward Beartown State Forest (yikes!) and lovely Benedict Pond instead of East Mountain. Route 23 was a pretty reliable barrier against our hypothetical pursuer, and what were the chances of encountering a second bear? On balance, I decided that we had had enough excitement for one day, and I think the dogs agreed, because they were completely out a few minutes after we got back on the road, all curled up with each other even in the heat.

Julee was too impressed by Millie's courage and the way she handled herself to be critical of what she no doubt viewed as yet another one of my misadventures in the wilds of Massachusetts. "It's a good thing we trained her," Julee said. "She might have just attacked otherwise. Good girl!" We had to get back to New York, and there was no time to formally upbraid me. I escaped with a few skeptical looks.

Back in the city we discharged our passenger on the East Side and drove home to the West Side and parked in our garage. Julee went upstairs while Millie and I headed to a corner store for milk and a few sundry things. We weren't inside more than a step or two when Millie belly-flopped onto the floor, a pathetic look on her face. I rolled my eyes, wondering what was wrong with her. Was this some sort of delayed reaction to the bear? I didn't feel like dragging my ninety-pound dog on a 90-degree day all the way back to the dairy case. But Millie wasn't budging.

"C'mon, Mil," I said, giving the leash a slight tug.

Hassan, the store's owner and an old friend, chuckled. "She fears Angelina," he said of his twelve-pound calico cat perched quietly on a shelf at the back of the store. The cat was giving Millie the evil eye.

"Millie, up. Don't be silly."

No deal. She wouldn't even look at Angelina. She averted her eyes.

"I'll get what you need," Hassan said, and while he gathered our things, I recounted the events of that morning, shaking my head at the irony of Millie's poltroonery.

"And now she cowers like a puppy at the sight of a little cat," I said. "Who can explain it?"

"Well, my friend, sometimes it's the little things that get to us," Hassan said, bagging our items. "The big stuff we're able to step up and handle. But it's the little things that can kill us."

He handed me the bag and slipped Millie a slice of deli turkey, which she was not too freaked out to gobble gratefully, casting a wary look at Angelina.

NOW, YEARS LATER SITTING in the car with the ultrasound report that Dr. June had given me crumpled on the passenger seat, I thought about again what an elusive phenomenon courage is. Is it the absence of fear or the overcoming of fear? How could my dog face down a bear but cower in front of a cat? What were the bears and cats in my life? I've never thought of myself as a courageous person. Stupid and reckless during certain periods of my life, wandering around South America in my twenties in a stupor, barely avoiding incarceration and serious physical harm. Was I sober now all these years because I had the courage to face my addictions, or was I simply scared to death at what I was doing to myself? And what was faith? The courage to believe in something greater than yourself or the need to lean on a metaphysical crutch when the going got tough? Was God a refuge or an enabler?

One conclusion I'd arrived at was that I overreacted to the radiologist's bedside manner big-time because I was afraid of what she might find. Afraid of what might lie ahead. Afraid of my own feelings. Afraid for Julee. Afraid for Millie. Just plain scared. Yes, Millie was frightened by the way she was manhandled. That wasn't fair. And here I was vibrating with rage, my breathing elevated, gripping the steering wheel so tightly I'd squeezed all the blood out of my knuckles. I glanced in the rearview. Millie was sitting in back, looking calmly out the window. Her ears perked up at the sight of a dog being walked behind the clinic. Her tail twitched a little. She followed the dog's progress with great interest. I could almost read her mind: *That dog looks like a nice dog.* She gave others the benefit of the doubt, always.

After all, the injustice was done to her and not me. If this was how I reacted now, then how would I react when—or if—things got worse? My anger was a symptom of my fear. Was I going to allow fear to become my Higher Power? Was I going to allow the little things, like a vet's manner, to get to me and not be able to handle the bigger things? Whether God was my refuge or my enabler depended on the quality of my faith, not on God. God was there for me no matter what, and I had to believe he would be there for Millie. After all, I had been trained, too—by a spiritual program of recovery that taught me how to face my fears with something akin to courage.

I looked north up Route 7 and saw storm clouds advancing on a dwindling blue sky. If Millie and I were quick, we could get in a walk in the woods before the rains came.

THE STORMS DID COME and the power was knocked out for a bit that night, which was enough to send me to bed early. I was awakened well past midnight by Millie's snout plopping down on my pillow. *Oh no,* I thought. *Does she have to go out? Now? It's pouring!* As if on cue, the rain did a windswept paradiddle on the bedroom window.

Millie stood by the bed, her chin as high as the mattress, shifting her weight from side to side, her manner both urgent and expectant, and a little . . . disapproving. She only woke me when she had an emergency. Apparently, she was having one.

"Just a sec, Mil," I mumbled, grabbing my robe. "Good girl. I'll let you out."

Millie preceded me down the stairs as I rubbed the sleep out of my eyes. She stopped just two steps from the bottom and stared up at me, then down again at the landing by the back door.

See? she seemed to say. *It's raining inside.*

I did see. The old roof had sprung a leak over that area. Not a gusher, but the whole landing was soaked. I also finally noticed the wet paw prints on the stairs. I gave my dog an amazed look. She had first investigated the situation. How did she know this dripping ceiling was important enough to rouse me? It wasn't as if Millie minded the rain. She just knew it didn't belong inside.

"Smart girl," I said. She watched while I snatched one of her dog towels off a hook by the door and sopped up the water. Then I found a bucket and positioned it under the leak to catch the drips till morning, when I could call a roofer. Millie seemed satisfied with my work. I gave her a nice rub behind her ears before we headed back upstairs, where I slid under the covers and Millie lay down on the floor with a contented sigh, like she thought the place would fall apart if it wasn't for her. Just before I drifted off, I said a quick prayer of thanks for having been blessed with such a responsible dog. "Thank you, Lord, for making her so vigilant. That drip could have caused some real damage."

The next night, the night before her surgery when I didn't think I would sleep a wink but did, she woke me again with the same insistence. Except it wasn't raining. It was a beautiful early spring night and I'd left the bedroom window cracked. I could smell flowers blooming in the moonlit dark.

"All right, all right . . ."

This time Millie led me into the bathroom and sat down in front of the sink. I switched on the light, squinting until my pupils shrank a little. I saw a lazy drip from the faucet to the basin.

"Really?"

Millie shot me a stern look, as if I were some kind of negligent home owner. I wanted to tell her it was no big deal, but instead I tightened the faucet and put the cap back on the toothpaste while I was at it. Maybe I had been a little hasty going to bed.

Millie led the way back to the bedroom. This time I knelt and gave her an enormous hug. I could feel the muscles in her shoulders shift beneath her fur and caught the faint odor of grass and underbrush mixed with her underlying animal scent. She relaxed into my embrace, leaning her weight against me. I held her like that for a long time. "It's going to be all right," I said. "We're going to take care of you."

EARLY THE NEXT MORNING I skipped breakfast because Millie was not allowed to eat before her surgery and it didn't strike me as polite to eat in front of her. Besides, I didn't have much of an appetite. My stomach felt like one of those rubber stress balls they habitually give away at conferences, squeezed by someone who was really stressing out.

I brought her back to All Caring and handed her over to Dr. June. I'd pretty much gotten over the events of two days earlier. Millie had that effect on me. And so did Dr. June. I had total confidence in her. The radiologist had moved on. I walked out of the clinic, feeling pretty good about everything.

So good I thought I'd get a little breakfast in me. I was weary from worry and from being rousted from bed two nights running by my robust, overweight, and anxious golden retriever, and when I'm tired I crave sugar. Fortunately, the world's best donuts were a mere quarter mile away at the Home Sweet Home Doughnut Shoppe on Stockbridge Road. It was family run, family friendly, and faith friendly. One of the owners, Jeff, always said, "God bless you," every time I tossed my change into the tip cup, and I knew he meant it as more than just an expression. It would be a good place to sit quietly for a spell.

My usual was a cream-filled donut (not Boston cream, mind you—vanilla cream; I am a total vanilla freak). Not that I didn't like other types of donuts. I loved all donuts. But to control my intake, I would only allow myself vanilla cream, and if they were out, as they sometimes were, I would forgo my donut fix altogether. It was an act of Spartan self-denial, I know, but I was generally able to conquer my cravings.

Not this morning. I obtained several donuts and an extremely large coffee and settled at a table by the window. The shop wasn't crowded, but there was a steady stream of to-go customers fueling up for the day. I watched them come and go. A woman with a double baby stroller powered in. Both baby compartments were occupied. Millie would have been out of control. Babies sent her into a delirium. Not even one of her old dog friends made her that happy. Truth to tell, Millie was a baby licker. A week or so before, we were walking through Chelsea Waterside Park along the Hudson. There were an inordinate number of children in the area, especially toddlers and eminently lickable babies, which put Millie into a state of great excitement, and a couple of mothers didn't mind Millie's sloppy proclivity. "Good for their immune system"—Millie's or the babies'?—one mother said while her baby got licked.

All right, I'm certain you will tell me there is a perfectly prosaic explanation. Babies usually have food stuck to their faces. Of course, they get licked. This also explains the folklore about rats eating infants' faces. I swear, though, it was more than food for Millie. She licked some very hygienic, well-kept babies. No, it was a kind of ecstasy for her, a divine joy. Maybe it was some common mammalian scent. It made me teary sometimes, imagining what a good mother Millie would have been. I have never seen any dog happier than Millie kissing a baby. No politician can come close. I don't believe in reincarnation, but if I did, I would bet Millie was a reincarnated grandmother. In any case, I believe that Millie was an old soul.

Julee had gone back to New York the day before Millie's surgery. She had appointments she couldn't reschedule. Or at least that was what she was telling herself. We both knew better. If the worst came to pass for Millie, it would kill Julee. Her emotional attachment to Millie and all our dogs was deep and profound. And the deeper your feelings for a dog, the harder you grieve when they are gone. Grief is the price we pay for love.

And Julee paid deeply. She cried every time she saw a three-legged dog. One of her childhood dogs, Kelly, a red golden, had to have a leg amputated mid-life. Kelly went into a long, disturbing depression, a tailspin if you will, following the loss of her left foreleg. She was listless. She lost her appetite, unnatural in the extreme for goldens, who eat anything and everything. She lost her joy. Julee grieved the loss of her leg with her.

But Kelly pulled out of it. Eventually, she would proudly present her stump to be shaken. Julee remembers kicking a man who refused to do it. And to this day a three-legged dog summons up all those feelings.

So the thought of losing Millie at eight was almost unbearable for her. We talked about staying positive and putting Millie in God's hands, but I knew deep inside Julee was ready for the worst and for the pain that came with it. She had to prepare herself for that eventuality. She could not have endured seeing Millie, who had never been sick, weak and bandaged from surgery. She wasn't ready for that yet. When the time came, she would be there for Millie in every way possible. No one was willing to do more for a dog than Julee. Once, when Sally had painful dental work done late in life and couldn't chew, Julee chewed up bits of meat and hand-fed them to her. For now, though, she needed the space, to prepare herself for whatever was to come.

LETTING GO IS A hard concept, and I have had to let go of many things in my life to understand it. Nothing is harder than letting go of something or someone you love. Love is the gravity of the heart and nearly impossible to escape. You hold on for dear life. You hold on even when the thing you are holding on to is gone.

Yes, it is the hardest thing having a dog and knowing that you will outlive all but the last one. And yet if you are of a mind like mine, you do it. Like one of my favorite *Guideposts* writers, the passionate and poetic Marion Bond West, we can't help ourselves. We can't say no to a dog.

Whether she's writing about her marriage, her faith, her children, or her dogs, Marion always seems to return to the theme of relinquishment. In fact, I once came close to suggesting that she might consider relinquishing the theme of relinquishment in her writing, but that would have most likely engendered another story about relinquishment. I'm glad I held my tongue (for once). Marion may repeat her signature theme, but she never repeats herself. Her writing is filled with surprises. So many writers forget how important it is to surprise their readers. Marion never does, and her story "The Dog I Gave Away" is fine proof of that.

Her rarely ruffled husband Gene started it by confronting her one morning about a stray dog she'd rescued, bellowing at her like a demented drill sergeant in their very backyard in Watkinsville, Georgia, in full earshot of the neighbors. "Marion, get that dog back in its pen! She shouldn't be running loose like that." Then for good measure he added, "And don't start again about keeping that dog. She has to go. One dog is enough!"

"I will never get rid of Red Dog!" she screamed back.

Red Dog had wandered into their yard one day, which was not that unusual. Dogs in need seem to find Marion. It's as if these dogs have a communication system like the hoboes of yore did, a funky set of scent symbols that say, *This woman always has food to share. This woman will give you a warm blanket to sleep on. This woman might love you forever.*

The dog looked like a little red wolf, hence her eventual russet name, which was assumed to be temporary. She was as sleek and as smart as a wolf, too. As Gene and Marion pondered what to do with the stray, their next-door neighbors stopped over. They had a roomy outdoor pen their elderly house dog rarely used. They could keep the red dog there. Marion would run an ad and canvass all the area vets. This dog was too stunning to stay lost for long. Meanwhile, she'd be good company for Marion and Gene's one-year-old retriever mix, Lovey.

But no one claimed Red Dog. She and Lovey became fast

friends, romping in the yard, swimming in a pond around which Marion and Gene liked to take their walks. Finally, Gene suggested they fly Red Dog to Oklahoma where his granddaughter Kari and her husband, Jason, would give her a good home. They'd met Red Dog on a visit to Georgia and had fallen for her—almost as hard as Marion had.

Marion equivocated. She dragged her feet and changed the subject. Red Dog had turned circles in her heart and settled right in. Marion had no intention of sending her to Oklahoma or anywhere else. Gene's patience wore thin. After all, he and Marion had agreed to find a new home for the dog, not keep her. Now Marion was reneging. It had happened before, but Gene was determined not to let it happen again. That's what resulted in the backyard shout-down that day. Gene was stubborn, but Marion even more so. And Gene was generally a peace lover. Marion was ready for war.

She stormed into the house after returning Red Dog to her pen and already she could feel a wall building between her and her husband. *He started it,* she told herself.

Later, while Marion was working in her study, Gene came in, took a deep breath, and spoke softly. "Marion, look, I know you care about Red Dog. She's a fine dog. But I want you to help me find a good home for her."

"I really want that dog, Gene," replied Marion. "She thinks she belongs to us. Lovey needs her."

"I have to be tough with you about dogs," Gene said. "We would have a yard full if I weren't. Besides, you're trying to manipulate me."

Marion was too angry to answer. Manipulate? How dare

he say that! *That dog is not going anywhere,* Marion vowed silently and returned to her work, tapping the keys furiously.

The wall between them grew taller and thicker. The wall was stubbornness and the bricks and mortar were will and ego. They barely spoke for the rest of the day, and Marion was bound and determined not to be the one to break the silence, to climb over that wall. Except that Marion was a writer, a communicator. It killed her not to talk to her husband.

When she heard Gene's car in the driveway the next afternoon, she wanted to run through the garage to greet him. Often she wouldn't even wait for Gene to come inside and instead would dash out to his car, jump in, and tell him all about her day. This day Marion stayed put in her study and Gene didn't even poke his head inside to say hello. *Keep writing,* she told herself. *You do not manipulate. And Red Dog stays.*

Her resistance didn't last. Soon she marched into the bedroom where Gene was changing. "I want you to know I'm miserable," she said, unsmiling, arms folded. "This fight is no fun. I hate this wall between us."

Marion found herself focusing on Gene's dimple, which she adored. She turned away, willing him to respond.

Gene cleared his throat and buttoned his shirt. "Thank you for your honesty."

What kind of response was that? Marion exploded from the room and back to her study. She didn't continue writing, though. She was too upset. Instead, she stared out the window until she decided to go for a run.

She ran hard up a hill near the house, overlooking the pond the dogs swam in. The surface reflected the slanting rays of the late-day sun like a mirror. And as if looking into a mirror, Marion saw her own part in her feud with Gene, her stubbornness, which was prideful and willful, she concluded.

But Red Dog needs me.

So as she ran, Marion prayed. She asked God to soften Gene's heart about Red Dog. And almost immediately she asked herself, *Am I trying to manipulate God now?*

She was breathing hard. The harder she breathed, the harder she ran, her feet pounding a rhythm on the road. And in the rhythm of her pounding feet she heard a single word.

Yep. You guessed it. Relinquishment.

She slowed her pace, then sat in the grass under a white oak. She missed talking to Gene. Missed it desperately, almost as much as she missed talking honestly to God. Now she closed her eyes and asked for the strength to let Red Dog go. "Lord, the choice is between my way and your way. I see that now."

She picked herself up and circled back toward home, the wind at her back. She turned into her driveway, Red Dog and Lovey yapping a welcome to her, their ragged barks sounding for all the world like a song. Marion stopped and put her hands on her knees, drained of the tremendous energy required to continue her struggle with Gene. Then she went over to Red Dog, who sat politely in her pen, delighted to entertain company. "Everything is going to be all right, girl. You're going to live in Oklahoma. But that doesn't mean I won't always love you."

Marion went inside, walked to her study, and wrote RRD on her calendar, Relinquishing Red Dog. Then she called to Gene, and he knew from the sound of her voice what she had decided.

That night they called Gene's granddaughter Kari with the good news that they would be sending Red Dog out to them.

"Well," she said, "the thing is, Jason and I saw this awesome German shepherd puppy and we had to have him. Besides, we thought you'd never let Red Dog go."

This is a test, Marion thought, *a test of faith*. At the grocery store a few days later, the cashier commented on all the dog food Marion was buying. "Looks like you're feeding a pack," she said. Marion told her about Red Dog and the woman seemed interested. "I think I found a good home for Red Dog," she told Gene that night.

The cashier's husband intervened, however, claiming they lived too close to a busy road to have a dog. *You could always get her a nice pen,* Marion thought, but dropped it. Instead she called the man who had built Lovey's pen and offered Red Dog to him. He wanted her, but his wife felt the dog would be lonely during the day with both of them working.

Now Marion became as stubborn about giving Red Dog away as she once was about keeping her. She pestered everyone who had ever said an admiring word about Red Dog, asking if they wanted to have her. "We'll find someone," she promised Gene. She put up signs around town and on the community bulletin board, a picture of a happy Red Dog at the top. FREE DOG it said. She got no takers.

One night she saw Gene standing out in the backyard, just staring. At what, she couldn't guess. She went outside and slipped her arm in his. "What do you see?"

Lovey was carrying on like she always did when they were near her pen and Red Dog was yipping in the neighbor's yard because she wanted out of hers. Gene smiled slowly and said, "What do you think about having another pen built right alongside Lovey's? You know how lonely Red Dog gets without her."

What did Marion think? Thoughts came so fast they overlapped, but one thought fought through: sometimes we are allowed to keep what we must first be willing to give up.

And sometimes we must give up what we wish with all our hearts to keep.

I SIPPED MY COFFEE and bit into a second donut. If it was cancer it would not be our first experience with it. Because before there was Millie there was Marty, our giant white Lab, a dog who would change our lives forever.

We have loved all our dogs equally but differently. For Julee, Marty was her "soul dog." I don't think there are any limits on how much Julee can love a dog, but her connection with Marty was unique. Maybe that's because he had so many issues. Maybe that's because he needed her more than our other dogs had. In truth, Marty was a walking ball of bluster and insecurity, exuberance and fear, strength and weakness. Marty was complicated.

He came to us out of the blue, about a year and a half after we got Sally. It was a year and a half that Julee had mostly spent touring with the Bees, with only sporadic returns to New York. On one of those swings through the city when the band was scheduled to play some shows at Radio City before the final South American leg of the tour, Julee spent a few days at our apartment, although hotel rooms had been provided for all members of the tour regardless of whether they lived in the city. It was part of the contract, I suppose.

Initially, Sally was pleased to see Julee. She wouldn't leave her side, the sweetest, kindest dog in the world. They took long walks and went for ice cream in the afternoon. But things turned ugly at bedtime. Sally was not happy. In the middle of the night I awoke to Sally sitting at the bottom of the bed, glowering at me. If she could have spoken I imagined she would have said, "How could you?"

The next night Sally left a token of her displeasure in the middle of the bed. The third night Julee availed herself of the hotel room.

"I've been kicked out of my home by a cocker spaniel!" she said.

"Sally is just upset," I countered. "She's very emotional."

"What have you done to that dog?" she demanded. I didn't have an answer.

A few weeks later, Julee called from Caracas. "We're wrapping up the tour. A couple of us are going to Bermuda for a few days to decompress. When I get home, can we get another dog?"

I was silent. Sally was asleep on the couch beside me.

"Please?" Julee said. "I think that's just what Sally needs. I love that dog. I don't want her to be unhappy, Edward. Please."

"We'll talk about it when you're home." Which was pretty much a capitulation. We were going to get another dog just as soon as we were done talking about it. I was pretty sure of that.

That inevitable conversation about another dog actually took place not in our apartment but in a hotel uptown. Just a few days after Julee got home, Sally's acting out had become intolerable, even for me. She was tearing the apartment apart, marching around in the dead of night, barking angrily, nipping Julee in the rear end whenever the opportunity arose.

"I have holes in all my jeans! I walk around with a cocker spaniel attached to my butt!" Julee said. It was a bit of an exaggeration, but I didn't think I was in a position to point that out. It wasn't so bad when I wasn't around. Really, Sally and Julee got along famously. Whenever I entered the picture, though, the dynamic went south.

"Another dog is the only answer," Julee insisted. "It will settle her right down."

Julee stared. I said nothing. I noted the passage of time.

Finally, I gave in, as I knew I would, and honestly, the prospect of another dog, even within the confines of a New York City apartment, was exciting. Yes, two dogs would be twice the work but also twice the satisfaction. And what else were we going to do about Sally?

Julee had been thinking this through in more detail than she had let on. She was dreaming of a white Labrador retriever, the American Field Lab version, which was taller and lankier than the traditional Lab, whose body type was stockier and lower to the ground. And she had one lined up.

We called him Marty (officially Martin Jehoshaphat Grinnan-Cruise) and brought him home in a cab in a cardboard box configured to look like a dog house and immediately liberated him inside the apartment. The first thing that became apparent was that he had never experienced a rug or carpeting. He kept retracting his giant puppy paws until we assured him that rugs were safe and good. He was playful and goofy. He and Sally got along quite well, though at some point Sally had had enough. She sat down and gave me a look: *Isn't it time for him to go home now?*

Marty slept in the new kennel we'd gotten for him, right outside the bedroom door. He cried in the middle of the night and Sally went to him, concerned and confused, as if she had forgotten he was there, as if the big white dog had been a fantastic dream.

The first indication that Marty might be an unusual animal was housetraining him. We had gotten him at twelve weeks, so it would be another month before he completed his vaccinations and it was safe for him to go outside on the sidewalks of New York. At first I took him up to our roof terrace to do his business. This proved futile. We knew he was paper trained, so Julee cordoned off a section of the living room with baby gates and laid down papers. Marty was happy.

Eventually it came time to teach him to go outside. I didn't think this would be a challenge, except that he was growing bigger by the day—by the hour, it sometimes seemed—and carrying him down to the street in the morning from his kennel was a workout. The problem came when I got him outside. Nothing in heaven or on earth could induce him to go. We'd walk and walk and walk until finally I'd give up and go inside. Marty would dutifully head for his papers and go, with a relieved and self-satisfied look on his face. *I made it.* It took all my self-control not to reprimand him. It would only confuse him and he was confused enough already.

Instead, Julee and I would stand there saying, "Good boy pee-pee. Good boy poo-poo." Polly, our dog trainer, said that if we named the behavior he would eventually understand that we wanted it performed outside. So far weeks of walking around the block saying "pee-pee, poo-poo" hadn't produced a thing, except bemused looks from the neighbors. Some of them would add their voices as we walked by. Marty loved it, but I was humiliated.

Marty was not a dumb dog. Far from it. He learned most things lightning fast. He simply had a very rigid learning style. He learned so well that he had trouble changing. Tell me that doesn't ring familiar. Yet I was on the verge of a nervous breakdown every morning. I had a job to get to, places to be. Even dog-loving Van Varner, my editor, was growing impatient with my tardiness. "Van, he won't go," I would plead. He'd just shake his head and say, "I've never had that problem with a dog." How many hours could I devote to Marty's bodily functions? I had the terrible feeling that the longer I walked Marty in the morning without the desired outcome, the more I was training him to hold it. Marty was developing Herculean powers in that regard.

We removed Marty's beloved papers until there was just one, which I took outside and laid on the sidewalk. He looked at me like I was insane. "Pee-pee, poo-poo." No dice.

The morning routine grew more desperate. I would take a fresh paper and a bowl of food downstairs with us, hoping that a big breakfast might get something started. Nothing changed except that Marty got to eat al fresco, which he enjoyed immensely, followed by a nap in the middle of the sidewalk. On the advice of our vet, we added a glycerin suppository to the mix.

I was convinced this would do the trick and put a great deal of faith in the suppository. But it only made him more obstinate.

One morning I sat in front of our building staring at Marty, an otherwise terrific, lovable dog. A special dog with a very interesting learning style. I held the paper, limp and hopeless in my hand. He hadn't gone in twelve hours. I'd given him a double ration of breakfast and inserted two glycerin suppositories. All he wanted to do was say hi to the regal ridgeback two doors down who *was* doing his dog duty. I stood and threw the paper into the street. It landed on the windshield of a cab and earned me some choice words from the cabbie. But I was beyond caring. I was at a breaking point. Yes, my dog had broken me. "Pee-pee!" I yelled. "Poo-poo!" Pee-pee, poo-poo over and over again. People stared. Marty cocked his head, perplexed.

God, do something about this dog. Please! I know you have greater things to worry about than pee-pee and poo-poo. But I am about to lose my mind. Thank you for listening. Amen.

I dragged Marty inside, threw down a new paper, and said to Julee, "Call Polly. She is going to have to deal with this."

Polly showed up that night to take Marty out to her house in Queens where for three days and three hundred dollars she promised to persuade him to perform his functions in the great outdoors once and for all. Julee, Sally, and I stood at the curb, waving good-bye as Polly drove away, Marty looking forlornly at us from the back window until they disappeared in the night, Julee and I wiping tears from our eyes, Sally looking around as if she couldn't figure out what had happened to her big little brother. Gone, just like that. *And just when I was beginning to like him,* she probably said to herself.

I couldn't have felt like more of a failure. That night I dreamed of walking through a forest with Marty, the ground covered with paper as far as the eye could see. He still wouldn't go.

Three days later Polly returned Marty to us, and there was celebration and jubilation. I think Sally was more relieved than happy. She'd worried about him the whole time, sniffing his kennel and staring at the apartment door.

"How is he?" I asked Polly.

"He's great. I love this dog. He's got the whole business down pat now."

"How did you do it?"

"We stayed outside until he went, all day if that's what it took. And that's what it took. He's the most stubborn dog I've ever met. Smart but stubborn. But I'm more stubborn."

She gave Marty a rub under his chin, told him to sit, held out a treat, told him to wait, one second, two seconds, three, four, five. "Take it," she whispered, and Marty politely took the treat from her hand. A few days ago, he would have practically taken my hand off.

"He's all yours now. Let me know when you need me again. 'Bye, Sally Browne. You're a good girl, too." With that she was off, back to Queens where there was a whole city full of dogs needing to be trained, to be taught, gently and lovingly, what it meant to live among the humans. Polly always said that every dog she trained taught her something. I reminded myself to ask her someday what Marty taught her.

Julee and I called Polly "Magic Polly" and she earned her moniker that time. I don't know what we would have done if Polly hadn't stepped in. But I do know this: from that day on,

Marty would rather have died than go in the house, paper or no paper.

MARTY WAS NOT THROUGH with his puppy tribulations. Enter a burly black Scottie named, predictably, Angus, one of the few dogs I could ever say I disliked. Of course, I never actually met Angus.

I would hear about him from Julee. In the late mornings, Julee would take Marty and Sally to an apartment building that had a pretty little courtyard open to the public. There were trees and a fountain with a little pool that people tossed coins into.

Angus liked the courtyard, too. He never bothered Sally, but the first time he saw Marty, he barked at him and nipped at his neck, common dominance behavior. After that, whenever Angus made an appearance, Marty would fall to the ground and roll submissively onto his back while Angus stood menacingly over him, growling and nipping. Angus never actually hurt poor Marty, but he bullied him unmercifully.

"That nasty dog is back," Julee would say on her phone, calling me at the office. "The owner is oblivious, so I have to go over and referee."

I nursed a growing grievance against this dog, this Scottish bully. Wasn't this pretty much what some kids did in the playground or schoolyard? Wasn't this something society denounced? Was there nothing to be done when a grown dog bullies a puppy? I kept threatening to accompany Julee to the little park, but she said to let her handle it.

"You're too emotional, Edward."

"Of course, I am. Besides, Marty is probably bigger than that Scottie now. He can kick his butt."

"He doesn't realize that. I'll talk to the owner. Don't worry; Marty will man up. He's going to be huge."

That was for sure. I couldn't wait.

One morning Julee called me excitedly. "Angus pushed Marty into the fountain pool," she reported.

"That bully!"

"I know. But guess what? Marty *loved* the water. I've never see him so excited. It was just a bit over his head, so he taught himself to swim. He had this incredible smile on his face. I almost cried."

That night when I took the dogs for their walk, I told Marty that sometimes blessings can be discovered in adversity and humiliation. I was certainly proof of that. He looked at me as if he had all that figured out, as if he hadn't stopped thinking about the amazing sensation of being in the water, the cold, wet ecstasy.

From that day forward, we were on a quest to find places in the city for Marty to swim. Usually we took him up to Central Park, which necessitated a cab ride and other chances for the dogs to get into trouble and for me to learn a lesson.

Taking advantage of the perfect spring weather one Saturday after Marty turned one (and Angus had finally stopped harassing him and I stopped entertaining revenge fantasies, like hurling Angus into the fountain pool), Julee, Marty, Sally, and I piled into a taxi cab that we'd managed to get to stop for us and headed to the park. We were stalled in traffic when a white horse hauling a carriage full of tourists stepped up and inclined his huge head to the rear window of our conveyance. Marty came totally unstrung, howling and thrashing around the backseat. He landed on poor Sally, who shrieked and yelped. The terrified cabbie threw us out in the middle of Columbus Circle. I apologized miserably and gave him a huge compensatory tip. He was smiling as we left him.

In the park, we took our eye off Sally just long enough for her to snatch a hot dog out of a little girl's grasp. I bought her another hot dog while Julee tried to make things right with the mom. Meanwhile, the kid gleefully fed her second hot dog to Marty, who thought he deserved one after Sally's bounty. The little girl apparently agreed. "She's always been afraid of dogs, especially big ones like your Lab. Now look at her!" the mother exclaimed. The little girl was squealing and clapping her hands with excitement.

"Can I ride him?" she asked. "Like the merry-go-round?"

"Not today," I said, moving the dogs along.

We headed to the lake near Bethesda Fountain for some swimming and fetching. Technically we were breaking the law, unleashing our dogs into the water where boats, both life-size and toy, plowed the waters. One time Marty nearly capsized an elaborate model ship sailed by remote control from the shore. He couldn't find the dummy I had thrown for him to fetch and was paddling around frantically in search of it. As he closed in on the remote control ship the owners on shore began to yell and wave their arms, jumping up and down until Marty veered away at the last second.

But the swimming really tired him out and lately, as he matured, he got a little testy if he didn't get enough exercise. Maybe more than a little testy, which worried me. *A tired dog,* I told myself, *is a good dog.* An exhausted dog was even better.

So today we really wanted to give him a serious workout with the floating orange dummy. So what if we got a ticket? It wasn't like they could throw us in jail. I hoped.

I threw the dummy until my shoulder ached, Marty barking at me whenever the pace of my throws slowed. He would dive in and fetch while Sally scolded him from shore then dove in to fetch him, her little body trailing his big white one. Finally, I threw the dummy as far as I could. I have a pretty good arm from years of playing ball, and the dummy arced high into the air, spinning end over end, an orange blur in the blinding blue sky.

It landed in a rowboat, occupied by an infatuated young couple out for what is considered a romantic rite of passage in Manhattan—an afternoon rowing the waters of Central Park. They glanced about, puzzled. They'd been too busy gazing into each other's eyes to be fully cognizant of what had happened and the jeopardy they were suddenly in.

Marty homed in like a torpedo on the target. I had no doubt he would throw himself over the transom of the boat to retrieve his dummy, tipping the couple into the lake and sinking their vessel. They would probably call the police when they got to shore if they didn't drown first. Could they even swim? Why weren't they required to wear flotation devices, these oblivious young lovers?

"Marty!" Julee and I screamed. "Marty, no!" Sally ran back and forth on shore barking.

He was undeterred, focused like a four-legged smart bomb on the boat and the couple and his beloved orange dummy, steering with his giant tail as they desperately tried to get busy with the oars and escape. No power on earth was going to stop him, though.

"Throw it out!" I yelled. "Toss it in the water! Hurry!"

Marty must have been about a yard or two away from the target, ready to hurl himself into the boat, when the woman, collecting her wits, her boyfriend paralyzed by apparent indecision, noticed the sopping dummy, picked it up with her thumb and forefinger, a slightly disgusted expression on her face, and flipped it overboard just in the nick of time. Marty clamped it in his jaws and brought it ashore, oblivious to the drama he had caused and proud of his performance, which really was remarkably athletic. The couple waved to us, weak with relief. By now both dogs were soaking wet and trailing tendrils of muddy water weeds. But they were happy and rather pleased with themselves.

"Let's get out of here," Julee muttered. "We're pushing our luck."

Too late. Down a path from the direction of Tavern on the Green strolled a wedding party accompanied by their photographer eager, no doubt, to get some memorable waterside shots. The sky, the lake, the lovers in their boats sans flotation devices, the cute little fairy-tale bridge in the distance, like a Seurat canvas.

And the dogs.

They rushed to investigate the new arrivals, the bride resplendent in pure white, and prior to introducing themselves they shook out their coats quite vigorously, splattering the surprised bride and her equally surprised bridesmaids with tiny dots of mud. It was a disaster.

I was lightning quick with a prayer: *Lord, please don't let them kill us.*

There was a pause. Maybe it was the joy and the celebration of the day, but suddenly the entire wedding party burst into laughter. "We've already taken a thousand shots of me in this dress!" the bride laughed. So all was well, and Marty and Sally got their picture taken with the bespattered bride. Somewhere, in some couple's wedding album, are two wet, grimy, grinning dogs, delighted to be a part of someone's big day.

I was sweating as we left the park, still shaken by the various close calls. No chance of getting a cab with these bedraggled mutts. We wouldn't do that to a cabbie anyway. They had a tough enough calling as it was and many came from countries where dogs were not afforded the privilege of private transportation. So we had a long walk back to our apartment.

Along the way Julee sensed my subsiding panic. "Listen," she said. "Everything worked out—a smiling cabbie, a braver little girl who'll someday get a dog just like Marty, a couple of boaters who barely escaped getting dunked by a crazed Labrador, and a wedding photo for the ages. They'll remember that forever!"

I took a deep breath. Julee said maybe God was training us a bit, teaching us to take the little potential disasters in life in stride and not to panic. I was in no position to disagree. I was just very grateful we hadn't caused more havoc than we did. And a part of me was grateful that in the greatest city on earth, in the most famous park in the world, on a spring day that God had made perfect, Marty and Sally had stolen the show.

*   *   *

SHORTLY AFTER THESE EVENTS, we moved back to the West Side to our old apartment on Thirtieth Street, where Sally had spent the first months of her life with us before our temporary relocation to the East Side. Marty did not take the move in stride. In fact, it seemed to unnerve him, leaving the only home he had ever really known for some strange new apartment in a larger building full of strangers with strange dogs like Freddy, a rescued terrier mix who lived with our neighbor Cynthia down the hall. Maybe Freddy's terrier genes, reminiscent of the bully boy Angus, caused Marty to go into a rage at the mere scent of him. Or maybe it came from the fact that Freddy was inexplicably unfixed, something I never understood in a rescued dog. If Marty saw him, he would launch an attack, jerking you off your feet if you didn't plant your weight, take the leash in two hands, and counteract his lunge. Whatever the case, it was a problem.

It became a bigger problem as Marty grew to a muscular one hundred pounds by his third birthday, almost the size of Julee, whose safety I was beginning to worry about. Not that Marty would ever intentionally hurt Julee. He was utterly devoted to her. But when he went into a rage, there was no telling the collateral damage. Even I had trouble holding on to him. And it wasn't just the unfortunate Freddy who set him off. Most terriers did it. He was unpredictable, which was the greatest mystery of all.

Except for these meltdowns, Marty was the sweetest animal. So many people loved him. Julee understood his vulnerabilities and grew to be tremendously protective. She was vigilant for situations that would trigger him. She would take him down to Saint Francis, light candles for him, and ask for the friar's blessings. I looked into a condition called hyperadrenalism, where the adrenal gland is triggered but lacks the hormonal mechanism to shut itself down. Marty certainly fit the bill. But we couldn't find a vet who knew how to treat it.

One beautiful evening in early September we decided to take the dogs out for dinner. Or rather take them with us while we ate at an outdoor café on Columbus Avenue. The dogs loved this since invariably they would score some table scraps, if not from us then from fellow diners. New Yorkers are like that. We secured Sally's leash to one of the chairs and Marty's to the table itself, which had a wooden top and a heavy metal base. The waitress took our order and brought a bowl of water for the dogs.

We were halfway through the meal when a lady passed by walking a dog that may have been part Scottie. That was enough for Marty. He went berserk. He leapt up, roaring like a rhinoceros. I tried to grab his leash. Too late. He pulled the table over, food flying and glassware shattering. And then he was off in pursuit of the enemy dog, dragging the table behind him, moving in a kind of slow-motion gallop up fashionable Columbus Avenue. The woman with the dog looked back in horror and ran. People scattered. The table banged up against a parked car, setting off the alarm. I finally caught up to Marty and wrestled him to the ground and tried to calm him. It was as if he were having a fit.

A busboy came to retrieve the table. I'm not sure what country he was from, but I was pretty certain he had never seen anything like this. Because of the nervous looks on our fellow diners' faces, I was reluctant to walk Marty back to the outdoor dining area so I kept him at a distance while Julee tried to assuage the owner and pay for the damages. He would hear nothing of it, insisting insurance would cover it and, by the way, the meal was on the house and—unspoken—please take your dogs away and never bring that crazy one back again.

Marty was as sweet as an angel on the walk back to the apartment. He strode more like a lion than a dog. He made friends with folks who stopped to admire his magnificence, said a friendly hello to several dogs he found absolutely no objection to. Still, once back at the apartment, Julee buried her head in her hands and said, "We have to do something."

So again we turned to Polly. She had never failed us. This time would be the first. "I'm not really an expert in this kind of aggression," she said, sitting on our couch the day after the incident and giving Marty a hug (Marty adored Polly ever since he spent that weekend with her when he finally lost the great battle of wills—he respected his conqueror). "And frankly, Marty now weighs almost what I do, which makes it hard for me to work with him from a physical standpoint."

But she did have an idea, Dr. B., out in New Jersey. "He's not your ordinary dog trainer," she said. "I'll give him a call."

In fact, Dr. B. was a noted professor of clinical psychology at a New Jersey university. During his grad student years when he did the grunt work in the laboratory, evaluating behavioral experiments carried out with a variety of animals, he grew more interested in animal psychology than in what makes humans tick.

"The animals trained me!" he told us on our first meeting at his house in a woodsy Jersey suburb on a crisp fall day that smelled of apples and burning leaves. "They're more interesting than humans." Which was how Dr. B. became an animal behaviorist working in a university psychology department. "You can't understand an experiment unless you understand the psychology of the animals being used in that experiment." He sighed. "Sometimes my colleagues can't grasp that concept."

He poured us coffee and read his notes from his conversation with Polly.

"I think Marty's aggression is almost certainly fear-based rather than an overzealous desire for dominance or antisocial behavior. I can tell he is a very bright, friendly dog," he said. "I strongly suspect his inappropriate behavior is triggered by fear, like many people's. It's not so different."

Julee wiped away a tear, and I gave Marty a pat on his massive neck.

"I would like you to leave Marty with me for a while."

"How long," Julee asked. "Like a day?"

"No, this will probably take weeks. I want him to live with me so I can get to know him. At night, he will sleep in my garage. Don't worry, it's heated and carpeted. It's very nice, very comfortable."

"But he'll get so lonely!" Julee cried.

"After the work we will do, Marty will need some time to himself. Dogs need their privacy, too."

"When can we see him?"

"You will have weekend visitations."

I detected Julee's hand twitching and curling like she wanted to snatch Marty's leash and escape with him. She'd once threatened to run off with Marty to the most remote spot in North America she could find. "I'll wait tables in a diner in Idaho. I'll live in a trailer. I'll do anything to protect this dog." I believed her, too.

"This isn't something we can correct overnight, Julee," Dr. B. said. "It's going to take work. Please trust me."

Dr. B. was a big guy and Marty had taken a clear liking to him already, which finally helped Julee relax. A few minutes later after agreeing on a price for his services, we stiffened our upper lips and handed over our beautiful and beloved white Lab to Dr. B.

"I'm going to have to sell some recording equipment to pay for this," Julee said on the way back to Manhattan. I told her that wasn't necessary, we'd figure something out. "No, I think I should," she insisted. As if it were some kind of penance.

"It wasn't anything you did, Jules," I said. "Don't beat yourself up."

"Maybe it was. Maybe Marty feeds off my own fear. Maybe I did this to him."

"Don't be ridiculous—" I started to say before it was too late.

"Don't say I'm ridiculous! I know that dog better than you do, Edward. I know Marty better than anyone. Remember that."

We rode the rest of the way home in silence.

For the next four Saturdays, Julee and I rented a car and drove to Jersey to work with Marty and Dr. B. It was not lost on me the similarities between this and family weekends at drug and alcohol rehabs I'd been a patient in. I hoped Marty didn't think he had done anything wrong, the way I did in those situations. No matter how many times they tell you in rehab that it's no use feeling guilty, you always do.

How happy Marty always was to see us! Yet clearly he was enjoying himself in the New Jersey woodlands. "He's collected just about every stick on the hillside," Dr. B. said. "This dog loves the outdoors and he wants tons of exercise."

"We walk him four times a day in the city, at least," Julee said, a bit defensively. "I take him everywhere."

Dr. B. made no response to this.

On those Saturdays, we worked with Dr. B. and Marty on anticipating trigger events and how to avoid them, or once they occurred, how to short-circuit Marty's response by redirecting his behavior and lavishing him with praise and reassurance. We worked on giving him confidence and a sense of security. In two of the sessions Dr. B. required Sally's attendance so he could evaluate her effect on Marty. For her part, Sally seemed eager to demonstrate that she could learn things quicker than Marty could. She loved showing off, and she was a crafty little dog to say the least. And I had the strangest sense that she knew exactly what was going on with Marty and Dr. B. She sometimes had a contentious relationship with her brother, but she also had great empathy for him. You could tell by the way she barked and worried and paced the shoreline every time he dove wildly into some lake. You could tell now when she watched him work with Dr. B., there was something in her eyes and attentive posture that said she wanted Marty to be okay for the sake of our little pack. There was sibling rivalry, of course, but there was sibling love, too. I wondered what one would ever do without the other.

After a month, we got Marty back. Sally barked and nipped at him for being away. We threw him a little party with his favorite delicacies—filet mignon, shrimp, and ice cream, in small portions, of course. Julee and I ate the leftovers, with a few bites for Sally.

All that winter Marty was on his best behavior. We had a couple of close calls to be sure, but we were ever vigilant for situations that might set him off and were ready with Dr. B.'s countermeasures. Julee did some touring overseas that spring, and we hired a big strong dog walker to handle Marty while I was at work. Our main requirement was brute strength, and the guy we hired, Blake, moonlighted as a bouncer, which was just about a perfect answer to prayer.

Everything came crashing down on July Fourth. We were walking the dogs early, before the fireworks started. The streets were crowded. People were setting off firecrackers. The air crackled with energy. Maybe all the commotion made Marty nervous. We took him around a corner, hoping to get away from the crowds. He practically collided with another dog who was extended well out on a flexi leash, a small terrier with a big star-spangled cape, all dressed up for the festivities. Marty snapped. Instantly, he had the dog in his mouth. It was like something out of *Mutual of Omaha's Wild Kingdom* with Marlin Perkins from Sunday nights on TV when I was a kid. I didn't know what else to do but slam him with my fist between his shoulder blades until he dropped the dog.

Julee and I were horrified. The terrier's owners were in shock, their dog bleeding on the sidewalk, likewise in shock.

I could not say a prayer fast enough—for the injured dog, for Julee, for Marty. *Please don't let this dog die.*

Julee and I put the owners and their dog in a cab and sent them up to the Animal Medical Center, then took Marty and Sally home before heading to the Medical Center ourselves. We found them in the waiting room. Their dog was in surgery having a scalp wound stitched up and other injuries attended to but he was expected to be all right after a night in the hospital for observation. The dog's name was Mookie. "He's very traumatized," one of the owners said. We didn't know how to begin to apologize. Mortified wasn't a strong enough word. "We'll pray for him," I said. "We'll pray for you and your dog, too," they answered. We stopped by the cashier on the way out and had them run our credit card to cover the dog's expenses. I prayed we had enough room on our credit line.

The streets were crazy. Cabs were impossible to get and buses were packed. It was a beautiful night, so Julee and I decided to walk back to our apartment. I stopped by a deli to buy a cold bottle of water, not because I was thirsty but because my hand hurt from punching Marty, though I was sure he was just fine. I could have hit him with a tire iron and it wouldn't have fazed him.

As it happened, we walked by the little courtyard where Marty played as a puppy, where Angus used to lord it over him. "You know he'd actually roll over and pee, he was so scared of that dog," Julee said. We sat on the low wall of the fountain where young Marty had first experienced the joy of swimming. Julee broke down in sobs.

"Edward, I'm afraid we're going to have to put him down. I can't stand the thought of him hurting another dog."

"We're getting way ahead of ourselves, Jules," I said.

"No. What if they report him? They have our names. What if the city takes him away? I'd rather we do it ourselves with our own vet. And if we give him away, who's to say he isn't going to hurt another animal? Or get killed in a fight on some farm somewhere? You don't know how much I pray for that dog. I pray for Marty every day, begging God to keep him safe, pleading. I hardly pray for anything else anymore."

I put my arms around her. "You always said that Marty deep down inside was a good dog, a misunderstood dog, a dog that wanted to do right, that he was more your dog than any other dog had ever been. I just don't believe you're ready to give up on him. I'm not. God's not."

"Those owners bear some of the blame," Julee said, standing up. "Flexi leashes are totally irresponsible in the city. They put that dog at risk. I'm going to tell them!"

"I agree about the flexi," I said, resuming our walk, "but let's just focus on helping Marty."

The dogs were waiting for us. I sensed a pall over the apartment. Marty was down. He barely greeted us. Sally, who was a witness to the mayhem, stayed curled up on the couch, though eventually she brought me a toy. When it was time for bed, we all crowded into the bedroom together and turned out the lights. There were rumbles in the night but I couldn't tell if it was fireworks or thunder.

I wandered into the kitchen at about 3:00 a.m. to find Julee drinking coffee. She seemed pretty wired.

"I know what we're going to do about Marty."

"What?" I said, half dumb with sleep.

"We're going to buy him a house."

"We are? What, a doghouse?"

"No, a real house. It's the only solution."

Julee and I had always dreamed of moving up from our one-bedroom rental to a larger apartment of our own. There were some good deals coming on the market in our Chelsea neighborhood, which was on the way up, according to the *Times*. And I'd recently been promoted to editor-in-chief of *Guideposts*. Still, a little vacation place in the country seemed far in our future.

We occasionally borrowed a house in the Berkshires of western Massachusetts from a friend, Amanda, who was the Juilliard-trained keyboardist for 10,000 Maniacs and frequently on tour with the band. If she couldn't rent her place out, we got to use it; and it was true, Marty loved the country. He was a different dog there. He loved the hills and the streams and the lakes, and he taught me to love them, too, reconnecting me with my formative years in Michigan.

In the weeks that followed, Julee and the dogs, using the absent Amanda's cabin as a base of operations, roamed the Berkshires for the perfect place. I joined them on the weekends. One day Julee called me at the office. "Marty found his house."

"He did?"

"He loves it. It's a little funky, a hand-hewn post-and-beam built into a hillside. All peg construction, not a nail in sight. Not the usual layout, so I'm not surprised they're having a little trouble moving it. We'll have to paint and put in a heating system—"

"We'll what?"

"Marty just ran around in circles when we got here. He practically knocked the real estate broker on his butt. It comes with thirteen wooded acres, not developable, so they're more or less throwing it in. But it's a kingdom for him. There's some kid poet squatting here now, a dropout from Simon's Rock College who's into Gary Snyder—there's pictures of him everywhere—but he's happy to move on. He says he's been waiting for us to come. He's already communed with the dogs and is writing a poem about them and their new house. Edward, this is perfect."

"What does Sally think?"

"She wants what Marty wants at this point, I think."

Which is how the Berkshires house came to be ours, or the dogs', rather. My mother had recently died and left us enough money for a down payment. Julee said, "This is exactly what Estelle would have wanted us to do with the money. I know this is her doing." At the closing, Julee asked if Marty's and Sally's names could be added to the deed. She was only half-kidding.

THIS PARADE OF MEMORIES came back to me sitting in the Home Sweet Home Doughnut Shoppe. By then I must have eaten a dozen, foolishly waiting to hear something about Millie's surgery. Dr. June promised she'd be the first on the operating table but realistically I wouldn't hear from her until late afternoon. So I returned to the house and sat out on the back porch, where there was a memorial stone to Marty that had "Athlete and Mama's Boy" engraved on it with his dates.

Our big crazy Lab had done well living in the hills. The house was a blessing. Even his behavior back in the city improved. Maybe it was because he was getting older, but I always thought that in the back of his mind he knew he had the house to go to and this calmed him. Oddly enough, he even made friends with a young Scottie that moved in up the block.

When he was ten and a half, his health suddenly declined. He was diagnosed with lymphoma, too far gone to treat. We were devastated. Ten years was too short a time. Julee was inconsolable. She'd grown up back in Iowa with a vet who'd gone on to national prominence, and now she consulted him regularly on Marty's cancer. He promised to tell us when it was time to take matters into our own hands and do the right thing for Marty. And his advice, when it finally did come, came at a difficult time.

Julee had long been committed to performing a three-show date at Joe's Pub at the Public Theater featuring material from her newest album. It had been sold out for weeks. Rehearsals with the band were in full swing just as Marty began his final decline.

"I have to be with him all the time now. I'm pulling out of the shows," she said. "Call them and tell them I'm canceling."

"Don't put me in that position, Jules. You can't pull out. You know that."

"Call them!" she screamed. "Call them!"

We stood staring at each other for a long time, Marty sleeping at our feet. Julee was shaking. Her face was white. Then she buried her head in my chest. "Sometimes I just hate the choices we have to make," she said. "These are the two things

I've always prayed for, and now both are making me miserable."

Julee did the shows at Joe's, and the next day, Sunday, we drove the dogs up to the house and called the vet we were using at the time to come out. Marty was so very weak, but he still had his appetite. Nothing surprised me about that dog. We fixed him some steak and shrimp on the grill and a little Berkshire Ice Cream, vanilla, his favorite flavor. At sunset when the light was turning a soft mossy green and a mountain chill snuck into the air and the owls were hooting, we laid him down on a blanket in the backyard and said our good-byes. Sally, too.

Afterward, Julee went upstairs to call her mother. I tried to lose myself in a Yankees game, staring blankly at the screen, Sally's head in my lap. Suddenly the announcers went crazy. The Yanks had just hit three back-to-back home runs, practically unheard of, all of them into the right field bleachers at the stadium. That could only mean one thing. Three consecutive home runs by left-handed hitters. Even more of an odds-beater. Like winning the lotto. I smiled, then started to laugh, remembering how a vet had once told me that Marty was a dog of considerable rarity. "He's left-pawed. Don't you see? Your dog is a lefty!" When I told Julee about the three left-handed big flies, she screamed and laughed and jumped up and down and waved her arms at the heavens.

Yet Julee's grief at losing Marty ran dark and deep. Sally did what she could, but she was getting older, too. So was Julee's mom. "Everyone is dying on me," she said one night.

It wasn't until quite recently that people began to take seriously the grief one feels over the loss of a pet. In fact, our friends the Franciscans were among the first to establish support groups for grieving pet owners. At the time Julee and I had few places to turn, really. I had my twelve-step program, but even there the death of a pet was not exactly what people wanted to discuss unless you were going to use it as an "excuse" to drink or to use drugs.

It would be over a year before Julee began to finally let go of her grief. She grew ever closer to Sally. Cocker spaniels were her mother's favorites, and Julee took after her. And then, one bitter January morning before the sun had come up, Julee got a call from the nursing home in Iowa where her mother lived that Wilma Cruise had died of a stroke.

The most helpless feeling in the world is to be unable to console the inconsolable. Julee was a self-admitted mommy's girl. Early in her life, like so many daughters, she had a difficult relationship with her mother. Julee joked that the Cruises sometimes treated their dogs better than they treated one another, and they did love their dogs. In later years Julee and Wilma tried to make up for it. When I met Julee, she was talking to her mother on the phone virtually every day, sometimes for hours, as if they were desperate to recapture the lost years and the lost love, to unfreeze that emotional permafrost. And in large part they succeeded. I remember a performance Julee did at the Cannes Film Festival. She was the star of the night, performing a song on the beach under a perfect moon. There was a major after-party packed with global A-listers. This was the dream, living it up on the French Riviera with international movie stars and the paparazzi, cruising like piranhas. All this for a girl who had come to New York from the Midwest and waited tables until she got her break. But all Julee wanted to do was hurry back to the fancy hotel suite and call her mom in Iowa, who waited up all night to hear how the show went. They were still talking when I fell asleep in my tux.

Wilma had suffered a major stroke five years before the one that killed her. Julee was already packed when I got home from the office the day it happened. So were Marty and Sally.

"You're taking the dogs?"

"I need them. So does Mom. Especially Sally."

Julee had Sally's flight kennel ready, but Marty had long outgrown his. He wouldn't fit no matter what we tried. This was all making me very nervous.

"Look, I know what I'm doing. I know what Mom needs."

At LaGuardia the airline informed Julee that Sally could fly in the luggage compartment under their new Priority Pet program. She'd get a boarding pass and everything. The document would be presented to Julee once Sally was safely on board. Julee was using her miles to upgrade to first class. She thought it would get the dogs better treatment.

But Marty was just too big to go Priority Pet. He would have to be shipped air cargo and at a considerably higher cost once you factored in the huge cage that had to be rented. He would be in a different compartment from Sally but just as safe, the airline promised.

They changed planes in Minneapolis for the flight into Des Moines and the luggage was transferred expeditiously. Julee got Sally's boarding pass ceremoniously presented to her in the first-class cabin, which Julee later told me gained her maybe six extra inches of leg room and a cocktail she didn't want. What she did want was confirmation that Marty was on board.

"We don't really track the air cargo, ma'am. You did say he was going air cargo, right?'

No doubt it was the deep-down anger and fear over her mother's stroke that bubbled up to the surface of Julee's consciousness like a boiling spring, not that my wife doesn't have a bit of a temper to begin with.

"I want to know where that dog is. I want confirmation he is on board."

The flight attendant disappeared toward the cockpit and spoke into a microphone. She came back in a few quick minutes. "I'm sorry, ma'am. We can't confirm that. But I'm sure he'll be on the next flight if he's not on this one. Or the one after. In fact, we can arrange to have him delivered to you."

"Let me off this plane."

"I'm sorry, we've secured the doors. The pilot is about to pull back."

"I don't care," Julee said, standing up and grabbing her carry-on. "You lost my dog. I'm getting off. And so is my other dog. Tell your luggage handlers to get busy. She's a Priority Pet named Sally. Here's her boarding pass."

"And what would the other dog's name be?"

"Marty!"

With that, Julee stormed up the aisle toward the cockpit. Another flight attendant intercepted her.

"Ma'am, please take your seat."

"Not till I talk to the captain about the dog of mine you seem to have lost. How can you take off not knowing what you did with him?"

Cooler heads eventually prevailed. Or should I say dead heads. A sympathetic pilot flying to his next flight city intervened. They opened the door, let Julee off, brought Sally out of the hold while all the passengers on the terminal side of the plane stared (a few clapped and cheered, Julee said). By then Julee was at the boarding gate, trying to keep it together, telling a customer service rep that her mother was in a coma and that the airline had lost her dog.

"This is the worst day of my life."

"I can only say a prayer for your mother, honey, but we're going to find that dog of yours, I promise."

"Thank you," Julee said.

Eventually they located Marty at the far end of the airport inside a giant air cargo hangar where he had somehow been misdirected. Julee heard his bark from one of those little open-air trucks she and a cargo supervisor were making the rounds in. Inside the hangar Julee discovered Marty had been paroled from his cage and was playing fetch with the cargo guys, barking deliriously in between throws. The space must have been the size of two football fields and the guys were having a contest who could throw the ball farther. Marty was having a blast. The cargo guys were sorry to see him go. "He's a great dog," they said.

"I'll personally make sure he is on that next flight with you, ma'am, and I am truly sorry about your mom," the cargo supervisor said as they drove back to the terminal, Marty back in his giant cage.

Julee put her head on the supervisor's shoulder and sobbed. Later, when her mother had regained consciousness but not her speech or much movement, the story so tickled her there were tears streaming down her cheeks. Julee told it to her again and again.

Now her mother was gone. Marty was gone. And soon Sally was as well, a year or so later while Julee was doing a concert in Germany and I went up to the house with our beautiful girl and spent her final days chasing the sunlight. Life felt like it had darkened. Our parents were dead. The dogs that had been so much a part of our marriage and our lives had gone on. Our careers were good but they were what they were. Our faith felt obscured by grief, like you had to fight through a fog to find God.

And then like a shaft of light from heaven, Millie appeared. As if all those dogs—Rudy, Pete, Marty, Sally, Kelly, and countless others—had conspired with the angels to send us the exact dog we needed and who needed us. A big, strong, gentle, kind, beautiful animal sent to lead us farther down the path of life. We were lost and she found us.

And now, eight and half years later, here I sat wondering how much longer we would have her and begging God for every second.

CHAPTER 7

———— 🐾 ————

I spent the afternoon on the back porch, staring at Marty's stone and waiting for the phone to ring, watching the sky go gray. I was too unsettled to do much else and feeling more than a little sick from the donut binge. When the phone did finally ring, I nearly tumbled over my bloated stomach running to answer it (there's no cell coverage where we are). But it wasn't Dr. June with the good news that Millie had pulled through like a champ and everything was going to end happily ever after. Instead it was a friend in New York, Chris, someone I knew well from my twelve-step program.

"Any news?" he asked.

"Not yet. I thought this might be them. Or Julee."

"Sorry . . ."

"No, no, thanks for calling."

"How're you holding up?"

"Fine."

"Really? So how badly do you want to have a drink?"

I paused. That was certainly a shot across the bow.

"Not at all," I said. I hadn't had or wanted a drink in many years, not consciously at least.

"So everything is hunky-dory says the alcoholic who nearly drank himself to death over failed relationships and painful losses and love that went astray and failures and malignant resentments, who was hospitalized and institutionalized and homeless and lost and crazy—"

"Okay, okay, I get it. Enough."

Chris laughed. "I'm not trying to give you a beatdown, bro, I just know how easy it is for us to conveniently forget that we're powerless alcoholics prone to reverting to our previous disease state, especially in big-time trigger situations like this."

"I haven't thought about a drink in a long time—"

"Neither have I. But I still *think* like an alcoholic. I act like an alcoholic. Who did you get mad at recently for no good reason? And don't tell me you didn't."

I thought about my rage at the heartless radiologist, that coldhearted shrew. I was still mad at her, truth to tell, nursing that grudge at the breast of my resentment, as if it were her fault Millie had a messed-up spleen and maybe something worse that I didn't want to even think about.

"And I bet you're still mad at them for no good reason. Probably just someone doing their job, right?"

I laughed again. It was a relief to talk to a friend, someone who understood my feelings, and yes, I needed to let go of this resentment, to hurl it right in my Higher Power's face. A sponsor once told me that holding a resentment was like drinking poison and expecting the other person to die.

"Chris the Amazing AA Seer has another prediction: You acted out. Probably with food. Probably sugar, knowing you, which is a kissin' cousin of alcohol, the next best thing for some people."

I had mindlessly gorged on coffee and donuts, that was for sure. I kept stuffing my face long after I wanted to stop, and I was paying the price in terms of gastric distress.

"I have a third prognostication. You ready for it?"

"Lay it on me."

"You're projecting like crazy. Not just whether Millie has cancer but how you will feel about it, how Julee will react. That scares you even more. The emotion. The uncertainty and lack of control. I know. I've been there. You know I've been there, and you said the same stuff to me. So now I'm giving it back, bro. We don't know the future, and our projections are almost always worse than the reality. We control nothing and for us life is a day at a time and God is in control at all times. And his will is as immutable as his love for us. So relax, my friend, and stay present in the moment. That is where you belong, and where you will do the most good, especially for Millie. And Julee. That is where sobriety lives. That is how you stay alive. Because as you and a million other people in the program have told me, our choices are a matter of life and death. Sobriety is a gift that can slip away from us with the tip of a glass. And the drink or the drug is the end of the slip, not the beginning. Our downfall is always in our thinking. But you know all this. Gotta go. You hang in there and call anytime, day or night. I mean it. And lay off the donuts or whatever you're eating too much of."

Chris clicked off, but his voice took up residence in my head. There wasn't anything he told me that I didn't already know, and yet I needed to hear it. I needed to hear it because it is so easy for alcoholics not to listen to themselves, to willfully ignore what they know, to disregard their own advice and hard-earned lessons. That's why we have the slogans, as simplistic as they might sound to some: Keep It Simple, Live and Let Live, A Day at a Time, Easy Does It, But for the Grace of God. The first time I saw those sayings plastered on the wall of a dismal church basement I was dumbstruck. How could anyone expect to stay sober on the strength of this kind of trite spiritual boilerplate? They had to be kidding. Who came up with this stuff? What was this, the Mickey Mouse Club for drunks?

Yet at one point or another every one of those slogans—to say nothing of those church basements—had saved my sober butt, sometimes on a daily basis. Their very strength is in their simplicity. Their mysterious power lies in how they cut through all the convoluted rationalizing and self-justifying we alcoholics are cripplingly prone to, all the manipulative, psychological jujitsu. (Do you know how exhausting it is trying to manipulate yourself?) But most mysterious of all for me is that last slogan, *But for the Grace of God.* It was that saying that preemptively saved my life one summer night in New York years before I got sober, long before I saw it tacked to a basement wall. And it involved a mysterious dog who may have stood between me and oblivion.

That summer, the summer between my first and second years of graduate school, I was more or less on my own. Not such a good thing, though it felt wonderful at the time. Liberating. The woman I'd started seeing was studying in Europe, and I was living in a graduate student dorm for close to free. I had a work-study job with the drama school that had seemed like a good idea to me at first. And I'd promised just about everyone that I would do something about my drinking.

The job involved working at the old Yale University Theatre, not technically part of the drama school, assisting one of the third-year production students, inspecting the rafters, catwalks, rigging, and other upper regions of the sixty-year-old building and repairing things that needed repairing, mostly old rivets.

What I thought would give me valuable insight into the technical aspects of theater turned out to be brutal, suffocating drudgery, mostly due to the individual overseeing our shared labors, David P.

David was aggressively cheerful, especially early in the morning as we made our way up to the rafters, several stories above the old stage. He talked almost without pause, mostly about tools and my habit of being late. Once we were in the rafters, he'd break out the power drill and other implements and we'd get to the deafening business of drilling through steel. He liked to talk to inanimate things with tools. "Let's talk to that overhang with a hammer. Let's talk to that beam with an eight-inch bit."

It was a hot summer that year but a mild one wouldn't have made much difference up in those airless rafters, where it always felt twenty degrees hotter than it was outside. Before our first coffee break, I was drenched in sweat, often tinged with alcohol vapors still transpiring from my person because of the previous night's campaign, a phenomenon that was usually remarked upon. But the worst thing of all—and I know of no better way to say this without offending readers' gentle sensibilities—was that David P. was chronically and, perhaps most maddeningly, politely flatulent.

By that point in my life I had long since forsaken prayer, but pray I did to be delivered from this asphyxiating hell. Every accompanying "excuse me" and "so sorry" drove me one step closer to madness. I'd stare far down at the stage where Paul Newman and Robert Klein and Stacy Keach had trod the boards in the years before the famed Yale Repertory Theatre on Chapel Street had been established by Robert Brustein, converted from an old Baptist church, I should add. I tried to will myself to believe that I was breathing in the dazzling history of theater production at Yale instead of working in the aging beams of a theater from a previous era with a partner who was in no position to be complaining about the alcohol vapors rising from my pores. I've held several brutal, backbreaking jobs in my life, perhaps in an unconscious attempt to pay for my sins, but no blot on my soul ever demanded a penance like this.

These were hard dues to pay for my education, but I accepted them. The end of the project brought me into a kind of euphoria. I treated myself to a baseball game at Yankee Stadium, a reward for the agonies I had undergone. My beloved Detroit Tigers were in town. I was still a diehard Tigers fan at the time. My mom was sending me the Motor City sports pages (both papers) nearly every day. Later that would change as she declined. She would send me the wrong sections of the newspaper, business instead of sports. As she faded, so did my allegiance to the Tigers, as if I couldn't separate it from my mom's devotion to the team, as if that attachment died with her, a very weird form of sports codependence, I suppose.

I'd been reasonably sober in the weeks leading up to my trip on the Metro-North New Haven line into the city for the game. I'd been trying hard to control myself and I was almost afraid to wonder if it would last.

Grand Central Terminal, where the train discharged me in my Tigers cap with the Olde English *D*, always swept my breath away. I vaguely remembered it from passing through as a child, as if the sheer zeitgeist of the building had imprinted on some primitively impressionable section of my brain, soft clay stamped with iron. My heart raced a bit every time I stepped from the track into the grand waiting room, even if, at the time, the celestial ceiling was grimy with age and a huge, garish Kodak sign dominated the east side of the terminal like a giant slide projector screen. I half-expected to see my father's shots from some summer at the Jersey Shore appear suddenly, little Eddie with his outie and his concave asthmatic chest standing on the beach at Stone Harbor with his brother Bobby. I will confess to sometimes missing that giant commercial slab of Kodachrome. Just don't tell anyone.

I caught the 4 subway up to the stadium, bought a ticket in the lower deck in left field, and settled in to watch batting practice. I also thought it was a good idea to settle in to a hot dog and a cold beer. What's a ballgame without a beer? There could be no harm in that on this fabulous summer night.

Somewhere around the fifth inning some rowdies a few

rows behind me noticed my cap and began pointing and screaming, "Take it off! Take it off!" I immediately reversed it to afford them a better view of the Olde English *D*. This just incited them more, of course, and things might have gotten out of hand if a beer vendor with megaphonic lungs hadn't materialized and diverted everyone's attention, including mine. By now I was on my third or so. More like so.

The Tigers pulled off a late-inning comeback, as I somewhat recall, with a home run by Lance Parrish and a bases-clearing ground rule double by Lou Whitaker that careened into the stands a few rows in front of me. I left the stadium happy but wary due to my cap, which drew hostile stares all the way down the exit ramps.

It was still early, at least by my clock. No reason to rush back to moribund New Haven. I rode the subway down to the Village in search of adventure. The train was not air-conditioned, and the roar and the hot dirty wind poured into the car as it rocked and slammed down the track to Astor Place, where I got off. I drifted from one bar to the next, like a cork bobbing on the bay, each location a little hazier than its predecessor, occasionally joining little knots of people, occasionally talking to a woman. One, a psych student at NYU, asked me about my brother's death when I brought up my family. "Was it natural causes?" she asked, an awkward phrase if ever there was one, with its voyeuristic undertones. Her lowered voice was laden with practiced empathy and she leaned in closer.

"It depends on who you ask," I said. "They never really closed the books on it."

"What do you think?"

"It is what it is, like most things, don't you think?"

The conversation kind of died after that, a natural death, I would say. By two o'clock I found myself stumbling through the East Village, at the time decidedly less salubrious environs than the Village proper and therefore decidedly more seductive. I followed some people into a cavernous place with a deafening band that sounded like Sonic Youth with blown amplifiers. From there I migrated with a loose group of revelers further east into Alphabet City, where the avenues become letters and drugs were as available as drink, on every street corner and in every bar bathroom. Literally anything you wanted. And by that point in what was dangerously close to becoming a full-blown binge, there was a lot I was willing to consider as long as my cash held out. All I needed was enough to get back to New Haven.

Bars close legally in New York at four in the morning. Caught serving booze after last call and you get your license and livelihood yanked. Your children might starve. But that doesn't mean people aren't still willing to do business. The underbelly of Lower Manhattan nightlife was the after-hours clubs. I'd been to a few. Some were nicer than others, and some were not very nice at all, where I usually ended up. All of them were illegal if alcohol was served. They tried to get around the law by having you "join" the club for a nominal fee, turning what was in essence an illegal bar into a private club. The place I ended up that night in the electric hours before dawn dispensed with such pretense. You were surreptitiously ushered through an unmarked door in an alleyway and down some rusty metal steps into an open area with a distinctly temporary feel. There were stools and chairs and some old couches and tables haphazardly arranged and a bar that looked like it could have been rolled in from your Uncle Joe's knotty pine basement party room. There were all sorts of uninhibited activities taking place, and drugs were everywhere. If the cops busted this place, we were all going to jail.

The place was like a big, makeshift living room. I collapsed onto one of the couches next to an impossibly thin woman with indigo hair who was wearing shoes that had soles like two-by-fours covered in glitter. I tried to regain my focus, both visual and auditory, forcing my brain cells to regroup, trying to lasso those neurons into functioning units again before the synapses became abysses. I had by then lost track of exactly what I had introduced into my bloodstream over the last several hours.

The atmosphere was dark and suffused with a smoky ruby glow. There was a tape being pumped out over the sound system, another derivative band of wannabes, while simultaneously a hapless guitarist with a gouged Fender Telecaster that had probably spent half its life in a pawnshop tried to play without falling off his stool. Someone kept yelling at him to tune his guitar. It might have been me, for all I could tell at that point.

And suddenly, out of that cacophonous, fuliginous murk came a dog, a fabulous dog, who sidled up to me to make my acquaintance. It made perfect sense that a dog would be wandering around a transient joint like this. He was big and muscular and strangely, unsettlingly familiar, like something out of my distant memory or my imagination or both, that point when the two converge to become a single entity, where imagination and memory are one breathing thing. This dog, I had seen him before, touched him before, long ago, somewhere.

"I think his name is Shadow," I thought I heard the stick woman next to me say. When I looked at her, her lips were not moving.

The dog and I said our hellos, and he settled at my feet while I nursed a drink that had come from somewhere. Directly across from me was the single provided bathroom facility, which I felt I would need to use soon for a purpose other than its primary function. It had a wide door and seemed to be a fairly large room with a toilet and a sink and a chair or two. Every so often someone would go inside, there would be the click of a hook and eye lock, and a few minutes would pass before the person emerged or rather exploded out the door, sometimes reeling, sometimes laughing, sometimes just staring straight ahead, zombie-like.

As I regained my focus, I discerned that there was a woman stationed in the bathroom and I realized what she was doing, and it wasn't handing out fresh towels. She had long, tattooed arms and hands that handled the hardware deftly—a couple of syringes, some spoons and lighters and matches and lengths of rubber tubing and the usual detritus of a mobile shooting gallery.

I figured she was charging probably twenty bucks per speedball. A speedball is where you crisscross junk and coke, two drugs with opposite effects that when combined produce the best of both worlds—if it doesn't kill you, as it eventually did John Belushi at the Chateau Marmont, which this dive definitely was not. The spectacle of people going in and exploding out of the bathroom was nonetheless mesmerizing and in and of itself addicting. It stirred something in me that wanted more, that wanted danger and the prospect of never coming back. It was like some kind of call of the wild.

I'd done the minor-league version of speedballing on a pool table in the backroom of the Gypsy, a graduate student drinking club next to the drama school. I'd snorted the drugs, one designated line up each nostril. But the real way to speedball was to slam it. Everyone knew that.

The woman next to me on the couch tottered to her feet, seeming more frail now than fashionably emaciated, and went inside the bathroom, maybe for her second round from the looks of it. I decided I would go next. This was something I wanted. As soon as I tried to rise to my feet, my canine companion rose, too. He had herding genes in there somewhere, I concluded, because he kind of pushed me back in place. I lost my spot as the woman with the platforms floated toward the couch and settled back in with a sigh that was more of a rattle, closing her eyes, her mascara running all over the place. I tried again in a few minutes only to be blocked once more by the dog. This strange dance repeated itself several times, me unsteady on my feet to begin with and the dog strong and determined. I would have to fight my way past him if I wanted to get into that bathroom, hand over my twenty, and get hit up before the needles on the syringes she was using got too dull.

"What's up with you, boy?" I said. He looked me directly in the eyes and for a moment he locked my gaze in place and held it there, like a test of wills, his eyes impossibly bright in the gloom, his ears pointing almost heavenward.

The next time I looked up, the woman was packing up her gear and moving out of the bathroom, disappearing through a door behind the bar, off to her next locale presumably, leaving me with a crumpled twenty in my fist and feeling frustrated but a little relieved as well, though I couldn't tell you why. There is nothing quite so deflating as the high that gets away.

Eventually I said good-bye to my mysterious canine compadre and made my woozy way back to Grand Central, which now looked drab and oppressive in the stark morning light, dirty and decrepit, a crumbling relic of a finer era, full of people from the Twilight Zone. I didn't look at the Kodak sign. What if I saw my own debauched visage looking back at me? Instead I squinted at the departures board and stumbled onto an early train back to New Haven and slept for about a day, awakening with a full-blown case of the heebie-jeebies that it took a few more days to shake.

It wasn't long after that strange night that stories about a mysterious virus sickening and killing IV drug users, among other afflicted groups, proliferated in the media. A year or so later, the AIDS epidemic in New York was full-blown. *But for the grace of God go I.* Did I dare imagine that I managed to dodge this deadly viral bullet because of a dog that seemed to have emerged from my memory? I thought long and hard about that, many times, especially a few years later the night I turned thirty in a room full of men, many of whom had not been so fortunate.

IT HAD BEEN A great personal satisfaction that Millie had never seen me drunk or high. To many people that might seem like an empty source of pride. What would a dog care? Could they even tell? What did it matter as long as you fed them?

It would have mattered, and Millie would have known. I'd seen her shy away from drunks stumbling down the street. Dogs discern more about us than we can possibly imagine. They understand that they have a purpose, a reason for being sent to us. Had I ever taken a drink, she would have understood that it was dangerously wrong. Others could but I couldn't, she knew. I noticed whenever we were around people who were imbibing she sat near me, like a protector.

So as I sat there on the porch, waiting on the call from Dr. June, I closed my eyes tightly and spoke silently from my heart: "I'm not making a deal here, Lord. What happens to Millie is the will of the universe, the course of nature. But I know that it is your will that I do not pick up. I would rather die than have that dog see me drunk."

I heard the phone ring and ran inside to answer. Dr. June. Millie was doing exceptionally well post-surgery and I could pick her up as soon as I wanted, which meant immediately. I set out a fresh bowl of spring water and grabbed my keys.

Millie was ever so slightly out of it when I took her behind the clinic to pee but not so dopey that she didn't give me a long grateful look as she emptied her bladder. She had a belly wrap that covered the bandaged incision like a girdle. Thankfully an e-collar was not called for. I was glad. I hated the cone. I gave her a kiss on the head as I helped her into the car.

I called Julee as soon as we got in to tell her how well Millie was doing. "No more spleen. But she's as hungry as a school-girl," I said, recalling some old phrase I'd once read or heard.

I'm sure I was trying not to sound nervous. Julee, I knew, was holding back tears.

"Did Dr. June say anything?" Julee asked. "Could she tell anything from the mass?"

"No. It could be a week before we get the biopsy results. Maybe longer."

"That's so cruel! Why can't they do it sooner?"

I didn't answer. Instead, I said, "Remember, Millie has a fifty-fifty chance the mass is benign. We have to stay hopeful." Then I hung up because she was staring at her food bowl like it was going to magically produce her dinner all on its own.

The fifty-fifty odds were what Dr. June had originally said, like the flip of a coin. But I'd gone online and found out that was only partly true, the way statistics can paint a broad picture. Golden retrievers, Millie's breed, were particularly susceptible to cancerous masses in the spleen, along with other large dogs like German shepherds and Labs. And with a golden of Millie's age, the odds went up even more. So it was not a coin flip. It was a roll of the dice.

That night I slept downstairs on the couch and blocked off the stairs so Millie wouldn't be tempted to climb them in the dark. She liked to conduct night patrols, but they would have to be suspended for forty-eight hours. I made her an improvised but very comfortable bed, Julee instructing me on the phone and making me text a picture for her approval. When Julee was finally satisfied, we turned off the lights and turned in, one of the hardest days of my life behind me with more, I feared, ahead.

I lay in the dark thinking of a *Guideposts* cover story from 2009 by the novelist Dean Koontz, known more for scaring people than inspiring them. But he had a different kind of story he wanted to share with our audience that began, "My wife and I were married for thirty-two years when we finally decided to get a dog. Our lives would never be the same. I write books for a living, but it took a dog named Trixie to teach me what living was about."

Dean and his wife, Gerda, were virtually inseparable. While he wrote bestselling novels, selling nearly half a billion copies worldwide, Gerda worked down the hall, managing their finances, doing book research, handling requests for her husband's time . . . fielding anything and everything that might divert his fingers from the keyboard and impede his prodigious imagination. They never had kids and they both worked seventy-hour weeks. Their life was their work and each other, and it made them very happy and very prosperous.

"We had always promised each other that we would get a dog someday," Dean wrote in our October issue, "but we realized that a dog requires almost as much time as a child, so we hesitated to take the plunge." They thought about it and dreamed about it and imagined the kind of a dog they would want. Never could they have imagined, though, the dog that would transform the way they saw their lives.

Dean and Gerda had been generous, longtime supporters of Canine Companions for Independence, an organization that raises and trains assistance dogs. The people who ran Canine Companions had tried to convince Dean and Gerda to adopt one of their dogs who for one reason or another did not finish the training program. Year after year they demurred, citing the demands of their work. Finally, one night Dean said to

Gerda, "You know, we'll be ninety and too busy or too old. We should just do it and make it work."

I'll let Dean tell you how it went down.

Trixie had taken early retirement due to elbow surgery. Joint surgery will force the retirement of any assistance dog because, in a pinch, it might need to pull its partner's wheelchair. When Trixie met us, she was a highly educated and refined young lady of three. We were standing with others, but she came right to us, tail swishing, as if she had been shown photographs of us and knew we were to be her new mom and dad.

It was love at first sight. She had a good broad face, dark eyes and a black nose without mottling. Her head and neck flowed perfectly into a strong level topline and her carriage was regal. Beauty, however, took second place to her personality. Well-behaved, with a gentle and affectionate temperament, she had about her a certain cockiness as well. In a picture of her CCI class, 11 of the dogs sit erect in stately poses, chests out, heads raised, each holding the end of its leash in its mouth. The twelfth dog sits with legs akimbo, grinning, head cocked, a comic portrait of a clownish canine ready for fun. Did I say refined? Not totally.

In the beginning, Trixie seemed to accept the Koontz household's tireless work schedule, which kept Dean and Gerda at their respective desks until seven in the evening. But this did not sit well with her. And after she had become securely settled in her new home, she began a campaign.

"One day," wrote Dean, "promptly at five, she came to the farther side of my U-shaped desk and issued not a bark but a soft woof. After telling Trixie it was not yet quitting time and that she must be patient, I turned my attention back to the keyboard. Fifteen minutes later she issued another sotto voce woof. This time her head was poked around the corner of the desk, peering at me. Again, I told her the time to quit had not arrived. At five thirty, she came directly to my chair. When I didn't acknowledge her, she inserted her head under the arm of the chair, staring up at me with a forlorn expression I could not ignore."

And thus it began, a new life for Dean Koontz. Within a month, five o'clock became the official quitting time. The ensuing hours passed in a blizzard of tennis balls. "I would throw and Trixie would retrieve until either I had no more strength or she dropped from exhaustion. The shimmer and flash of her golden coat in the sun, the speed with which she pursued her prey, the accuracy of every leap to catch the airborne prize . . . she was not just graceful in the physical sense. The more I watched her, the more she seemed to be an embodiment of that greatest of all graces we now and then glimpse, from which we intuitively infer the hand of God."

Trixie filled Dean's life and heart where he had once thought there was no room. "I found the innocence of her soul to be a revelation," he wrote. She wanted nothing more than to love and be loved, to be the very essence of devotion. Dean even found that Trixie lent him greater confidence in his writing. He undertook his greatest writing challenge yet in a complex novel— *From the Corner of His Eye*, which went on to sell six million copies.

The most poignant anecdote he told our readers was the night Gerda and he were watching a movie on their big-screen TV. "A character rolled into a scene in a wheelchair, which electrified Trixie. She stood and watched intently, and even approached the screen for a closer look. I'm absolutely certain she was reliving a time when a person in a wheelchair needed her, and when she served ably."

Why do dogs break our hearts? Is it because they bring such wonder and joy to our lives that the thought of living without them becomes nearly unbearable? That creatures so pure and beautiful do not seem mortal?

It was a Friday morning when Trixie was eleven that she refused her food for the first time in her life, just like Millie had. She refused even to take a bite of her favorite treat, an apple-cinnamon rice cake. Gerda and Dean rushed her to the vet. An ultrasound revealed a mass on her spleen. "It could burst at any time," he said. "You have to get her to surgery right away."

Gerda and Dean sat holding hands in the waiting room while Trixie's spleen was removed. They must have gone through an entire box of Kleenex. When the surgery was over, it was clear that the mass had spread. A week later Trixie died at home on her favorite couch, on the covered terrace where she could "breathe in all the good rich smells of grass and trees and roses," Gerda cradling her body and Dean holding her head, gazing into her eyes. "As always she returned my gaze forthrightly. I told her we were so very proud of her, that we loved her as fully as anyone might love his own child, that she was a gift from God."

*   *   *

AS I LAY THERE the night of Millie's surgery, the same surgery
Trixie had undergone, the passage I recalled most from Dean's
incredible piece for *Guideposts* was what he said about the night
of Trixie's surgery: "I never went to sleep but spoke to God for
hours. At first I asked him to give Trixie just two more good
years. But then I realized that I was praying for something
I wanted. And so I acknowledged my selfishness and asked
instead, if she must leave us, we be given the strength to cope
with our grief, because her perfect innocence and loyalty and
gift for affection constituted an immeasurable loss. So even in
my pain and confusion, Trixie helped teach me to pray." Dean,
in fact, would go on from that night to write a wonderful book
called *A Big Little Life,* memorializing Trixie and inspiring the
Guideposts story he shared.

What would Millie teach me? In a perverse way, grief is
the most selfish emotion. We are consumed by our own sense
of loss. It is a morose solipsism if we allow our pain to eclipse
God's presence. Yet I was unsure that if Millie's days were
indeed numbered I could accept her passing and retain my
faith and trust in God.

Millie was breathing easy, and I let that comforting rhythm
lull me to sleep, like it had so many nights. I dreamed of Millie running out of a brilliant sun through a field of tall grass
toward me, always toward me.

CHAPTER 8

On December 11, 2014, I was awakened in our New York apartment by a cold nose gently touching mine. I opened my eyes. "Millie," I said groggily, "are you saying happy birthday?" I smiled, gave her a scratch, and checked the time on my phone. It was 5:59 a.m., exactly one minute before the alarm was set to go off. Who said dogs couldn't tell time?

I wanted to tap snooze and steal a few more minutes of sleep, but Millie just stood there staring at me. "What?" I groaned. "It's my birthday. Let me sleep in a little."

It was strange because Millie definitely wasn't a morning girl. She rarely stirred from her slumber until I grabbed some coffee, checked the news, weather, and sports, and fussed around a bit. Finally, as soon as I put my shoes on, she'd rise, yawn, and stretch luxuriously in preparation for her walk.

Not this morning. There was an urgency to her, a nervousness. And just at that moment the phone rang. It was Amy Wong. "It's Winky," she said, her voice somber. "I think it's time."

Winky, now nearly fourteen, had been battling two types of cancer for the past year or so. She'd had surgery, radiation, and chemo. Plus, an emergency procedure for an episode of bloat that would have killed her if it wasn't for Amy's quick thinking. Even then the surgeon told Amy that she might be better off putting Winky down. "That's what I would do if she were my dog," he said as Winky lay anesthetized and intubated. Amy declined the advice. She trusted her gut. And her heart. Winky came through with flying colors and rallied in her cancer treatments.

In fact, Winky was the star of the animal hospital where she was being treated. On days when she was getting chemo or radiation, they would let her roam free for a bit. She'd check up on the other patients in their cages. The clinic workers said Winky was making her rounds. She'd visit the sicker dogs, or the ones who were frightened, and reassure them. There was just something about her presence, her posture, that confident gaze even when she herself was sick. And those amazing ears that pointed straight up. She'd visit the cats, too, though most of them objected. "We had to tell her not to bother the cats too much," one of the technicians informed Amy. Winky just wanted to see that everyone was okay.

Why? Why did she assume such responsibility when she herself was so ill? Because Winky was a true alpha, a term that is so often misunderstood and misused. Many people assume only males are alphas. It's just as likely a female dog will achieve that status. The term is wrongly associated with aggression and dominance. Not true, not in a well-adjusted alpha dog. They use their eyes, body language, facial expressions, and movement. And Winky was a good alpha.

In my opinion, female dogs make better alphas than males. They don't seem so uptight about the natural authority God has given them. I loved watching Winky at the dog run with Millie. While Millie would play and visit with her friends, Winky kept a wary but wise eye on the proceedings, like a true peace officer. She'd break up fights, warn off aggressive dogs, and protect the weaker ones. And always she kept her attention on Millie, for whom she had assumed great responsibility, as if she thought I didn't quite understand enough about dogs to do the job completely myself. No dog would ever hassle Millie while Winky was around. Not that too many dogs wanted to mess with a ninety-pound golden, no matter how sweet-tempered. For her part, Millie could stick up for herself, especially when certain boy dogs tried to take liberties with her. But Winky always kept an eye on her.

Winky was at her alpha finest one summer weekend when Julee and I decided to have a dog party up at the house. We invited Amy and Winky, naturally, and Millie's walker, Christa, and her two pugs, Ollie and Hank, and a dog she was watching for a client, Bella, a rescued Lab mix. It was a full house, and nothing makes Julee happier than a house full of dogs.

A weekend in the hills with all those dogs called for a serious venture into the woods. I picked one of my favorite and most challenging Berkshire trails and Winky, Millie (who was not much more than a puppy at the time), Bella, Amy, and I set off. The pugs stayed home. The breed doesn't do well exerting themselves in the heat and elevation, in part due to their foreshortened snouts, which make it hard to breathe. Julee stayed with Christa to keep her company. I also think hiking those hills with a dog brought back too many feelings about Marty, whose death she was still getting over, though Millie was certainly helping her, even then.

So Ollie and Hank were put in charge of overseeing the grilling for when we returned.

Bella was an unusual dog. Her owner suspected she'd been neglected or abused before she landed in the shelter from which he and his wife adopted her. Her social skills were a little miswired. She had an unfortunate habit of baring her teeth. She meant no harm. She was a gentle, sweet dog. It was more of a tic, a nervous habit. I don't think there was an aggressive bone in her body. She'd been too mistreated. But every so often, apropos of nothing, she'd curl her lip.

Winky would not tolerate this. It was viewed as very poor behavior. Winky would bark and nip every time poor Bella pseudo-snarled. Even charming, peace-loving Millie got in on the act, bullying Bella in her own puppyish way, much to my considerable chagrin. Millie was supposed to be a saint, an angel.

Bella adopted me as her protector that weekend, since I always jumped to her defense and backed Winky and Millie off. So when it came time to navigate a steep ravine choked with underbrush and the going got tough, it was me to whom she turned. As the four of us stood on one side of the shallow, rushing stream at the bottom of the ravine, Bella remained on the other. I stood there sweating and breathing hard. Suddenly it occurred to me that the dog had probably never been out of Manhattan. She'd spent half her life in a cage in a shelter. No wonder she was absolutely frozen with indecision. Another blunder on my part. This dog was not a wilderness dog. She wanted desperately to stay with us, but she couldn't bring herself to descend the ravine and cross the stream. She barked softly and looked at me across the tangled divide. *Help me.*

In a moment of despair, I thought, *Am I going to have to climb back down and carry this fifty-pound scaredy-cat of a dog all the up the other side? How much more of this will there be? Do we have to turn back?*

Just then Winky came up beside me. She'd been taking it all in—assessing, judging, strategizing. Before I could go into action, she went back down the ravine, stepped across the water, trotted up to Bella, and touched noses with her. There was some kind of dog conversation between them, however they do it. We'll never really know. Winky placed her chin across Bella's neck, which is a gesture of both dominance and reassurance. She nudged Bella with her long, slender, elegant snout. And then shoulder to shoulder they came down the ravine. Bella crossed the stream, Winky dropping behind her in case she lost her nerve. Bella bounded up the other side and we were all together again, and wet and happy Bella was wagging her tail like crazy and jumping up on me, as if I had anything to do with her retrieval. Winky kept a close eye on Bella the rest of the hike, especially on the steep approach to the summit, our final destination. When Bella's courage faltered, Winky was right beside her, fulfilling her alpha obligations, as she had not so many months before when she helped Millie find the courage to navigate the turbulence of Manhattan. That was Winky. And when we reached that summit, breathless with exhilaration, I saw Bella gaze out over a sight I am sure she had never seen or dreamed, the rolling green hills stretching to the sun-washed horizon. Her eyes blazed with astonishment, with joy. Winky did that.

Over the last year Winky had become too weak to make the trek all the way over to the West Side and join Millie at the Chelsea dog run, such a big part of their friendship. Late that summer on a hot, beautiful afternoon when the sky was the color of faded denim, Millie and I headed east to rendezvous with Amy and Winky at Madison Square Park, close to where they lived. I had a feeling it would be the last time the two friends saw each other in this world.

"Want to go see Winky?" I'd asked. Millie had jumped up and headed to the door as she always did when the name Winky was spoken.

It was a subdued encounter. Mostly they lay side by side in the shade of one of the great old elm trees the park is known for, panting gently. They played a bit, Winky still letting Millie know that she was her big sister and had to be minded. They got to split a ceremonial hot dog, always the high point of their get-togethers. And then they stood together one last time. Millie bowed her head and curled her body and let Winky put her chin over her neck. I pulled her away gently and we headed west, Millie looking back over her shoulder one last time at Winky sitting by Amy's side.

Winky had been losing her cancer fight ever since, until this day in December when Amy called to say that the end was here. As long as Winky still enjoyed her food, played with her toys, and looked forward to her walks, Amy was committed to keeping her alive. In the past week, though, Winky's interest in those things that are so central to a dog's existence had faded, and Amy made arrangements to have a vet who specialized in doing in-home euthanasia on call.

That morning over coffee Julee and I talked about what we should do. "I think you should be there, Edward," Julee said. "You were always a father figure to Winky."

I would have laughed at that notion under any other circumstances. Being a father figure to a dog sounded ridiculous. Still, Winky was very special to me. I loved her. I loved her for how she loved and protected Millie, even when Millie grew to be considerably larger than her. I loved those weekends when Julee and I would kidnap her and speed off to the country. I loved her God-given confidence. I loved how she could be as silly as she was smart when she wanted to be.

"But I think Millie should stay here with me," Julee continued. "It would be too confusing for her. She already knows what's happening. Why else would she have gotten you up?"

For what seemed the millionth time in my life I asked, *How do they know, Lord?*

Later that day I walked over to Amy's apartment. It was warm for December and foggy and dreary. The sidewalks were gritty and damp from a predicted snowfall that never became more than a dirty drizzle. Everything seemed gray. A hazy shade of winter indeed. Despite being very weak, Winky made a valiant effort to greet me. I had her lie back on her bed and preserve her waning strength. "Good girl," I murmured. She eased her head back down and breathed out.

While we waited for the vet, who was blessedly running late, Amy and I talked about all the wonderful Winky and

Millie moments. For the Guideposts website they'd conducted a video tour of the editorial offices, introducing our editors to our audience. They'd tested dog products and reenacted Winky teaching Millie to walk the streets of Manhattan. It was a tour de force. The dogs could actually act! For a time, they were the stars of our site. They got fan email.

Then Amy's buzzer sounded and we stopped talking, almost as if someone had pressed a mute button. Neither one of us moved. Winky didn't even bark. It was one of those eternal, agonizing minutes. I watched Amy's body language. She didn't want to move. She didn't want to answer that buzzer. She knew what it denoted. But eventually she did because it was her responsibility. It was as if at long last she'd done all she could do for Winky, and this was the final act of mercy.

The vet was a kind and lovely woman from Australia. I briefly considered what a ghoulish calling it was to go around delivering death like you would deliver a pizza. Yet as I watched her prepare Winky and Amy, and even me, I realized how humane and decent what she did was, what courage it must take. Vets, no less than physicians, are taught to heal. Easing an animal through a gentle and painless passing took a remarkable kind of human, one who could resist the basic instinct to preserve life and approach the act of dying as a form of healing, of becoming whole again. It takes great strength to do that.

Winky was administered a mild intravenous sedative and the sick addict in me envied her. Was it the high I envied, that cosmic sense of euphoric release, or just the protection from my feelings? I was relieved to see the pain and apprehension drain from her eyes. Winky was drifting, drifting away. Watching us from halfway into another realm as the vet took a cast of her right forepaw for Amy.

I whispered in her ear the name Millie and told her how incredibly grateful I was to her for being such a loving friend and teacher. The three of us sat on the floor around Winky, very quiet. Amy stroked her neck and I held one of her paws in my hands. The rest of the sedative was administered and very quickly Winky was at peace. Suddenly it was as if the mute button had been released. I heard cars honking, buses groaning, a distant jackhammer, like a giant metal woodpecker pulverizing asphalt, the city's ceaseless serenade through life and death and everything else.

I left shortly after and got a cab downtown, where I was supposed to be at a meeting. I was wiping tears from my eyes when the cabbie looked in the rearview and said, "What, you break up with girlfriend?"

"No," I muttered, "a dog."

His eyes widened. "With a dog?"

"No, a dog died. A friend's dog."

"Very sad, mister. Very sad."

"She was my dog's best friend."

"Best friends? Really?" He emitted a small, disbelieving laugh, as if he may have come from a culture where dogs were not ascribed such emotional complexity.

"You got kids?"

"Yes. They want a dog. Someday, maybe."

"Then someday you will understand. And you will love."

I got out a few blocks from my destination to give myself a chance to regroup. The cabbie said, "I am very sorry for your loss, mister." He did a nice job with the phrase.

That night Julee told me that Millie had been very clingy all day and not her usual upbeat self. "I know she knew," she said. They took a nap together and Julee thought she heard Millie cry in her sleep. "I don't know. It might have been my imagination. But she wasn't herself all day, I know that."

When I left, Amy and the vet was gathering up Winky, she apologized for ruining my birthday. Not ruined at all, I told her. It had been a gift to be with Winky, a blessing I would never forget, to say good-bye to such a loving and well-loved dog. Perhaps I, too, was being prepared, as Millie once may have been, on that muddy day she found Buzz.

ON THE MORNING AFTER her splenectomy, four months after her friend Winky died, Millie awoke surprisingly full of vigor, her eyes bright and lively. My heart broke a little seeing her in her hospital blue belly wrap. It made her waddle a bit. But it didn't seem to bother her at all, so I let her out. I'd bought some wee-wee pads just in case, but it was clear I could dispense with them. She trotted to the place in our yard where turkey buzzards often congregated at dawn, in case it was necessary to evict them. It wasn't. They'd long since scattered. They knew all too well about Millie. It was a fun way to start the day when the opportunity presented itself, though, scaring off those ugly things. She checked out the apple tree to see if any deer had disturbed it. It was a little early in the season for that, but Millie was always prepared. That's where Julee had scattered Mick's ashes and I think Millie knew it was sacred ground. It was her job to oversee it. Then she padded in and devoured her breakfast. *This dog cannot possibly be sick*, I told myself. *We should go for a walk in the woods*.

But I thought better of it, of course. Dr. June had banned any vigorous activity for a few days and there was no telling if Millie might take off into the bush and hurt herself chasing a chipmunk or something. So I contented myself with sitting outside on our stone bench, still cold and damp in the morning shade of an ash tree, watching her play in the yard and marveling at her God-given recuperative powers. *Lord, what a strong dog you gave us. Please keep her that way. Please . . .*

I heard the phone ringing inside the house and ran to get it. It was Julee.

"Bring her home," she said. "I have to see her."

Julee was in the process of canceling some upcoming obligations. I knew she was preparing for the worst. I checked with Dr. June. She said it would be okay to travel with Millie if she was doing as well as I said. And the belly wrap could come off the next day. So I packed up the Jeep and headed back to New York after making an appointment to bring Millie up the following week to check the incision and hopefully get the biopsy results. I administered Millie four milligrams of Xanax, eternally guilt-ridden that I had turned my dog into a dope fiend.

We took Route 22 instead of the faster Taconic Parkway. I kept the speedometer at 55, the speed limit, and sometimes slower. We rolled through little towns along the way: Copake, Millerton, Amenia, Dover Plains, Pawling. To the east the Berkshires dissolved into gently rolling farmland being prepared for spring planting. Cars passed me, which was unusual. I was trying to slow down time. I was trying to make time last.

Millie bounded up to Julee when we got in: the full booty wag, knocking over things on the coffee table in the living room and practically everything else that wasn't nailed down, then rolled on her back as if to say, *See? I'm all right!* I could see Julee trying not to cry and I could see Millie trying to overwhelm her with joy. I think she understood the role she played in my wife's life. Julee had endured the loss of Marty, her mother, Sally, Mick. One wave of grief on top of another, one blow to the heart after the next. Her health had suffered and her soul had suffered. Millie helped restore her. Millie had been there at her darkest moments to pull her through the way no human could. I believe Millie knew this. In a strange way, then, Julee may have been better prepared to accept Millie's fate than I was, come what may. They had come to peace with so many hard things together.

The belly wrap came off the next day. Millie danced around and tried to play tug-of-war with it, but I couldn't throw the thing down the trash chute fast enough. It had become second only to the dreaded cone in my list of veterinary unpleasantries. It probably should have gone in with the recyclables, but I thought I could be forgiven this one ecological indiscretion.

That Saturday I took her on one of our long weekend walks. The day was warm and cool all at the same time, the way spring days can be, but I brought lots of water along for Millie and a book for me. Normally we would have gone to the Chelsea dog run on Eleventh Avenue so Millie could catch up with all her friends—Max, Ollie, Buddy, Snoop, Nico. She only rarely made new friends these days, though when she made one it was a friend for life, always to be greeted with maximum enthusiasm. But her old friends, the ones she grew up with at the dog run and in our neighborhood, held a very special place in her affections and she always showed it. We never give dogs enough credit for the complex relationships they form, for the variety of love and bonding they experience. We think they just like to sniff each other. Millie recognized her old friends and treated them accordingly, more decently than a lot of humans treat their friends.

Today we would have to forgo the run. She wasn't cleared for play. So we wandered around Chelsea for a while. It's hard to exaggerate what a star Millie was in the neighborhood. All the shopkeepers knew her and invited her in even if they adhered otherwise to a strict no-pets policy. We could barely go a block without someone stopping us. Tourists took pictures with her. People wanted to share their pizza.

We headed for Chelsea Waterside Park and Pier 64, one of our favorite spots in all Manhattan. I thought we'd spend a good part of the afternoon there, just sitting on a bench and watching the river go by. Millie and I loved rivers.

We'd been coming to Pier 64 since Millie was a puppy. The first time one of the big cruise ships that docked a little further upriver steamed by on its way to Europe or the Caribbean, blasting its horn and making a commotion, everyone crowded topside to get a good gander at the Manhattan skyline sliding by, Millie jumped and barked so boisterously I thought she was going to leap off the end of the pier. It was the horn that set her off. The passengers pointed and waved to her and got their cameras out. It became a kind of ritual whenever we were at the pier and a cruise ship went by. There must be thousands of people all over the world with a picture of the big white golden retriever giving them a send-off.

Today we sat quietly on a bench. As the afternoon slipped away I read my book while Millie watched the boaters out on the Hudson, lapped water from her pink porta-bowl, and gave a woof to the occasional duck bobbing by. We were like a comfortable old couple. I thought of those Paul Simon lyrics, "And you read your Emily Dickinson, and I my Robert Frost." Except I hadn't read Frost since college, and I don't think Millie would have particularly liked Dickinson's verse. I'm not sure what she would have made of Emily's famous observation, presumably about her own dog, Carlo: "Dogs are better than human beings because they know but do not tell." All dogs have secrets, I would agree, little places they slip away to, treasures that they hide away from us, certain things they don't want us to know. I wondered what Millie's secrets were.

I'd caught her at one the previous summer. Julee and I had installed an invisible fence when we got Millie, one of those underground wires that carry an electrical charge. The dog wears a collar with a little receiver on it and if she gets too close to the fence a minor shock is delivered. Dogs hate shocks and the invisible fence worked like a charm. Millie, I assumed, had long since internalized her boundaries. I doubted she would ever venture off her electrically circumscribed territory, and Julee advocated doing away with the collar entirely. I used it more or less as a formality.

I was jumping back into the Jeep one morning after making a routine stop at our Quick Mart when a neighbor from down the road waved and said, "Millie stopped by to visit with Bosco the other night. That was sweet of her." Bosco was the neighbor's new puppy.

I smiled and said through gritted teeth, "It sure was," then drove away. Back at the house I took Millie aside. "What have you been up to?" She tilted her head innocently. *Who, me?*

I summoned the boundary fence guy immediately. Were we going to have to dig the whole yard up? He did some testing with a Buck Rogers–looking device that I was sure was more for show than anything else, and to justify his fee since I'd called this in as urgent. He explored the yard like a dowser as Millie and I observed. Millie was still acting as innocent as the Virgin Mary. Finally, the fence guy arrived at a conclusion: the battery in her collar receiver was dead, something I could easily have figured out for myself if I'd given it two seconds of thought. I hadn't because I'd stopped checking the battery years ago on the assumption that Millie was too pure of heart to ever violate her boundaries. He installed a new one, and I slipped the collar on Millie and went inside.

A minute later I heard a surprised yelp and a minute after that one indignant golden retriever marched into the house. She couldn't believe she'd been found out.

"It's for your own good, Millie, because we love you."

I was able to make everything all right with a slice of turkey.

I couldn't help thinking about her visiting Bosco. It was sweet of her to look in on the puppy. I think dogs always want to make sure we humans are doing a good job of caring for their kind. There was another dog once who lived just on the other side of her boundary, Simon, her first love. Millie was maybe a year old and Simon, a smallish black Lab mix, was at least five with a touch of gray on his muzzle. Millie fell head over tail in love with him. You could barely restrain her from jumping out a window when he was around. She'd whine to be let out and pine for him when he didn't appear. She'd chase him through the yard, yipping and whimpering in a way she only did for him. If Simon took off up into the woods Millie would await his return patiently behind her underground fence. She would wait for hours. Simon was a bit of a wild boy. He was known to range far and wide, and to even get into a little trouble from time to time. Once he was brought home in a police cruiser. That only made Millie like him all the more. What good girl doesn't have a weakness for a bad boy?

I remember arriving at the house one crisp fall afternoon and watching Millie run to the end of the yard just short of her electric barrier. I'd barely had a chance to put her zap collar on her. She sat politely waiting to see if Simon and his owners had come up for the weekend, too, her tail sweeping the carpet of leaves. I wonder what goes through a dog's mind when she's in love? Probably the same thing that goes through ours. An intense longing that is part pleasure and part pain, a mad ecstasy as powerful as any feeling we are likely to ever have, and a contentment we cannot find with anyone else.

"They must be up," Julee said.

"Probably just got here," I said. "Simon will stop over soon enough."

An hour passed. No Simon.

"It breaks my heart to see her wait like that," Julee said, peering out the kitchen window while we made guacamole. The sun was dipping below the hills, pulling the afternoon warmth with it. Millie would want her supper soon, but I didn't think she'd come in unless I made her. Love can make us as patient as it can passionate. I made a little appeal for Simon to appear: "She's in love, Lord! Don't you see?" I even wondered if I should turn off the fence. Just this once. For love.

A bit later, as I was carrying in some firewood, I caught a black streak out of the corner of my eye, a white streak right behind it, and that familiar happy whimper.

Simon and his owners eventually moved on, though for a long time Millie would wait for him. He's old now if he's even still with us. But I don't think that would matter to Millie. Her love was a constant. Simon didn't break her heart. He taught her that she could love, that not even boundaries could stop it. Indeed, they sometimes deepen it.

"TIME TO GO AND have supper," I said to her on the pier. "Your mama's going to start wondering." We packed up our stuff and headed home. On the way, we saw a dog that looked a lot like Simon but wasn't, I'm sure. Millie said hi anyway. Julee had her supper waiting, and that night Millie slept long and deeply. Once or twice she yipped in her sleep and slapped her tail on the floor. In my imagination, I saw her running and playing with Simon, young again and in love. Her first love, in a life of love.

*   *   *

THE HEART BREAKS SLOWLY sometimes. Mine had started that March Friday when I came home to that cosmic anomaly—Millie not eating. I didn't know it then but something in Julee's eyes told me she did. Now I was waiting in an examining room at her vet's in the Berkshires a week after her surgery while Dr. Maddie examined her incision. I tapped my foot nervously. Millie, lying cooperatively on her back while the doctor got down on the floor with her, wagged her tail. Despite the ordeal she'd been through with her spleen, she still loved the vet's. Such a trusting and forgiving soul. Plus, she knew she'd get treats. That helped.

Dr. Maddie was the third and youngest vet at the clinic. I liked her a lot. She patted Millie and gave her a kiss and the compulsory treat. Two in fact.

"She's healing quite nicely, but I'm afraid the biopsy results were not good. It's cancer."

I moved my mouth, but words deserted me. Maybe for the first time in my life.

"We had the sample tested twice," Dr. Maddie said softly.

"What kind?" I managed to ask. I wanted a name.

"Hemangiosarcoma."

Now I knew who the enemy was. The thing had a name. No longer an anonymous demon.

"It's not terribly responsive to treatment," Dr. Maddie said.

"How long?"

"Three to six months typically. I'm so sorry."

And she was. She'd put her own dog down due to cancer just that winter. It's no easier for a vet. It's not easy for anyone.

"Is there anything we can do?"

"Sometimes chemo can help. We don't offer that here, though. You could try the Animal Medical Center in the city. There's also a therapy I've heard about that involves a mushroom extract that has reportedly shown some promise. We don't provide it, though. You can go online and find out more. But mostly these things extend the dog's life at best. This is usually a fatal cancer."

I had a question I wanted to ask but couldn't bear to. Dr. Maddie must have read my thoughts.

"It's generally not a painful cancer."

I put Millie on her harness and led her out into the reception area. The staff behind the counter, Katerina and the others, looked on silently. I almost stopped to weigh Millie, which was usually mandatory. Then I figured it was pointless. She could eat as much as wanted.

BACK IN NEW YORK Julee and I went into full research mode. Hemangiosarcoma is a blood-borne cancer that particularly afflicts goldens, German shepherds, and boxers. A ruptured spleen is often the first sign. And the last. It usually indicates that the cancer has progressed too far to be successfully treated. Some dogs don't live much past the first bleeding episode. That's probably what happened to Trixie, Dean Koontz's golden. Somehow Millie had survived the early bleeds. As I've said, she was an unbelievably strong dog.

The cancer lives in the lining of the blood vessels. By the time the spleen is affected, cancer cells are already loose in the circulatory system. It is only a matter of time before they find another organ to attack, often the heart.

Chemotherapy didn't seem promising. But we came across a clinical trial that was under way at the University of Pennsylvania, testing the mushroom extract Dr. Maddie had mentioned, isolated from the *Coriolus versicolor*, or Zhi, mushroom from China. There were three test groups: dogs that got just the mushroom, dogs that got just chemo, and dogs that got both. I called immediately. Yes, Millie was perfect for the study. She could go into any group. We would have to drive her back and forth to Philadelphia every Friday.

I explained about the car and the storm and the panic attacks and the Xanax. I was practically in tears when I finished because I knew what they'd say and it was my fault.

"The required travel sounds like it would be too stressful for a dog with cancer," the clinician said. "I'm afraid it could do more harm than good."

I thought about how brave Millie had been swimming to shore in the thunder and lightning, swimming for her life. How that came back to haunt me now!

"However," the clinician said, "I can give you the supplier of the extract we are using in the test and explain the dosing. You can put her on the mushrooms yourself and keep us updated."

I ordered the stuff by the gross. Millie required thirteen capsules a day, which meant more than four hundred a month. I was constantly reordering. Sometimes there were shortages. I was obsessed with having enough of the extract. I put all my faith in the mushroom. There was strong anecdotal material suggesting that it significantly extended a dog's life. There were even claims of a cure. I checked online every day for anything new.

Meanwhile, Julee made plans to move up to the Berkshires house with Millie for the summer. She thought the environment would be better for her. I agreed. I'd schedule time off and take long weekends. I would miss them during the workweek, but I knew how much Millie loved the hills. And Julee needed time with her.

Julee also made contact with an old friend from her hometown, Larry Tilley, a vet who had gained a worldwide reputation as an animal cardiologist. Larry had advised Julee when Marty got sick and he had just lost his own beloved golden to the same cancer Millie had. The fatal tumor took root in the heart and now Larry was deep into writing a paper on it. He'd heard about the mushroom extract and agreed it couldn't hurt. He and Julee would stay in touch.

"I can't imagine what it must have been like for him not to be able to do anything for his own dog."

I stayed silent. I could imagine it. More than imagine it.

THAT SUMMER OF 2015 was perhaps the most memorable of my life, full of highs and lows and little in between. Through the years Millie had been my most popular blog topic on Guideposts.org. She'd gained a large and loyal following. So when I wrote about her cancer, prayer requests were posted by the thousands. I can't tell you how much that lifted us. And how much it helped me to write about her, as if writing about her would keep her alive somehow.

She was doing remarkably well. Every weekend we hiked her favorite trails. By August the Berkshires were full of vacationers. She got to meet and greet lots of kids. One day we gave a young couple thru-hiking the Appalachian Trail a lift into town. They said they would pray for Millie. And for Julee and me.

I tried to pray like Dean Koontz wrote in *Guideposts* that he had, to embrace that lesson, to pray for the strength to endure what was likely inevitable. But I could never stop myself from asking God for a miracle. I would not let go of that prayer, that desperate hope. I held on to it like I was hanging on to the edge of a cliff.

One weekend in early August, Julee had a recording session she was unable to cancel. She'd be gone for the night and she would be taking the Jeep with her. I knew it killed Julee to leave Millie even for a night. It brought up all those regrets about the last week of Marty's life. Yet I also believed she knew I needed time alone with Millie, just the two of us. That made it easier.

Without transportation, Millie and I were limited in where we could wander. At sunset, we walked over to the little enclave across the road where we had encountered Buzz back in March. We hadn't been over there since.

The road was dry now. The smell of outdoor barbecues hung in the air, voices and laughter. I looked up to where the vacation house of Buzz's owner, the podiatrist, was, but I couldn't see any lights through the trees. Millie and I walked to the other side of the lake where the houses were fewer. We sat up on a bluff overlooking the water while the sun set behind us and I told her again not to hold on for us.

"We'll be with you, no matter what," I promised her. "All we want is to take care of you." I looked across the lake and for just a second the road on the other side appeared muddy and covered in icy slush. A beautiful white dog was making its way up the hill to the podiatrist's house. I blinked and looked away. The next time I looked the road looked as it had before, dusty and summery.

One evening later in the month I got a call at the office from Julee. "Millie's outside lying in the grass. She won't come in. She wouldn't eat. Edward, I think she wants to die. You've got to come now. I know she's waiting for you."

I rushed to Penn Station. I had been planning to come up the next day anyway so I switched my ticket and barely caught the last train out. All the way up I stared out at the Hudson, a rolling ghost in the night, praying for Millie to hang on. I took a cab from the station in Hudson so Julee wouldn't have to leave Millie to pick me up. Fifty-five minutes later, a little after one in the morning, I was in our driveway in Massachusetts. A second after that I heard one of the sweetest sounds I knew. A bark from the dark. Not her usual big bark that reverberated like a cannon shot. It was soft and welcoming. I ran up and found her in her favorite spot where she had a good view of her surroundings, her kingdom. She stood and came to me. Happy as always but in a different way, I sensed. Relieved more than joyous.

Julee was inside. I thought I'd find her in tears. Instead she had managed to unearth some Yunnan Baiyao, a Chinese herbal coagulant we'd used for Millie's spleen bleeds while we were waiting for her surgery. Despite my skepticism, it had worked wonderfully. We gave Millie a triple dose and all slept together on the ground floor. I put up the baby gate at the foot of the stairs so Millie wouldn't be tempted.

In the morning, she was almost 100 percent better. She wolfed down her breakfast, having skipped dinner the night before. Her bark regained its power. The medicine had worked. And that wasn't good. Almost certainly a new tumor had formed, one she wouldn't survive.

We went through the motions at the vet's. Dr. June this time. She took X-rays and put the images up on the light box. She didn't even have to show us. I saw an egg-shaped shadow in Millie's stomach, right along the margin of the liver, like an incubating demon, and I felt anger—no, hate—rear up within me. At that moment, I hated cancer more than anything I had ever hated in my life. I wanted to smash my fist through the image. Instead, I took Julee's hand and dropped my head in defeat and despair. We had done everything for this dog since she was a puppy. For eight blessed years, we had loved her as much as any dog had ever been loved. But we couldn't save her.

The Yunnan Baiyao would work for a while, like it had with her spleen before the surgery. Yet there was nothing more to be done. Dr. June apologized that she couldn't be more specific about the timeline. "She's an awfully strong dog," she said. There would be nothing left to do but the kindest—and hardest—thing when the time came. This time I didn't thank God for giving us such a strong girl. I didn't thank him for anything.

The time came quickly. I was there the following Thursday night, Labor Day weekend. Millie was peppy, practically bratty. In the morning, we hiked a portion of her favorite stretch of the AT. I didn't want to go too far because I didn't want to tax her and she looked at me questioningly, as if she remembered Dr. Maddie saying we should let her do as much as she wanted to do. *Dr. Maddie said!* I could imagine her thinking.

Again that night, though, she wouldn't eat. She was bleeding internally, slowly, and nothing was going to stop it now. She went down to the end of the yard near the spot where she used to wait for Simon and lay in the deep, cool grass. I followed and lay down next to her. We stayed that way for a long time, just breathing. I stared up at the sapphire sky. The moon was waning and the starlight was impossibly lucid, light poking through from heaven. Sirius, the dog star, was ascendant. I planned to just sleep out there all night, but eventually Millie rallied and we walked slowly up the hill to the house where Julee had been watching. She gave us both a long hug, mine a little longer and a little harder. Early on she'd said she was worried how I would handle this. I did, too. I always thought we'd have Millie for a long time, far more than eight years. It was that that hurt the most. I felt cheated. Why would God do that? Why create such a beautiful being and then cut her life short? She had been nothing but a blessing to us. This was not the Old Testament where God was allowed to be seemingly capricious and punitive. What sin had I committed to deserve this? What had Millie done? I tossed and turned all night with those questions. Millie slept peacefully by my side of the bed.

Dr. Maddie came in the morning. We'd been able to hand-feed Millie little bits of poached chicken breast. That was about it, and I think she was only eating for our benefit. She was very tired. We laid a blanket on the grass at her favorite spot, where she always waited for me, where she had waited that night the week before when we thought we were losing her, and I heard her quiet, poignant bark, the sound of which I will never forget.

Julee and I lay down beside her, our heads against hers, while Dr. Maddie administered mild sedation. I didn't want her to be scared. I would rather die myself than see her scared right then.

It was a beautiful, God-given morning, the old hills bowing to the sun, tufts of clouds drifting high across the sky. I could almost feel the earth turning. We both whispered to her: "You'll see Marty and Sally, and Winky, and Rudy and Kelly, and Sparky and Pete, maybe even Simon, and all the other dogs. You will never be sick again or scared of the car. We love you so much, Millie. Thank you for being here for us. We love you."

We said we were ready, though really we would never be. Dr. Maddie gave her the second shot. Millie's eyes half-closed and she took one long, final breath. Yes, the heart breaks slowly.

THERAPISTS LIKE TO SAY we process our feelings. I've always disliked that terminology. It reminds me of processed meat or maybe a word processor. I didn't feel much like processing anything. I felt numb but not numb enough, and I certainly knew how to make myself more numb. I had been very good at that at one time. It had been long ago, but it could come back in a second. I had all the excuse I needed. Yet I couldn't.

I couldn't dishonor Millie. They say you will never succeed staying sober for someone else's benefit. You stay sober for yourself. And that's true. Except on this night. On this night, I stayed sober for a dog whose life deserved no less.

All that night the anger and sadness and helplessness kept bubbling to the top of that numbness. A short time before Dr. Maddie had arrived, I'd logged onto the Guideposts system with my password to tell a few people what we had finally decided for Millie and to ask for prayers. Afterward, I went back inside to log on again and let people know and to thank them. Maybe I could post a quick blog. Instead I got a message on my screen: Access Denied.

I tried again. Denied again. My password had expired. Without any notice whatsoever, mind you. And way sooner than it should have. Poof. Access denied. Now my tears were tears of fury. I could not reset the password remotely. I was locked out. And who could I call? It was the Saturday before Labor Day. I fired off a livid email to some poor person on our IT team via my private account. I did not, as they say in the Big Book, exercise restraint of tongue and pen. How could they do something like this? How? Didn't they understand?

All day I'd ricocheted between grief and rage. I am not a complete fool. The two emotions were intertwined, I knew, like a riptide just below the surface of rational consciousness, and I was helpless to stop them. That night I tried once more to log on, typing my password very carefully: MILLICENT. Millicent. Millie. Maybe I am a fool, because at last it struck me. My password had expired at the very moment Millie had left this world. The IT guys weren't to blame. This was a message from heaven—let go.

* * *

SUNLIGHT WOKE ME ON Sunday morning. Sleepily but auto-matically I hopped over the spot where Millie usually slept by the bed. That would go on for a while, I suspected. It could go on forever as far as I was concerned. Today I wanted to get an early start and stay ahead of that aching void that was already forming on the first day without our dog.

Yesterday as Dr. Maddie and her assistant were leaving, I remembered something at the last minute and caught up to them before they pulled out of the driveway. I wanted to have a few clippings of Millie's fur. Dr. Maddie said that the crematorium would send us a beautiful braid along with Millie's ashes, but I said I needed a few tufts now. Dr. Maddie got out and raised the trunk. Millie was all curled up in a blanket. Dogs don't close their eyes when they are euthanized. Maybe because it's so quick. Millie's were half-open. What a terrible shock to see no life in a place where so much life had been. At last I let myself go. I sobbed. Dr. Maddie took the scissors and plastic baggie from me and clipped out the tufts herself.

I got dressed in my hiking gear and retrieved the baggie with Millie's tufts of fur. I also had a baggie of Winky's fur. I zipped them into a small shoulder pack with some water, started up the Jeep, and drove to Monument Mountain. It was another perfect late summer's day. Here and there I could see just a tree or two starting to turn. I always wondered about that. Was this something natural or were these trees just anx-ious and excitable?

There were only a few cars in the parking lot, which was good. I'd wanted to beat the weekend crowds. I started out on the Indian Monument Trail, which paralleled Route 7 until it turned into the reserve. At the first juncture, where Millie and I always took a water break, I turned onto the Squaw Peak Trail, the rugged ridge trail with sweeping views of the Southern Berkshires. Millie loved to climb all the way up to the promontory called Devil's Pulpit where we'd gone after her first visit to the vet's. I didn't turn off there, though. I kept going all the way to the summit.

There I stood at its highest point, alone with the view, catching my breath. I hadn't been up there in eight years. I'd kept my promise to Julee after Winky had infamously plunged over the edge and had miraculously survived. I sat down and pulled out the baggies from my pack and dug a little hole in the crevice between two of the summit boulders. I took some of Millie's fur and all of Winky's, buried it together in the hole, and covered it with dirt. I found a small rock and wedged it over the spot so nothing would blow away.

I headed down the Hickey Trail on the north side of the mountain. There was one more spot I wanted to visit and rest a bit, a beautiful waterfall Millie loved. She would go right up to it and watch the water stream down a rock face into a pool below. Below that was another pool that Millie loved to splash around in. Except for the car accident when Millie had to swim for her life, she'd never been much of a water dog, despite the noble heritage of her breed and her webbed paws. She hated baths. She acted like I was trying to waterboard her. Once, at a swimming hole on the Green River, I hurled both Millie and Winky into the water, which was over their heads, and dove in after them. They practically drowned me trying to get out, and for the rest of the afternoon wouldn't come within twenty feet of me. It took burgers and franks on the Weber to set things right again.

But in this lovely little pool hidden high in a wooded cleft, Millie loved to splash and wade, as long as her paws touched bottom and she could breathe. I took the last tuft of her fur, put it in at the edge of the pool and blew it out into the water. Then I found a small boulder to sit on and do what I should have done much sooner.

I had a conversation with God that started with "I'm sorry." I said how deeply grateful I was for the eight and a half beautiful years he had given us with Millie and how ashamed I was of my anger that nearly obscured this heavenly gift. I thanked him that Millie's last months on this earth were healthy and content, and that she lived a month beyond the most optimistic prognosis. A month is a long time in a dog's life. He had brought a dog into our lives, a wonderful, loving dog, as an instrument of healing. She had brought us incalculable happiness, happiness that outweighed my grief like this mountain outweighed a feather. I speculated he must have gotten some advice from Marty and Sally, because as much as we loved them, they had been quite a handful at times and could be instruments of destruction, so they concluded we needed a wise and peaceful addition to our family. I thanked him for Rudy, who had brought Julee and me together and who was my buddy while I regained my sanity and sobriety and found my way in life again to a place called *Guideposts*. I gave thanks for Pete and all those asthmatic nights he sat with me in the dark with the vaporizer spewing fumes he must have found quite noxious. I thanked him for Sparky, technically my sister Mary Lou's beagle, who nevertheless demonstrated how hard a dog's life can be when he isn't shown how to fit into a family. Dogs need families just like we do. They yearn for a family. We have conspired with nature to make them that way. I thanked him for dogs whose mysterious appearances comforted and protected me more than I would probably ever know. I thanked him for loving the creatures we humans love. I could not imagine God not loving Millie and all the dogs that share our planet.

I thanked him for Winky. Everyone needs a best friend, and Winky was Millie's. Now they were together again. I knew that for sure.

Finally, I stood. I looked all around me at beauty I might not ever have stopped to see and love without dogs to teach me. I saw Bella in ecstasy when she reached a mountaintop. She couldn't believe what she was seeing, and I was so grateful to have witnessed that moment. An old-timer in the program once told me that gratitude is the antidote to grief. It would take a while to work on me, I thought, but I would try to let go. Still, I wondered if a part of me would always hold on to Millie, to have her always by my side. And I knew the answer was yes. Our dogs never leave us completely. They wait for us, as patient as love itself.

AFTERWORD

Grace Note

I was standing on a long, narrow path through the woods, the tall grasses of a dry marsh rising up on both sides, fanned by the autumn breeze. The trees were nearing their peak, kaleidoscopic against a seamless sky. A flock of geese honked overhead.

The six-month-old puppy at my side looked up. I wondered what she saw. Movement? Flapping shadows? Or could she see the very bones in their wings? At that age a dog's instincts are incredibly intense, sharpened by nature and breeding. I felt blind and deaf by comparison.

"Sit."

She sat, ears up, nose aquiver. I held tightly to the leash, feeling her vibrations through it. But not for long. We'd been walking this flat stretch of trail a lot lately but always on leash. Today would be the test. Today I would let go.

THERE WAS NEVER ANY doubt Julee and I would get another dog to love and be loved by. Life is too short. The longest we'd ever been without a dog was three weeks, after Sally died and before Millie came up to New York on that plane from Florida, scared to death of all the metallic slamming and banging but ecstatic to find us in that waiting throng at the airport. And that delay was only because Julee was finishing a tour in Europe, and I certainly couldn't seek out a new dog without her.

We weren't trying to replace Millie. No dog is replaceable, especially not Millie. Sometimes it felt as if she were still with us, as if she were occupying a spiritual space in our life. Julee thought Millie wanted to connect us with our next dog. "Then her life will be complete and she can move on." I wasn't sure how onboard I was with that concept, but I truly sensed that there was a dog out there waiting to be loved by us, chosen somehow for us.

The search for our next dog lessened the grief of losing a dog we thought we could never live without and who was taken too soon. We started almost immediately and with urgency. Grief can cause confusion and second-guessing. We bounced around from website to website, looking at breeders and rescue organizations. We filled out applications that were never responded to, or maybe never received for some reason. We were getting nowhere. Some breeders asked for substantial deposits on litters yet to be born. If they ended up with more deposits than puppies, your money would be kept back for the next litter. It could be a year before you got your dog. Julee said, "Our marriage won't survive a year without a dog, Edward."

In some cases, the breeder chose which pup you would get. Not happening, I said. We were getting frustrated and a little panicky. That void Millie left was expanding. Finally, a friend suggested we check with our local Golden Retriever Club. Maybe they could help. I found their contact info and sent them an email.

I rarely remember my dreams but when I do, I remember them vividly, as if I've dreamt in HD. That night I had a dream so vivid, so convincing I thought I might wake up in it. I stood in an endless field of tall grasses. There was no ground but there was solidity. Then in the distance I saw a golden tail, fading in and out of the swaying green, zigzagging closer. I caught a glimpse of something more than the tail. Millie? Was it Millie? At once it was her and then it wasn't. It was small, but not quite a puppy, not like she had been at ten weeks. Then it was Millie again, then the puppy, ever closer, so close I heard panting and woke up.

That morning I got an email from a representative of the Southern Berkshire Golden Retriever Club. She knew of no puppies available for rescue or sale on our side of the river, but across the Hudson there was a small breeder who had a female golden, an older puppy, four months old purportedly, the last of the litter.

"That's an old puppy," Julee said. "Will she even bond with us?"

I contacted the breeder immediately. She was a little hazy on the details of the dog's age and said that she had intended to keep her for breeding given her superior attributes but had changed her mind for reasons she didn't explain . . . or at least I couldn't understand. She was anxious, however, to inform us that the puppy's brother was already competing to become the New York State junior agility champion.

"Can you email us a picture of her?"

It came instantly and Julee stared at it for a long time then said, "Let's go."

The breeder urged us to hurry because she had to get the puppy's all-star brother to agility class that night. Julee frowned. "I bet that dog gets ignored because of her brother."

"That's just a guess, Julee."

Two hours later we were at the breeder's house in a nondescript subdivision, having stopped only to buy a bright red collar and matching leash and to cash a check, since the breeder wouldn't accept any other form of payment except the old-fashioned kind.

She ushered us inside. The house was a mess, with overtones of an old hippie crash pad. There were boxes and bags strewn about, the contents of which I was afraid to know. There were paintings everywhere, some of which would have been quite good if they had been finished. Julee pushed right past the baby gate partitioning off half the kitchen, where a skinny puppy with eyes that shone like melted chocolate and a coat the color of the inside of a banana peel sat, all paws and legs and a huge head. An instant later Julee was on the floor laughing, and the puppy had her hat in her wet, oversized mouth.

"She's the one," Julee said. "Absolutely she's the one. I know it. Let's go."

At which the suddenly liberated puppy launched herself into the chaotic living room, tearing open a baggie of dog food, kibble going everywhere, then flying into my arms, all forty-two pounds of her. I held her close. I felt her heart pounding inside her chest. I stroked her head and looked into her eyes. Those eyes said only one thing, *I've been waiting for you.* This was not my mind playing tricks on me. Certainly, my heart wasn't.

Maybe Julee was right. Maybe Millie had sashayed into heaven and told the powers that be that we couldn't live without the love of a dog, a perfect dog. And this puppy felt perfect.

I didn't want to let her loose, so I struggled with one hand to extract the cash from my pocket while Julee put the collar and leash on her. I finally put her down, to collect her official papers and vet records from the breeder, whose expression betrayed a wisp of sadness at having to let such a splendid creature go. It must be hard even for professionals.

The puppy didn't look back once as we led her from the house where she was born to the Jeep. Apparently, she didn't feel the need to bid adieu to her jock brother. She climbed in back with Julee and settled in, curling up in Julee's lap.

"She's not four months," Julee said with a little "umph."

As I drove back toward the river, Julee flipped through her papers. Her vet records showed that she'd been exceptionally well taken care of—"If ignored," Julee opined again—that she had an outstanding pedigree, her father being some kind of Hungarian champion, and that she was almost six months old, unhousebroken and basically untrained in any way.

"Her brother got all the attention," Julee said.

"Not anymore," I shot back.

"We have to give her a name."

The one she came with I won't even mention.

I had thought about Ada. The golden retriever is a fairly recent breed, developed in Scotland in the mid-nineteenth

century as the ultimate hunting dog by—I kid you not—
Baron Tweedmouth. The first recognized dam, the ur-mother
of all goldens, was named Ada, which has such a lovely Celtic
pitch to it. Then I thought of mitochondrial DNA and hemangiosarcoma and feared Ada might have carried it in her very
genes, which is ridiculous, I know, but I am given to occasional
superstitions, like all Celts. I thought of Millie again and wondered how things had changed so quickly and we had this
other dog now.

"I've never seen such an affectionate dog, Edward," Julee
whispered from the backseat.

"She needs love," I said.

"No, I think she needs to give love. She needs a family."

On cue, she jumped out of Julee's lap and licked the back
of my neck. I almost drove off the Kingston-Rhinecliff Bridge
as we crossed back over the Hudson.

"I think we should call her Grace, then," I said.

By the time we finished crossing the Hudson we were also
calling her Gracie and a few miles further, Googoo, because of
her prodigious drooling. And because we loved to say it.

WHATEVER TRAINING SHE LACKED when she came to us,
Gracie learned quickly. She was as smart a dog as I have ever
known. She loved to learn, and any dog of mine needed to
learn the woods. Which brought us to this moment of truth on
this autumn afternoon.

Gracie quivered at the end of the leash. She knew this was
going to be her test. I gave her a soft pat on the neck. She was

staring straight ahead, like a little soldier standing at attention. *Okay, Lord, I'm letting go. This one is in your hands now. P.S. Don't forget that Julee will kill me if I lose her.*

I unclenched my fingers, unclipped the red leash and laid it down on the trail beside her so she could see it, like an offer of trust. She got up, took a few steps, gave me a look, then shot off like a comet, her coltish hind legs kicking up dust and leaves as she streaked up the trail at a speed I couldn't have imagined for such a skinny, leggy thing. It was like she had been dreaming of this all her young life, like she would run too far to ever find her way back.

In a matter of seconds, she disappeared, the trees closing in on her. I waited a bit. Waited some more. Tried to stay calm. Then I yelled, "Grace!"

No Grace.

"Grace! Grace, come!"

In the distance I saw a blur of white, and in an instant, she blew by me at a full gallop and disappeared in the other direction. I was about to call her again when she reappeared, coming at me faster, if that was even possible, tongue out. Up and down the trail she went, like a dervish, her movements like her name, full of luminous beauty and power. I felt something inside me give, something that had been clenched since the moment in March when my golden girl refused her food and my heart began to break. I didn't know how tightly I had been holding on till this moment. I felt a flood of relief and joy in the wake of Grace's ecstasy.

Eventually, she expended every atom of energy she had and flopped down at my feet, all rubbery and disconnected the way puppies are. I opened my water bottle and filled a porta-bowl that her dear predecessor had left her. I think more of the water landed on the ground than in her mouth, what with the wild way that she lapped it. Slowly her breathing eased and she rolled over on her back to have her belly scratched.

I'd have to put the leash on her again when we got close to where I'd parked our ride. She would understand, I felt. After all, the hard part had been letting go.

ACKNOWLEDGMENTS

First and foremost a most grateful nod to my two brilliant and patient editors, Amy Wong at Guideposts and Beth Adams at Howard Books. Considerable thanks must also go to Jonathan Merkh, the publisher of Howard Books, and to John Temple and the senior management at Guideposts for their encouragement and guidance.

I could not possibly have written this book without being blessed with the greatest magazine staff in the business, especially Rick Hamlin, Colleen Hughes, Celeste McCauley, and Adam Hunter. Particular thanks to Guideposts creative director Kayo Der Sarkissian for her great work on the cover; Lenore Lelah Person for getting this book off the ground; Keren Baltzer, Michelle Rapkin, Stephanie Samoy, and the whole staff at Guideposts Books for all their help; and to Ansley Roan and her group at Guideposts digital media for same. Thanks to Doug Snyder. Special thanks to Jessica Chin and Patty Romanowski for their excellent copyediting.

Thanks to my sister, Mary Lou, for filling in some childhood memory holes, and to my brother Joe for convincing me she was right.

For inspiration, wisdom, and their love of all things dog: Jane Kopelman, Polly Hansen, Toni Grinnan, David Matt, Jennifer Gates, Dean Koontz, John Guare, Marion Bond West, Monty Mayrend, Sharon Azar, Peggy Frezon, Dana Apple, Matt Pasqua, Bryan Welch, Kim Allen, Bob Young, Richard Blake, Lisa Pohl Davis, Lynn Schriner, Judi Blankenbaker, Evelyn Freed, Len Horovitz, Christine Firefly, Ari Benjamin, Christa Ackerman, Dick Hopple, Bob Waller, and the denizens of the Chelsea dog run, one and all.

To the good dogs, friends past and present: Jake, Oscar, Max, Kelly, Della, Brooks, Ike, Ollie, Cody, Penny, Jack, Sasha, Hounder, Laddie, Daisy, Roger, Velcro, Coco, Coqui, Trixie, Buzz, PoohBear, Chili, Nico, Buddy, Scruffy, Sunny, Rosie, Doctor, Morticia, Elvis, Lucille, Apache, Zoya, Snoop, Charlie, Hank, and Bogie.

To the wonderful veterinarians at All Caring Animal Hospital in Great Barrington, Massachusetts: Drs. Phillips, June, and Maddie; and the staff, Romana, Katerina, Rachel, Mary Jean, Donna Lynn, Hollie, Angie, and Ashley.

My EQ crew: Gregg, Nyree, Sabrina, Jillian, and Eniko.

Perpetual thanks to Debbie Macomber for her support of *Guideposts*, aspiring writers everywhere, and this one in particular.

And most of all to Julee, who taught me more about the love of dogs than I could ever teach myself.

Through no fault of their own there are people who should be here but aren't, primarily due to my own oversight. But you know who you are even if I can't remember. Many anonymous thanks.